OCCUPATIONAL ALCOHOLISM
PROGRAMS

OCCUPATIONAL ALCOHOLISM PROGRAMS

Edited by

RICHARD L. WILLIAMS, M.S.
Former Occupational Program Consultant
Mississippi State Board of Health

and

GENE H. MOFFAT, Ph.D.

C H A R L E S   C   T H O M A S   ·   P U B L I S H E R
Springfield · Illinois · U.S.A.

Published and Distributed Throughout the World by
CHARLES C THOMAS • PUBLISHER
Bannerstone House
301-327 East Lawrence Avenue, Springfield, Illinois, U.S.A.

© 1975, by CHARLES C THOMAS • PUBLISHER
ISBN 0-398-03282-3
Library of Congress Catalog Card Number: 74-13783

With THOMAS BOOKS *careful attention is given to all details of manufacturing and design. It is the Publisher's desire to present books that are satisfactory as to their physical qualities and artistic possibilities and appropriate for their particular use. THOMAS BOOKS will be true to those laws of quality that assure a good name and good will.*

Printed in the United States of America
W-2

Library of Congress Cataloging in Publication Data

Williams, Richard L
  Occupational alcoholism programs.

  1. Alcoholism and employment—Case studies—Addresses, essays, lecture.   2.   Alcoholism—Treatment—United States—Case studies—addresses, essays, lectures. 3.   Alcoholics—Rehabilitation—United States—Case studies—Addresses, essays, lectures.   I.   Moffat, Gene H., joint author.   II.   Title.   [DNLM: 1.   Alcoholism— Therapy.   2.   Occupational health services. WM274 W72530]
HF5549.5.A4W54   658.38'2   74-13783
ISBN 0-398-03282-3

This book is dedicated to the thousands of employees who have been reached by the unselfish efforts and service of persons devoted to the establishment and maintenance of industrial alcohol programs.

CONTRIBUTORS

Fern E. Asma, M.D. (Loyola University). Assistant Medical Director, Illinois Bell Telephone Company.

Rev. Msgr. Joseph A. Dunne, M.P.A. (City University of New York). Chaplain, New York City Police Department.

Daniel W. Edwards, M.P.H., Ph.D. (University of Michigan). Chief Program Evaluator and Assistant Professor of Psychology, University of California, Davis.

Otto F. Jones, M.S.W. (University of Utah). Director, Insight Program, Kennecott Copper Corporation.

Stuart H. Lindop. Commissioned Royal Military College, Sandhurst, England. President, Western Canadian Human Resources Institute, Ltd., Edmonton, Alta., Canada.

Jerry F. Lotterhos, M.S.W. (Louisiana State University). Associate Professor and Director, Alcoholism Training Program for North Carolina, East Carolina University, Greenville, North Carolina.

Iver S. Ravin, M.D. (Boston University). Medical Director, Boston Edison Company.

FOREWORD

THE PUBLICATION OF "Occupational Alcoholism Programs" is most timely. The last three years have seen this nation develop a belated, but healthy concern about the human and economic loss we suffer from alcoholism.

In addition, this nationwide concern has been translated into action—by government and private agencies. The most dramatic development, however, has been in the work place, where management and labor organizations are working together on this problem. That is what this book is about.

A few years ago, research and observation led investigators to the conclusion that training the supervisor to identify the "troubled employee" who manifests impaired job performance will result in getting the employee in trouble with alcohol to the treatment he needs much earlier (and with greater likelihood of success) than to train the supervisor to identify the "alcoholic employee."

Employers, public and private, have recently developed a healthy interest in combatting alcoholism among their work force—an interest which employers share with labor organizations. An insight into the problems and complexities of management control systems designed for this objective is revealed in the description of the programs now functioning in some of the giant corporations provided by the authors of this book.

The book is a valuable source of information and evaluation for anyone concerned with the well being and productivity of our work force.

DONALD GODWIN
Director, Occupational Programs
  Branch
National Institute of Alcohol Abuse
  and Alcoholism

PREFACE

T HIS BOOK IS intended to provide the reader with several relatively new organizational approaches to the problem of the "on the job" drinker. It is also possible for the reader to make comparisons with companies similar to his own and to make a critical evaluation of the advantages and disadvantages of each program. Each company may have its own method for dealing with employees who begin to function at lesser levels because of behavioral problems associated with alcohol abuse. However, these companies are unable typically to evaluate their own efforts from an unbiased position. It is unfortunate, but often true, that the more money a company expends on various "troubled-employee" programs, the more apt they are to defend the success of that program.

Our own opinion is that any program that attempts to alleviate these behavioral problems is, by the nature of its existence, successful to some degree. The existence of the program indicates that opinion has changed at one or more levels of management. The longer a program is maintained, the greater the likelihood of opinion change within the ranks of employees it was designed to help. Therefore, we believe it to be inappropriate to criticize any program or policy that has as its basic tenet the sincere attempt to alter an administrative position which may be adversely affecting employee morale and job performance.

The programs included in this book have been carefully selected: on balance, a greater number of programs deal with large companies. This is due in part to the relative ease in obtaining information from these companies as opposed to smaller companies. The final selection was based also on the type of industry and, most importantly, on the number of positive responses received from those companies initially solicited. We felt we could include only those organizations willing to share with us the frustrations and problems as well as the successes they had encountered in establishing their programs. Certain programs were not included because of their similarity to another program presented in more detail. We sincerely hope that the representativeness of the programs presented will provide the interested reader with sufficient information to develop an approach to a troubled-employee program which would facilitate the concerns of his company.

As with most edited books, the major credit must go to the authors of the chapters who agreed to become involved in this project and who have consented to our revisions of their work. Our most sincere thanks and appreciation for their efforts are extended to them.

We also wish to acknowledge and thank Miss Paula Jolly for her diligent and time-consuming work in preparing the final manuscript.

Finally, to our many colleagues and friends who consistently offered their support and guided us over many of the rough spots in our endeavor, we give our most heartfelt thanks.

R. L. W.
G. H. M.

CONTENTS

OCCUPATIONAL ALCOHOLISM
PROGRAMS

Chapter 1

HISTORICAL AND SOCIOLOGICAL PERSPECTIVES OF ALCOHOL-RELATED PROBLEMS

JERRY F. LOTTERHOS, M.S.W.

The material outlined in this total work represents two very important ideas: 1) this book is not a discussion of alcoholism, but rather, of people who drink and their relationship to the work world; 2) the contained material leads us to a total new chapter in the history of how we respond to our fellow man who relates himself in a self-destructive manner to chemical substances, predominantly alcohol.

This first chapter will endeavor to accomplish several things which can perhaps help to bridge the gap in thinking between what has represented our past mode of behavior aimed at dealing with alcohol-related problems in our culture, to a newer, fresher and more promising course of action which the content of this book represents. Certainly there is no intention of sounding as if this material offers any final solutions or utopian ideals, as it probably raises more questions than answers. Yet, the implications of the line of thinking elucidated throughout this book is certainly viewed as exciting and weighted with the expectation of great fruition in the future.

The first part of this chapter shall be devoted to an analysis of the problems in our society which are alcohol-related; the second part will concern itself with an historical view of attitudes and behaviors toward these problems which have characterized the nature of responses in our society in general and point to directions for the future; the third section will consider the specific history of occupational action regarding alcohol-related problems and provide a general framework of present philosophy concerning what constitutes most progressive thinking in the area of employer potential

3

*in coping with drug-relevant people problems. This should then
set the stage for the remainder of the book in which specific aspects
and approaches of individual programs are defined or explained.*

SO WHAT IS THE PROBLEM?

Today in America the consumption of beverage alcohol is
phenomenal. By practice, if not by absolute commitment, we
are a drinking culture. It is estimated that between 65 to 70
percent of our adult population are partakers of alcohol beverage.
That means that some 95 million Americans drink in some form
or fashion (Department of Health, Education and Welfare, 1971).
While most drinking generally results in pleasure (aside from
an occasional slight hangover), for some nine million persons,
use of this chemical results in problems from moderate life
difficulties to the throes of fully developed alcoholism or·addic-
tive drinking. Considering that each of these problem drinkers
affects an average of four persons, we have a total of some thirty-
five to forty million persons whose lives are in some manner
touched by abuse of the "magic spirits." These general considerations only state the overall problem in sterile terms. Let us
turn to more specific concerns.

We are presently in the grasp of an interesting social phenomena which may simply be called "drug abuse mania." We
have become extremely concerned about the use (and abuse)
in our culture of drugs other than alcohol. While the destructive
utilization of any drug by a society should be cause for alarm,
it remains true that the number one drug of abuse in our society
is the legal one—alcohol, Perhaps our relative lack of concern
for alcohol abuse stems from our long-term association with this
drug and says something about our attitudes which perhaps
prevent us from taking positive action toward alcohol-related
problems. Suffice it to say, at this point, that alcohol as a drug
is both highly used and highly abused in our society.

When one considers the consequences of alcohol abuse, it is
likely that thoughts of alcoholism or the alcoholic take preponderance. Typically the stereotype of the alcoholic in our
society is epitomized by the "stumblebum" drunk with a wine

bottle in his pocket sleeping under a bridge or the skid row derelict in our larger cities. It must be emphatically stated that this type of individual actually represents only 3 to 5 percent of the alcoholic persons in our society. The other 95 percent of the alcoholic population are very similar to you and me with similar problems but perhaps dissimilar solutions. This 95 percent are made up of persons who are family men and women, who are employed, who rear children, pay taxes and are citizens in a community. The 3 to 5 percent skid row type represents an end result of the severe abuse of alcohol and, like the end consequences of any of man's severe problems, is not a pretty sight. It is not, however, this 5 percent about whom this book is directly concerned. It is, rather, how we might begin to prevent the development of these human tragedies. It is our great concern that the problem drinkers now present in our culture be given a chance to avoid the progression into the tragedy area.

Let us consider the costs to our society of the problems which are alcohol-related. These shall only be related briefly, but a series of bibliographic references for further elucidation will be provided.

Economic Costs

It is estimated that alcohol abuse and alcoholism drain the economy of at least $15 billion per year (Department of Health, Education and Welfare, 1971). Ten billion dollars of this is within business and industry and public work forces. About $2 billion is spent in direct public and private health and welfare services to alcoholic persons and their families. The other $3 billion is devoted to such things as resulting property damage and corresponding medical problems, etc. The high costs of alcohol abuse to occupational systems is of primary impact since the successful functioning of any society's economic sector is crucial to its overall stability. As discussed by Roman and Trice (1972), work constitutes the central and crucial role of most adult American males and a disruption of work role performance can have significant consequences for overall societal functioning as well as individual stability.

Personal Costs

For most persons, the consumption of alcohol is generally pleasurable. Functionally, it is relaxing and a social lubricant for most of us, yet within the context of destructive use, personal costs are severe. The more intensive the problem, usually the greater the price paid. It can apparently demand any degree of psychological and/or physical dependence. It can rob an individual of his social role, his status, his prestige. It can intervene in the relationship of a man and a woman, and parents and children in a variety of degrees and manners. It can result in overwhelming negative self-imagery with intense remorse and guilt. It can cost the individual and his family in the economic sense and can rob one of any vestige of self-respect and dignity. The human misery and degradation associated with the abusé of the legal chemical is indeed one of the greater tragedies in our modern history. And it becomes even more tragic as we begin to realize that it really does not have to be this way. Other personal costs are associated with medical and physical complications which are often the by-products of excessive alcohol abuse. These include general deterioration from a lack of proper food intake, chronic gastric conditions, pancreatitis and, of course, liver disorders, as well as a greater general susceptibility to infectious disease of the chronic drinker. Perhaps the greatest personal tragedy is that typically, because of the negative stereotype prevalent in our culture toward the "alcoholic" and the ignorance and confusion surrounding proper responses to effectively deal with these problems, it is implied that the individual involved will typically not even be identified as a problem until he reaches a stage of the addictive process somewhere close to the skid row image. We will discuss this in more detail later.

Accidents and Alcohol

It is well known that alcohol has a direct effect on such physical responses as the ability to react rapidly to a given stimulus, the ability to coordinate gross muscle responses, poor judgment, etc. In a society in which man has developed and is the victim of so many extensions of himself, such as his machines and rapidly moving transportation vehicles, it is clearly seen that he places himself in considerable jeopardy and sets up a great potential for accidents when he consumes alcohol. This drug plays a significant role in highway accidents. It is estimated that some 28,000 deaths in a recent year were the result of the man-alcohol-auto triad. Many of the alcohol-related traffic fatalities are youth from sixteen to twenty-four years of age in which the proportion rises to six of every ten highway deaths (Department of Health, Education and Welfare, 1971). At least 50 percent of all fatal automobile accidents are related to the consumption of alcoholic beverages. A high percentage of airplane accidents are the result of alcohol consumption. Boating accidents are thought to be related to alcohol use. Certainly, in any task in which a high degree of coordination and judgment is required, accidents are likely in the presence of consumed alcohol.

Costs to Occupational Systems

It is difficult to some extent to estimate the real cost of alcohol consumption and abuse to private and public industry. Estimates of the number of alcohol abusers or problem drinkers in any work force range from 3 to 4 percent (Roman and Trice, 1972) to 10 percent (Department of Health, Education and Welfare, 1971). There are conservatively four and one-half to five million employed persons with alcohol-related problems in our society today, and the vast majority have been on the job from ten to fifteen years (Chandler, 1972). Dollar cost estimates of these problem persons to industry range from $3 billion to $10 billion per year. The average alcohol problem person is said to cost $1,500 to $4,000 per year, to operate at 50 percent efficiency, and to average twenty-two days in lost time (Orr, 1972).

Let us consider specifically some important costs to the employer:

1. Absenteeism, whether in terms of actual physical absence or in terms of on-the-job absenteeism is one of the most costly concerns of industry.
2. Poor decision-making in white collar workers can result

in considerable losses when poor decisions influence large areas of activity and people.

3. Supervisory time spent in concern about the troubled employee is another cost factor (Roman and Trice, 1972).

4. The effect on other employees is also significant. The troubled employee often lowers the morale of other employees who see the alcohol abuser shirking his duty.

5. Since most employees with an alcohol-related problem are often fired after they become unuseful, the cost of training a new employee to fill the role can be exorbitant in comparison to what it might have cost to assist the troubled employee.

6. Another cost factor is the industry's efforts to do something about the problems of troubled employees, which in essence is just a drop in the bucket compared to the cost of doing nothing.

7. Other costs include accidents, early retirements, garnishments, increased benefit costs, lost sales, safety hazards and unfavorable public relations (Habbe, 1970).

Several studies have been done to consider the cost of alcohol abusers on the job. While none of the evidence is conclusive, there are strong indicators which support the notion of the high costs of these persons to industry (Babbitt, 1967; Maxwell, 1969; Pell and Alonzo, 1970; Pritchet, 1967; Workov and Bacon, 1965). In 1966, Winslow considered four areas of concern including cost of absenteeism, cost of health and accidents, impaired production, and interpersonal friction in a work force. He found that in all categories, alcohol-problem employees were more costly. In a report in 1970, the Comptroller General of the United States estimated that including all cost concern areas, it cost the United States Government some $275 million per year considering the present way we deal with alcohol-problem employees in our federal civilian work force.

Alcohol and Arrests

It is estimated that arrests for public intoxication alone account for one third of all arrests reported annually (Department of Health, Education and Welfare, 1971). If one includes arrests for charges such as driving while under the influence of alcohol, vagrancy and disorderly conduct, the percentage of alcohol-related arrests could range as high as 45 percent of the total.

Other costs worth mentioning are related to the welfare caseload where alcohol problems are a significant reality. The American Indian on some reservations has a rate of alcoholism ✓ as high as 25 percent of the population (Department of Health, Education and Welfare, 1971).

It is easy to see that the alcohol-related human problems and concurrent costs in our society are phenomenal. It is also apparent that these problems and costs directly or indirectly affect all persons in our society. It is an unfortunate reality, however, that most of our efforts to date aimed at dealing with this great social problem have been directed only toward the more seriously affected, full-blown alcoholics—the skid row type individual. Yet, as stated earlier, this comprises at most 5 percent of our alcohol-related problems. What this basically means is that we have not yet learned to respond to these problems until they represent total tragedies and fully developed addictions for the individual affected. In considering another illness, for example polio, this same line of thinking would lead us to delay treatment or assistance until the afflicted person was ready for an iron lung! Polio has only been dealt with effectively since we learned to respond long before the situation became chronic, in this case, even before the disease was contracted. No battle can be won against any public health or social problem as long as one deals only with the casualties. The key question then is how we can begin to relate effectively to the larger mass of persons who make up the remaining 95 percent of the problem, the alcohol abusers or problem drinkers from whom eventually evolve the casualties—the alcoholics. The material in this book is concerned with at least one approach to accomplishing this, an approach which has been called Occupational Alcoholism Programming. It has been realized in the past few years through the development of industrial related programs as characterized by Hughes Aircraft, Kennecott Copper and others, that effective means of relating to not only alcohol-related problems but other behavior problems can be accomplished when employers utilize the work situation as a means of identification of problems and motivation to do something about them.

In recent years the National Institute of Alcohol Abuse and Alcoholism (NIAAA) conducted a study of three hundred occupational programs and found that only twelve of these could be viewed as effectively functional in really reaching employees whose problems are alcohol-related. But in those situations which were effective, research indicates that a minimum of fifty-four of every one hundred identified problem drinkers could be expected to recover (return to normal job efficiency) as a result of such a program (Habbe, 1970). Some companies have indicated a higher success rate than this, reaching up to 60 and 70 percent recovery rates.

Comparing the above success with the success of our typical or average treatment program for the alcoholic, some very interesting comparisons can be made. The "best" figures quoted by treatment programs of the inpatient type are around 25 to 35 percent considering success in terms of ongoing sobriety. It must be stressed that what is available as treatment in our society at present only relates to the chronic, fully developed alcoholic. Most treatment services which do exist are separated from the general health delivery systems into vested-interest, reasonably isolated services. This of course implies that as a society we have not yet learned to respond to the problems we associate with alcohol within our usual health and social service delivery systems, even though we have tended to define alcoholism as a disease in recent history. Present programs dealing with alcohol abuse and alcoholism are accorded a low priority and remain unrelated to most of the health and social resources within the community (Department of Health, Education and Welfare, 1971). In general, it seems safe to say that the alcoholic is a true deviant in our society and is simply not dealt with in a manner most appropriate to either prevent the development of serious illness or to assist the afflicted person when he does become seriously ill.

It cannot be denied that the problems and costs in both economic and personal terms are very large. It is also true that much is known about how we can be effective in both preventing the development of serious illness by early problem identification and appropriate treatment, as well as treating the existing casualties of our past neglect and failure to respond. How can it be then, with the present knowledge we possess about what to do and the recognition of the enormity of the problem, that we have not been more aggressive and positive in dealing appropriately with these problems?

In a speech delivered at the National Occupational Alcoholism Training Institute in Pinehurst, North Carolina in June 1972, it was stated by the Director of Corporate Relations, Hughes Aircraft, "American industry is helping thousands of employees commit suicide every year . . . We unwittingly commit this grave error by administering massive doses of misplaced kindness that leads the disease-ridden alcoholic further along the road to a shattered, unproductive life and possibly death. In the process, American industry suffers fantastic losses in human potential, talents and money—losses that really need not be . . ." (Chandler, 1972).

The answers to why we are in this state of affairs concerning alcohol-related problems is very complex. It is bound up in our history, our cultural attitudes toward drinking, and our learned responses to the problem over a long period of time. In the next section we shall endeavor to provide a basic historical perspective of our responses toward alcohol-related problems and to define how some of the elements of reality in our present modes of thinking about these problems represent handicaps or barriers to fully responding appropriately. This material will not only help in understanding our past and present, but will help point the direction for the future.

WHAT IS OUR HERITAGE?

In order to begin to understand some of the complex elements which represent the present reality of how we respond in our culture to alcohol-related problems, it is necessary to consider the past. We must look at our history of drinking and drinking problems and our feelings and attitudes, values and thoughts about this chemical which occurs so naturally, yet which has been viewed so attentively, scrutinized, glorified and vilified over the years. This will not only give us a perspective for where we are in present time, but also perhaps help paint for the future a more reasonable, more mature approach to the use of this drug in our society and toward the problem drinker.

History is full of references to alcohol. One of the earliest known references to its use by man is contained in a poem taken from a Sumerian cave dated around 5,000 B.C. (Dancy, 1967) which describes the introduction of a boy (Gilgamish) to the chemical and its effects on him in a reasonably positive way. Historical references are as often positive as they are negative in presenting the drug. Alcohol has been referred to as "the water of life" and the esteem in which it has been held is attested by its use in toasting extremely important human events such as birth, betrothal, death, contract signing, etc.

Man's relationship to alcohol, being his companion through many centuries, is described in many contexts with many meanings. Anthropologists say it is possible that man's pursuit of wine helped change him from a nomadic existence to a more settled creature since it took a long time to cultivate the grapes (Chafetz, 1965). It is suggested that during World War II, American troops on the front lines had some form of alcoholic beverage as an almost constant companion. Songs of many cultures are replete with references to the magic substance in toned feelings ranging from light and happy ("Tiny Bubbles") to bawdy (Irish drinking songs), to romantic and seductive, to comforting in the face of bad moods or of harsh weather. Man has been a user of alcohol for a long time. It would appear that the utilization of this "aqua vitae" is and has been in most respects positive and pleasurable for man although the problems associated with its abuse are also alluded to historically.

Let us turn to the use of alcohol in our society. When the arrivals from Europe came, they brought with them the values and attitudes of their cultures toward the use of alcohol. Basically, the early English settlers were alcohol users. The ship Arabella in 1629 arriving at the Massachusetts Bay Colony had on board forty-two tons of beer and beer-making equipment (Dancy, 1967). In 1637 the first brewery was built in the Massachusetts Bay Colony, and soon after brewing became the third most important industry in the colonies, surpassed only by milling and baking. The use of alcohol during the early years was positively viewed and accepted by the general community (Lender, 1973). The primary concern was how to deal with misuse. Alcohol was strongly condemned in terms of its misuse. Public drunkenness was not sanctioned, but the images of intolerant Puritan attitudes are distortions according to Lender (1973). The use of rum from the West Indies was an instant success even though our gain was based on propagating the, slave trade and promoting the disruption of other societies (Chafetz, 1965).

Liquor was a part then of our earliest social interactions and was held in high esteem. Its use spread westward, and as our country began its inexorable move from a rural and agrarian culture toward the complex industrialized and specialized system we now know, there sprang up in the midst a somewhat new expression of attitude. Alcohol itself began to be attacked as being "of the devil," "bad," etc. This beginning of the Temperance Movement in our culture is seen to be a part of a larger effort to maintain the status quo and fight against the new order and to slow down urbanization (Gusfield, 1962). Prominent groups which arose to propagate the prohibition of alcohol were the Prohibitionist Party and the Women's Christian Temperance Union (vestiges of which are still with us). These efforts gained great momentum with most religious orders "falling in" and supporting the nonuse of alcohol beverages. The final result, or the great orgasm of this social movement was the realization of Prohibition, which, like all orgasms, only lasted a short period, and like some orgasms, had some long-lasting results. It has left a notable influence on the thinking and attitudes toward the use of alcohol in our culture. During prohibition of course, the use of alcohol, though illegal, moved merrily along through bootlegging and highly organized crime activities. It is easy to see how ambivalences about the use of alcohol in our society have developed and become ingrained. This ambivalence continues as a part of our attitudes toward drinking even though we have repealed prohibition and have at least partially reintegrated the use of alcohol into our culture.

This ambivalence can be related to one of the basic value orientations characterized by the concept of individual self-control. Ideas of self-control, productivity and achievement are a part of our American character (Williams, 1970). When the Barnum and Bailey Circuses first began, it was difficult to attract audiences in the more rural areas as this much pure fun was a considerable amount to absorb in one setting. Circus business picked up, however, when the regular circus acts were coupled with a sound temperance lecture (Kendall, 1971)! That these values to some degree are at odds with the use of alcohol, which is associated with pleasure-seeking, and escape from worries and responsibility (Roman and Trice, 1972) is easy to see.

Drinking in American society seems to be characterized by pragmatic justification; i.e. it is all right to drink if one has had a hard day, if one "deserves" it. It is interesting to note that within the youth "pot" culture, there is a different philosophy toward the use of marijuana. There is no need felt for pragmatic justification to smoke pot; rather, the value of "feeling high" is the end in itself. So it seems that alcohol users (and abusers) actually "hide" or cover the basic reasons for drinking and our culture reinforces this in its attitudes, thereby setting up basic cultural and personal circumstances for ignoring the development of problems (Roman and Trice, 1972).

Alcohol, as a chemical with certain properties, may be said to serve certain functions for the individual (Bacon, 1962). It can reduce tension, guilt, anxiety and frustration. It can also reduce operational efficiency below the minimum necessary for social survival; alcohol can make possible an interpersonal activity which may ordinarily not occur; it can allow an escape valve for socially frustrated individuals which is relatively safe, and can also break down individual participation in associations, thus weakening them; it can impair the exactitude of behavior patterns and socially valuable ideas, and can impair foresight (Bacon, 1962). By considering these effect potentialities of alcohol use for social man, one can see many possible interpretations and many possible value orientations. Bacon (1962) has also stated that the more complex a society and the more socially isolated persons are from each other in a culture, the greater the potentiality of dramatic effect of alcohol on the individual. This is certainly the case in our present society where the use of alcohol is seen to serve the function of social lubrication, of easing tension, of making social relationships easier; even though we are somewhat ambivalent about its use for fun or escape, we have learned to use it in that fashion.

Another idea concerning drinking in our culture is that there are no clear-cut norms for what constitutes "appropriate drinking behavior" (Fraser, 1967; Jellinek, 1962; Roman and Trice, 1972; Snyder, 1956). This would seem to represent one element of our culture which might promote or enhance the potentiality for drinking problems to arise. As a contrast, the Jewish culture has an extremely low rate of alcoholism as noted by many researchers (Glatt, 1970; Jellinek, 1960; King, 1961; Simmons, 1968). This is generally attributed to the close association of the use of alcohol to religious sacramental significance and the existence of clear, definitive and powerful sanctions against excess in the use of alcohol. We have no comparable clear guidelines for use in our culture.

Before going further into the discussion of cultural considerations, let us turn our attention to the definitions of problems associated with alcohol use in our society. We have stated earlier that some nine million persons in our culture have alcohol-related problems. We use alcohol to have fun, but we also use it (although basically denied) to assuage frayed nerves and as a means of avoiding negative feelings, such as depression. Severe and destructive addictive attachments to alcohol in our society do occur; they are typically not helped until their disintegration becomes extremely severe. The terms "alcoholism" and "alcoholic" are used by professionals and laymen to describe a variety of things. We have said that alcohol abuse does accompany alcohol use in most situations. Drunkenness or intoxication produces a high potentiality for social disturbance. Drunk persons behave in ways likely to disrupt the normal functioning of any society

(Roman and Trice, 1972). Certainly the complexity of this culture provides a large set of social balances which the intoxicated person can begin to bump into or bend, for example, the drunken driver who runs a red light and causes property damages, or the white-collar worker who misses an important meeting on Monday morning because of a hangover.

What any society calls a problem and how it is ultimately labeled depends to a great degree on the value orientations and thinking about what "the problem" represents. If one believes that a certain bit of behavior is determined by some devil, then one might define behaviors associated with that as "of the devil" or "sinful." We have a cultural heritage which has defined immoderation in anything as "sinful." Drunkenness and "immoderation" have been viewed as sinful or as illegal in our culture (Roman and Trice, 1972). Public drunkenness is a crime in our society today and continues to be viewed in large part as representing criminal behavior even though we have begun to apply different criteria of judgment primarily centered around an illness or disease model. In 1954 the American Medical Association simply stated that alcoholism is a disease. E. M. Jellinek (1960) wrote a book outlining a conception of alcoholism as a disease. Jellinek viewed the progression from occasional intoxication to frequent and habitual intoxication to a stage of physical and psychological dependency on the chemical.

This definition of alcoholism as a disease was the greatest motivating force for a change in social policy concerning how we deal with alcohol abuse in our society since the beginning of Alcoholics Anonymous in 1935. Whether or not "alcoholism" is really a disease, this definition did promote our conceptualizing the problem as representing something other than criminal behavior and implied newer responses other than punishment measures which have represented our typical approach to dealing with any deviant behavior. The Christian value orientation, which set the stage for what we call humanitarianism, with its built-in idea of man having the right to be wrong and to try again, of transgressing with the right to forgiveness, was a fertile ground for the acceptance of the concept that what we call "alcoholism" is a disease. Since this line of thinking has been accepted as reality, there has evolved a great movement to take the social responses to alcoholics out of the hands of legal institutions and to place them in the hands of medical or health and social service institutions (Milford, 1970). Therefore, deviant drinkers have been pushed toward medical treatment rather than through the "revolving door of prison." We now have revolving doors relative to medical programs. While it is indeed true that the acutely ill chronic alcoholics can have a variety of physiological and medical complications, the simple acceptance of the disease model can have very serious and potentially negative consequences in attempting to deal objectively with the total problem of alcohol abuse in our society. It is becoming increasingly recognized that the simplistic notion of "alcoholism" as a disease just does not hold water in explaining all the associated problems of a person who is labeled an alcoholic (Cahalan, 1969; Roman and Trice, 1968; Seeley, 1962; Steiner, 1969). Since the arrival of the "disease concept" the problems associated with chronic heavy drinking have come under the microscope of most all professional care-givers in the health and social arena. Each area has its own peculiar "explanation" for the development of the problems and each usually propagates this or that approach for solution of the problems. Of course, there are no absolute answers to what causes alcoholism and the attachment to any simplistic or singularistic mode of explaining or dealing with the problem(s) will neither offer startling insights nor produce significant change in their development. There are theories of physical causation, psychological theories and sociocultural theories. Out of these, often very specific and narrow theoretical frameworks come bits of knowledge which are operationalized in terms of being put into a program to help afflicted persons. So often, these "programs" are so narrow as to be ludicrous. The literature contains a reference (Shiloh, 1961) concerning the treatment of the alcoholic by the use of lemons. A prescription is offered which requires 249 lemons. Though not quite as sour, there are any number of applications and remedies presently being propagated which come close! While it is apparent that elements of all these studies and theories are valid and relevant, it also is true that they must be viewed together, collectively, to accomplish a total view of man's relationship to alcohol. There are no simple, singular causes (Snyder, 1962).

We seem to always be both the victim and the benefactor of much of our knowledge and its application whether in the technological arena or in our understanding of ourselves and subsequent action based on that understanding. We benefit from the knowledge we have gained about the atom, yet are victimized to a degree by its application in destructive potential.

As our knowledge of our social problems grows, we operationalize that knowledge into action which usually appears better than what has gone before. Yet often we later find that what we have done has uninvited consequences. This is a normal course of development and raises no peculiar cause for alarm unless we fail to recognize its existence. For example, there are negative results from the definition of alcoholism as a disease, even though the positive results in terms of alcohol abusers being more humanly treated is recognized. These negatives have been discussed by several writers (Cahalan, 1970). One of the most serious problems is that the medical definition of alcoholism takes the responsibility for the behavior away from the individual (Roman and Trice, 1972). Actually medical labeling may make deviant drinking irreversible by absolving the drinker of responsibility for his behavior (Roman and Trice, 1968). The simple statement that alcoholism is a disease is misleading since it is too narrow and conceals the fact that a step in public policy is being recommended, not a scientific discovery announced (Seeley, 1962). Steiner (1969) challenges the disease concept by viewing alcohol problems as representing a series of learned social transactions aimed at obtaining personal advantage. It is felt in general that the word disease tends to foster needless dependency and to some degree prevents looking for real causes and other implications such as the social, cultural, psychological, etc. It also sets up conditions which foster the avoidance of responsibility by the general society who see the existence of "treatment facilities" as evidence that "the problem(s) is/are being taken care of."

We have previously commented that positive responses to alcohol-related problems do not occur in our society until they become so obvious that something "has to be done." This does indeed represent our heritage and implies that we aim our efforts at treatment toward the skid row type individual. Concern for this individual with the advent of the disease concept has resulted in the creation of what has been referred to as the "alcoholism industry" by Roman and Trice (1972). This is made up of all the helpers, alcoholism workers, designers of alcoholism programs, and solicitors of funds to support alcoholism programs. Almost every type of deviance in our society is surrounded by a group of "vested-interest" helpers. Specific agencies, occupations and semi-professionals have been developed to deal with the aged, the poor, the alcoholic, etc. (Roman and Trice, 1972). Each of these respective interests vie for tax dollars to support public programs. Each group makes strong efforts to influence positive legislation in their direction by claiming to have the "worst" or "most" problems. The interest being generated by the "drug-abuse industry" presently demonstrates this phenomena quite well. This is not meant to demean the motivations, nor the good done by these organizations. However, as has been pointed out (Roman and Trice, 1972), the irony of the specialized division of labor into various problem industries functioning as formal organizations and specialized professions is that their very existence effectively precludes to some degree the elimination of their respective problems. This kind of response to problems in our society is a very interesting phenomena.

Bacon (1969) suggests that there are two broad issues in utilizing a social approach in looking at problems. First are considerations of the actual problem (alcohol-related problems which do exist), and the second, the emerging social responses to the problem. After the problem is named and identified and it has been decided something should be done about it, policies and programs for action are made operational and responsibility delegated. In regard to alcohol-related problems, these kinds of efforts have typically been unsuccessful and these problems have been neither controlled nor alleviated. The resulting emerging type two problem or issue mentioned above involves argument and contention that the established means of handling the original problem are not acceptable and maybe even damaging and bad for a society. Social factions begin to argue about the program rather than keeping their eye on the problem which actually leads to neglect of the original problem, denial of responsibility and rejection. The reactions to alcohol problems by such institutions as religion, medicine, education and government are examples of the type two problem. Bacon states that alcoholism will appear in larger numbers and will persist longer in direct proportion to the weakness, uncertainty or avoidance reactions which appear at the level of societal response. He further suggests that efforts should be directed at understanding the responses of these social institutions and forces which actually prevent the successful control of such problems, rather than continuing to study alcoholism and drug abuse directly.

These ideas, of course, support the notion that the vested-interest "alcoholism industry" to some degree prevent the acceptance of true responsibility by a society for positively dealing with its problems. It would appear then, considering all these factors, that what we have done in our concern to be helpful to the problem drinker is to help crystallize his deviance outside the regular norms of social responsibility. That is, we are using the image of the skid row alcoholic to justify our conceptions of the problem as representing a disease, a severe psychological malady, or a concern of only the vested interest alcoholic industry in very nearly the same manner as the Women's Christian Temperance Union used the skid row image as an example to demonstrate their concepts of the "evils of alcohol." And the degree to which we allow this state of affairs to continue is the same degree to which we must hold ourselves in contempt of a responsible approach to these kinds of problems. Problem drinkers are people—people who have a variety of human and social problems and who happen to use alcohol as a supposed means of help. They are not "different" and the skid row bum doesn't start there. The skid row image does provide, however, a "boundary maintenance" function in our culture (Roman and Trice, 1972). By accepting the skid row image as the identification of the alcoholic, this serves to prevent those of us with lesser drinking problems from having to admit it. One can feel that he is "not that way." This idea not only works for oneself, but also prevents early identification of problems in others.

In addition to this, another relevant concept evolving out of our competitive social processes and achievement or "winning" orientation is that we need negative reference groups to which to say, "I'm better than you." (Rubington, 1962). Roman and Trice (1972) describe realistically and effectively the process through which deviant behavior develops and how the ingrained cultural responses of society assist in the development of the deviant drinker. It is accepted that alcohol can serve a variety of needs and functions for man in both symbolic and concrete ways. Therefore, it might be simply stated that man has suscepti-bility or vulnerability factors to alcohol in his physical, psycho-logical and social-cultural existence. These vulnerability factors for some men may be greater than others and offer a greater potential for trouble to develop around a more "intense" relation-ship with the drug. There are no simple, clear-cut, known absolutes, but it is considered that the physical, psychological and sociocultural factors can be weighted in different degrees for different problem persons. The failure of finding specific, absolute causal factors is one aspect which has resulted in severe questioning of the disease concept (Cahalan, 1970).

Several more specific vulnerability factors seem appropriate to mention before going into a discussion of the development of deviance (Roman and Trice, 1972):

1. Psychological or emotional dependency.
2. Poor self-identity (Conner 1962), i.e. by drinking heavily, a negative image is developed which may be better than nothing.
3. High anxiety or strong depressive feelings.
4. Very pleasant sensations brought on by alcohol use.
5. Having a deviant drinker in one's background with whom to identify either positively or negatively.
6. The mode of socialization into alcohol use. For example, a socialization process which identifies alcohol use with symbolic proof of masculinity. Alternatively, drinking may

be viewed by one's culture as a means of dealing with anxiety and bad feelings or as an escape mechanism and thereby set the stage for potential trouble.

These above vulnerability factors alone will not necessarily result in problems unless certain opportunities or pressures for involvement with alcohol are present. This includes, in general society, opportunities for alcohol abuse as a social alternative, stress which cannot be otherwise relieved, boredom, lack of personal fulfillment, absence of specific responsibiilty or low social visibility (e.g. the housewife). In addition are suggested in the work world (Roman and Trice, 1972) such opportunities and pressures as absences of clear-cut standards of work evaluation, freedom to set work hours, work addiction, occupational obsolescence and occupational mobility.

In considering the development of deviant drinking within this context of vulnerability-opportunity-pressure, one is not attempting to define etiological or causative considerations, but rather to look pragmatically at the social responses to the behavior which will either enhance or negate the possibility of the behavior being repeated (Roman and Trice, 1972). Labeling theory is the study of social reactions to deviant behavior (Lofland, 1969; Schur, 1971). This theory holds that deviance which becomes permanent occurs over a period of time, in stages, and can elicit social responses which either assure or promote continuation of the deviancy or promote stopping the behavior. This theory has a basis in the idea that we as social individuals are responsive to the social pressures exerted by our fellow man. Most deviant behavior eventually is recognized by others and this constitutes an initial social reaction. If one considers heavy drinking in our society in this context, observers who are heavy drinkers also would most likely react positively to an instance of heavy drinking since the exhibition of the same behavior in another tends to legitimize our own behavior in the same realm. It has been pointed out, however, that what is most likely to occur is neither a positive nor necessarily a negative sanction, but rather a normalization process (Roman and Trice, 1972), or attempts to ignore the behavior. Ignoring behavior which tends to imply a negative encounter is a characteristic of our culture. We simply do not seem to want to invite the discomfort we might generate by doing so. One may also invite the "boomerang labeling" process in which the accuser gets accused of being a "goody-goody," or he may find his own weaknesses exposed (Roman and Trice, 1972). Most persons take the stance that "Who or what represents deviance is none of my business." Bringing in the idea that there is a negative value placed on being an "alcoholic" (in the skid row perspective) in our society, it is easy to see how avoidance of the whole issue of alcohol-related problems is possible: "The exposure of your drinking behavior may cause me to look at mine."

Let us look at what might happen to the typical deviant drinker in our culture. He begins heavy drinking which gains reinforcement by heavy-drinking peers and even though this behavior might result in some lessening of attention to his wife, she does not respond with any positive confrontation. Therefore, no intervention occurs which might stop the process of problem drinking at this level. The denial and pretense go on until the deviant behavior becomes so bad that surrounding persons are "fed up." Now, at this point, a critical thing is about to occur in the development of the deviant. He is about to be rejected and to have his "negative image" reinforced tremendously. He receives a loud and insistent message, usually of rejection and anger or of coldly being ignored. No one responds well to anger or being ignored. There is no more severe form of rejection than being ignored. He is excluded from normal social drinking situations but no positive action occurs. The next move is toward a more compatible drinking group who have all undergone the same kind of exclusion. Thus, the deviant is becoming better defined, but even at this level of problem development, unless the person engages in some other behavior which puts him at odds with the law and gets him apprehended, he still may not be confronted by any positive action. He may still have a job and his co-workers may be playing the same ostrich game, for example. By this time, however, the heavy drinking and its rewards have become so important that successful intervention is already very difficult. The normal thing in our society would be for this individual to proceed in this exclusion process until his behavior is finally viewed as deviant and he appears before a "licensed" and sanctioned labeler, most likely a psychiatrist or physician, and receives an official label of "alcoholic." Getting the heavy drinker into the official labeling system is usually viewed as representing "success." He is finally "in treatment." However, it seems this is a real fallacy, since there are no really adequate psychiatric or medical mechanisms to change the complex, somewhat self-perpetuating, undesirable behavior. The person may begin to adopt the "sick" view and have a somewhat different self-image, but it only enables him the convenience of an excuse for his behavior, "I'm sick and therefore (by cultural definition in our society) not responsible for my behavior." If there exists some real treatment mechanisms for changing the behavior, this is not necessarily true; however, there are no mechanisms (visible to this author at any rate) of successful "treatment" within the medical or psychiatric areas which do much more than deal with the acute physical by-products of heavy drinking. Perhaps a part of the success of Alcoholics Anonymous is that it offers a mechanism of "redefinition" into society with at least some prescription for how to get there.

Labeling theory implies that the use of the 'sick" or "disease" label is a risky business and should be avoided if long-term consequences to society are to be minimized. Means of successfully avoiding labeling involve avoiding exclusion processes and avoiding labeling events which provide excuses for the deviant to continue his behavior (Roman and Trice, 1972). It may then be more useful from a pragmatic point of view to consider deviant drinking as simply representing inappropriate behavior rather than illness (Roman and Trice, 1972). This does not negate the fact that severe alcohol addiction involves serious medical problems which can most competently be treated by medical personnel. These concepts certainly lend credence to a broad perspective about alcohol-related problems arising out of the context of social interaction. It is becoming more recognized that these problems arise out of man's interactions in his society (Steiner, 1969) with all its cultural values and ideations (Reinert,

1968), and that what we presently refer to as "alcoholism" may not have to happen if we can disengage in methods not shown to be of value because of tradition, politics, inertia, economics, the "therapist's" person "set" and resistances, threatened egos and pocketbooks, and small, narrow thinking (Edwards, 1970).

The implications of all this and especially the "labeling theory" is that it offers a very practical method of thinking which allows us to see ways of plugging our efforts to deal with these problems into society rather than continuing not to face our responsibilities by allowing deviancy to occur. The key issue is whether we can make the knowledge we have available within the inter workings of society where the action is. The implication for this understanding is great and may have applicability in a variety of ways, such as within educational systems. Certainly there are implications for the work world as this represents a place in the real world where action can be initiated to prevent the evolution of serious deviant behavior which involves the use of alcohol. Our history must be left behind and we must face the issue squarely and promote early identification of these problems. The movement toward early identification must also include the willingness to stop exploiting the skid row image. Ultimate solutions to alcohol-related problems will only come about when society comes to grips with its ambivalence about drinking and accepts a positive, clear-cut definition of what represents appropriate drinking. We must learn to expect health rather than illness or problems and to emphasize our positive expectations to each other in an atmosphere of "caring" which recognizes the positive value of letting our expectations for behavior be known to each other rather than taking the easy way out by denial, coverup and ignoring problems. The work world offers an excellent kickoff point. The structured characteristics of the work world, if properly utilized, make it an ideal environment for identification of problems at an early stage of development, as well as providing motivation toward treatment (NIAAA, 1972). Work essentially involves a contract between the employer and employee, specifying that certain performance by the employee will obtain certain rewards from the employer and, should either party breach the contract, the other has a right to demand a change in behavior (Roman and Trice, 1972). It is obvious that the impairment of job performance through any behavior problem represents such a breach of contract. Having established some rationale as to where we can direct our efforts, let us turn our attention to a historical view of the efforts which have been made by occupational systems to deal with these problems.

✕ THE HISTORY OF OCCUPATIONAL ALCOHOLISM PROGRAMMING

American industry has come a long way in its relationship to its employees from those early days when the only concern of management was how much work could be squeezed out of a person in long hours with a low rate of pay. We are approaching a spirit of cooperation in the complex industrialized world of today in which management and labor work collaboratively for the good of man and an improved quality of life for all. Management has learned over the years that it has a real stake in its human resource potential as well as its physical resources. Predecessors of behavior problem programs are seen in company-based medical departments, insurance benefits, and other employee services which have come to characterize our modern companies and public service programs. It is in this context of concern for human resource potential and sound management practice that the present development of occupational alcohol-problem programs has been able to really begin.

The responses and attitudes toward alcoholism and alcohol-related problems in industry have of course been no different in the past than the typical attitudes and responses of the general society of which they are a part. One example of this is the Litchfield Connecticut Corporation. In 1789, in sympathy with early temperance activity, it pledged discontinuance of distilled spirits for members and their employees. The New York temperance society made increased labor efficiency the central point in its argument for limited drinking. There has existed by default in employer systems a policy toward alcohol-problem employees which might be characterized as: "We will pay you well and help you cover up poor job performance, absenteeism, etc., for ten to twenty years. When your poor job behavior becomes so severe it cannot be ignored, we will fire you." And, of course in the meantime, the employer pays dearly, the man pays dearly, his family and all of society pay dearly.

The first efforts at the development of programs within companies to reach problem drinkers were begun in the 1940's (Presnell, 1967). These programs were basically pushed by the existing National Council on Alcoholism and its representatives from 1944 to 1959 in some of the larger industrial cities in the country (Presnell, 1967). During this period, the "Yale Plan" for Business and Industry was developed by Bacon and Henderson as a general outline of suggestions on how to deal with alcoholism among employees (Presnell, 1967). From 1944 to 1959, there was no sharp increase in the number of companies who developed alcoholism programs. But even at this early stage, the companies which had developed some form of program were reporting recovery in over 50 percent of those persons who were identified and received treatment. By 1959, it is estimated that approximately fifty companies had developed some type of program (Presnell, 1967). About 1960, the National Council on Alcoholism took stock of what had been learned through early efforts and began looking for new approaches. NCA developed a specific department of industrial services and propagated a combined community organization–management consultation approach which by 1965 had helped increase the number of companies developing new alcoholism programs by 357 percent (Presnell, 1967). Nothing of significance occurred during this time except learning by trial and error, and the growth of a new approach to alcohol problems really began to emerge. Studies done in 1958 and 1968 by the National Industrial Conference Board began to sum up the developing knowledge (Habbe, 1970).

National legislation began to give considerable attention to alcohol-related problems, and the first large thrust at the federal level culminated in 1971 with the development of the National Institute of Alcohol Abuse and Alcoholism (NIAAA). Paying heed to the apparent success of some employee alcoholism programs, the NIAAA developed an Occupational Branch to promote program development in the broad area of occupational systems, both public and private. The Occupational Branch, under the leadership of Willard O. Foster surveyed more than three hundred companies with existing programs and found that only twelve could be said to be actually successful and operating efficiently (NIAAA, 1971). The factors responsible for success in these programs were evaluated and a general philosophy of approach began to emerge.

The positive results of these programs was so impressive that a decision was made in 1971 by NIAAA to promote the development of occupational alcoholism programs throughout the country by offering $50,000 to each state with which to hire two consultants to stimulate the development of programs within both public and private industry at the state level. Recognizing that the best available knowledge in philosophy and approach to accomplish the task rested in a few individuals and was scattered throughout the country and that the persons who would be hired in the states would not necessarily possess the needed knowledge and would actually be embarking on a totally new professional endeavor, another decision was made to require that the new state occupational consultants undergo an intensive training experience. A training grant was awarded in 1972 to the School of Allied Health and Social Professions and the Division of Continuing Education at East Carolina University to develop and provide the training (Byrd, Lotterhos and Waldrop, 1972).

In developing curriculum for this training program, experts from across the country representing the most up-to-date concepts in occupational programming were brought together by NIAAA to consult with the training staff from the university. One week was spent in clarifying the proposed role of the new consultants and in making decisions regarding curriculum content for the training program. The training program was then finalized by the East Carolina University staff and was to provide a total of six weeks of training, with an initial three-week training session in the summer of 1972 and three one-week follow-up training sessions to be held 1972-1974.

In the spring of 1972, the grants to respective states were awarded, with all but a few states accepting the challenge. The initial three-week training session was held in Pinehurst, North Carolina in June, 1972, with a total of 112 trainees representing most of the states and territories in attendance, and the "Thunderin' Hundred" as the new occupational program consultants soon came to be known, were on their way. The second training session was held in November, 1972. Initial evaluation reports of these first training sessions have been concluded and the results indicate a high degree of success in reaching the objectives of the program and providing necessary knowledge to the new consultants (Baler and Edwards, 1973). These consultants represent a tremendous investment in the propagation of sound knowledge and expertise in the development of occupational alcoholism programs. They are available as consultants to both public and private industry who desire their assistance in the development of this type of program. In some states, further program development has occurred with added personnel to assist the consultants. Indications are that these consultants are having considerable impact in promoting the development of employee assistance programs.

The Basic Ingredients of Occupational Programs

The early alcoholism programs which related to occupational systems suffered from some of the same attitudes, thinking and problems outlined in the earlier part of this chapter which have characterized the approach to this problem area in our general society. The tendency to view drinking problems only in light of the skid row perspective of the alcoholic and the fact that employers and employees alike (being members of this culture) share some of the same denial and coverup processes described earlier have represented considerable barriers to the acceptance of this type programming.

Early efforts to assist companies in the development of these programs often played right into these cultural realities with some negative results, usually placing the supervisor in the role of identifying alcoholic behavior on the job and basically trying to turn him into a diagnostician of illness, a chore which he both rejected and for which he was not prepared. These early efforts to "spot alcoholics on the job" and confront them about their drinking were often feared by the employees, disliked by the unions and received the uncomplimentary label of "witch-hunting." More than this, these efforts were also ineffective in identifying problems before they became severe, since the supervisor's perception of the "problem" was also tainted by the cultural image of the chronic alcoholic as representing the problem. Based on the concept of the Labeling Theory outlined earlier, it is easy to see the supervisor feeling considerable ambivalence in confronting one of his men about his drinking behavior. The end result of this approach was that company programs wound up relating only to the chronic cases of alcoholism.

Since the basic idea was to identify problems at an earlier stage to enhance the potentiality of full recovery and job maintenance, new approaches were sought. Efforts were made to engage the supervisor in training to provide him with knowledge of what were thought to be some early signs of a developing problem, such as absenteeism, moodiness, tardiness, etc. While it may be quite true that these signs could represent a developing alcohol problem, it was also true that they might represent other problems and this put the supervisor in an even more precarious position as a diagnostician. Out of these mistakes, however, came the understanding that the supervisor simply cannot diagnose behavior disorders. This knowledge was a real step forward in understanding and developing a more reasonable and proper role for supervisors. Today, the role of the supervisor is still considered to be the key to any successful occupational program (Lotterhos and Waldrop, 1972). The supervisor is asked to simply monitor job performance which has always been a significant portion of his job. By being sensitive to the employee's job performance and following appropriate confronting processes, he can be brought to a point of dealing with his problem whether it be an alcohol problem or some other problem (financial, emotional, family, etc.) which is having a negative effect on his job performance. Viewing the supervisor's role in this fashion implies that adding a troubled employee program to a company actually does nothing to change his role, but rather adds incentive to being a good supervisor since doing so is the best way to help prevent the downward spiral of such employee problems as alcohol abuse. Furthermore, this takes the uncomfortable role of diagnostician away from the supervisor and has the added bonus that by monitoring job performance, any behavioral problem affecting an employee will be handled. In considering the proper role of a supervisor in a program, Habbe (1970) offers several guidelines:

1. It is a supervisor's job to deal with personnel problems as well as production problems.
2. A confrontation with a worker who is falling down on his job should be in terms of job performance, not his personal habits or characteristics.
3. There is a better chance of obtaining positive results if action is initiated well before the situation has deteriorated to the point where suspension or discharge of the worker seem to be the only alternative.

Another consideration is offered that the supervisor should not attempt to counsel an employee with a behavioral or health problem, but should make a referral to the proper associated health, medical or counseling section of the company.

In considering the development of thinking and understanding that monitoring job performance as a mechanism of identifying behavior problems actually began to result in the identification of more early stage alcohol abusers (Habbe, 1970), it is worth noting that NIAAA published a position paper in 1972 supporting the notion of a "broadbrush" approach in employee systems which would include alcohol problems as only one of a number of problems that might be encountered (NIAAA, 1972). By deemphasizing alcoholism-centered program approaches, it is felt that the old stigma attached to the terms "alcoholic" or "alcoholism" can be avoided. Results seem to indicate that based on the approach outlined, indeed it can be expected that more problem drinkers will be identified in the early stage. It can generally be expected that about 50 percent of identified problems will be alcohol-related in such a program.

Having looked at some of the specific problems faced historically in the development of these programs, a general view of the philosophy which an occupational system can embody in such a program will be given. It is not intended that this will represent any hard and fast set of guidelines as each company is different; however, these general ideas should be helpful to anyone interested in developing such a program. Other authors in this book will present more specific information and more detailed examples of specific programs.

Several very general principles should be kept in mind when an employee assistance program is being considered. First, it is a reality that at least 3 to 5 percent of any work force will have alcohol-related problems. It is also true that perhaps another 3 percent will have other problems which effect job performance. These problems cost the employer and employee in many ways. It has been established that one of the primary reasons chronic alcoholism and other chronic behavior problems develop in our culture is due to the failure of adequately developed social response mechanisms which confront these problems at a point in the earlier stage of their development. It is recognized and has been demonstrated effectively that the context of the work world, within the established employer-employee contract offers an ideal point of departure for the early confrontation and identification of behavioral problems within the context of job performance. The purpose of such a program is to combine sound management principles with a humanitarian approach which will assist troubled employees and prevent the development of serious behavior problems.

It should be recognized that behavior problems and especially alcohol-related problems are no respecter of position within an employee system. These problems are as likely to develop in management and executive ranks as they are in lower-level line workers. Any program then, to be effective, should be a "total" company program and should be accepted by and implemented within all management levels.

Another consideration is the need for a cooperative approach by management and the union in both the development and implementation of an employee assistance program. Only if the company and the union fully accept the proposition that a strong alcohol program with early confrontation of declining job performance is in the individual's best interest can mutual cooperation be expected (Habbe, 1970). These programs are pro-people, not pro-labor or management.

The first activity which should be considered by a company is the establishment of a policy statement which clearly states the intention, commitment and philosophy of the program. A written policy statement is a functional device in beginning to dispel the old, unwritten policy of denial and coverup which characterizes our past.

Another consideration is the provision of an educational or training program for appropriate persons within the company. This training, while providing good information about behavior problems and their effect on the work situation, should be geared to give the supervisor a rationale based on an understanding of the progressive nature of behavior problems, which will enable him to act quickly and without undue hesitation in confronting deteriorating job performance. This type of training can enhance the potential of getting such a program off the ground.

The key ingredient of the effectiveness and success of such a program is within the context of the immediate interaction of the supervisor and employee. The supervisor is the key to the implementation of such a program. The supervisor simply confronts poor job performance and makes a proper referral to the counseling or medical department where appropriate persons can assist in understanding the problem. Communications between the supervisor and counseling department can assist in better handling of the problem in many instances.

A final, very important general consideration is the treatment and service resources available to identified troubled employees on a confidential basis. Obviously, it is necessary to have a wide variety of available types of assistance or treatment including such things as counseling and medical services. In a troubled employee assistance program, a variety of problems aside from those which are alcohol-related will be identified and help must be made available. Some companies which have adopted these programs have established a unit within the organization known as an "employee counseling or assistance service." Where these exist, they represent the point of referral by a supervisor for a person whose job performance is deteriorating. This counseling unit may be located either in the medical or personnel section or by itself. While location is not important, its proper function is greatly desired and is enhanced by being staffed with competent social behavior counselors who are aware and can make referral to necessary other service resources. In such an operation as this, what appears to gradually occur is that the employees soon learn to make self-referrals, especially when they understand the service is aimed at helping and is confidential. While the counseling service does not provide all treatment resources, it does make referral. In a few larger companies, there exist in-house resources; however, few smaller companies could possibly afford these services. Therefore, the successful implementation of such a program by one or several companies in a community obviously has tremendous implications for community health and service resources. There are questions raised as to the implications of these early identification programs for existing community services, especially in relation to alcohol-related problems since many existing services have typically shied away from these problems. At any rate, treatment or help, whatever it is, must be provided in such a fashion as to be acceptable to the person. There is some question as to whether existing services for alcoholics, which are geared to the chronic case, are acceptable to persons with lesser problems.

Companies must adopt a stance of concern for their employees, yet one reality must be clearly stated. The employee must understand that job termination is a possible consequence of his not taking proper action to improve his work behavior. It is only by firmly and wisely applying this principle that sound management practices can be maintained and a true atmosphere of effective confrontation can be established. This assures maximum success and is a must in any employee assistance program. It is possible that job discontinuation itself is sometimes the necessary confrontation to begin to bring about behavior change. To sum up, the following general elements of any program are seen as necessary to maximize its potential for success (Lotterhos and Waldrop, 1972):

1. There must be a company policy and procedure which is developed and supported by both management and labor.
2. There must be a clear understanding by the supervisor of his proper role in monitoring poor job performance and making quick referral for assistance when necessary.
3. There must be consistency in dealing with problems at all levels of the work force from top management downward.
4. Supervisors need training in their proper role and need to be provided with a rationale so they can understand how implementing the program will be helpful to the employee and the company.
5. Confidentiality should be assured all employees.
6. A company should take a neutral stand on the decision to drink alcohol and should remain concerned only about job performance.
7. Treatment resources either within the company or available in the community must be available and acceptable to the employee with a problem.

The program should bring the employee to the point of facing his poor work performance, with the decision to seek treatment left up to him. In this way, the company assures the person the right to make his own personal decision and maintains a company orientation to the problem only as it affects job performance. Proper referral by the company to appropriate resources for help can be accomplished by an in-house counseling office. The maintenance of confidentiality in the handling of job performance problems can help create an atmosphere of trust and perhaps more willingness on the part of employees to become self-referrals. The company must stand behind the employee in this process in a supportive, but firm manner. A company has every right to expect proper job performance. When the above elements of philosophy and procedure are incorporated by a company, they should create a set of circumstances through which early identification of poor job performance results in motivation to seek help or treatment.

The general approach outlined briefly here, offers great hope that we have developed at least a beginning understanding that

man's social behavioral problems arise out of his social interactions and circumstances and that we can take positive action
steps to identify these problems early, within the gut level
structure of our society—the work force. There are many questions concerning such issues as how small companies accomplish
these programs, how public employee programs differ from
private (if at all), what are the real implications of these
programs for community treatment services. Perhaps too much a
fantasy to say that these programs can represent an approach—a
beginning to a recognition that a positive combined private,
public and community health approach to man's problems within
the context of his everyday life can become a reality.

REFERENCES

Babbitt, H. H.: What does it cost to be an alcoholic? In Pittman, D. J.
(Ed.): *Alcoholism.* New York, Harper & Row, 1967.

Bacon, S. D.: Alcohol and complex society. In Pittman, D. J., and Snyder,
C. R. (Eds.): *Society, Culture and Drinking Patterns.* New York, Wiley,
1962.

Bacon, S. D.: Drug abuse and alcohol abuse: The social problem perspective.
*Prosecuter, 5:*32-36, 1969.

Baler, L. A., and Edwards, D. W.: Evaluation reports of the National
Occupational Alcoholism Consultants Training Program (Unpublished
report), 1973.

Belasco, J. A.; Trice, H. M., and Ritzer, G.: The role of the union in
industrial alcoholism programs. *Addictions, 16:*13-29, 1969.

Byrd, W. C.; Lotterhos, J. F., and Waldrop, J. H.: *National Occupational
Alcoholism Training Program.* NIAAA Grant to East Carolina University, Greenville, North Carolina.

Cahalan, D.: *Problem Drinkers: A National Survey.* San Francisco, Jossey-
Bass, 1970.

Cahalan, D.: News release, *Raleigh News and Observer.* Raleigh, North
Carolina, July, 1973.

Cahalan, D.; Cisin, I. H., and Crossley, Helen: *American Drinking Practices:
A National Study of Drinking Behavior and Attitudes.* New Haven
College and University Press, 1969.

Chafetz, M. E.: Alcoholism prevention and reality. *Quart J Stud Alcohol,
28:*345-348, 1967.

Chafetz, M. E.: *Liquor: The Servant of Man.* Boston, Little, Brown, 1965.

Chafetz, M. E.; Blane, H. T., and Hill, M. J.: *Frontiers of Alcoholism.* New York, Science House, 1970.

Chandler, G.: *An Effective Program to Combat Alcoholism in Industry.* Speech delivered at National Occupational Alcoholism Training Institute, 1972.

Comptroller General of the United States: *Substantial Cost Savings from Establishment for Federal Civilian Employees,* 1970.

Conner, R. G.: The self-concepts of alcoholics. In Pittman, D. J., and Snyder, C. R. (Eds.): *Society, Culture and Drinking Patterns.* New York, Wiley, 1962.

Dancy, D. R.: *Cultural Aspects of Alcoholism.* Paper presented at Third Annual West Virginia School of Alcohol Studies, West Virginia Department of Mental Health, Charleston, 1967.

Department of Health, Education and Welfare: *Alcohol and Health.* DHEW, 1971.

Edwards, G.: Place of treatment professions in society's response to chemical abuse. *Brit Med J, 2*:195-199, 1970.

Falk, G.: The contribution of the alcohol culture to alcoholism in America. *Brit J Addict, 65*:9-17, 1970.

Franco, S. C.: Problem drinking in industry. *Quart J Stud Alcohol, 15*:453-468, 1954.

Fraser, F.: Drinking and mass education. *Canada's Mental Health, 15*:30-32, 1967.

Glatt, M. M.: Alcoholism and drug dependence amongst Jews. *Brit J Addict, 64*:297-304, 1970.

Gusfield, J. R.: Status conflicts and the changing ideologies of the American temperance movement. In Pittman, D. J., and Snyder, C. R. (Eds.): *Society, Culture and Drinking Patterns.* New York, Wiley, 1962.

Habbe, S.: *Company Controls for Drinking Problems.* New York, National Industrial Conference Board, 1970.

Hughes Aircraft Company: *Program for Alcoholism and Related Disorders.* Program policy statement, 1971.

Jellinek, E. M.: *The Disease Concept of Alcoholism.* New Haven, Hillhouse Press, 1960.

Kammer, M. E., and Dupong, W. G.: Alcohol problems: Study by Industrial Medical Department. *NY State J Med, 69*:3105-3110, 1969.

Kendall, Elaine: *The Happy Mediocrity.* New York, G. P. Putnam's Sons, 1971.

King, A. R.: The alcohol problem in Israel. *Quart J Stud Alcohol, 22*:321-324, 1961.

Lender, M.: Drunkenness as an offense in early New England: A study of "Puritan" attitudes. *Quart J Stud Alcohol, 34*:353-365, 1967.

Lerner, J.: Chronic alcoholism: After 30 years, some second thoughts. *J Am Geriatr Soc, 15*:137-141, 1967.

Little, J. W.: Challenges to humanitarian legal approaches for eliminating the hazards of drunk alcoholic drivers. *Georgia Law Review, 4*:251-297, 1970.

Lookout, M. F.: *Alcoholism programs with emphasis on implementation.* Paper presented at Third Annual West Virginia School of Alcohol Studies, West Virginia Department of Mental Health, Charleston, 1967.

Lofland, J.: *Deviance and Identity.* Englewood Cliffs, Prentice-Hall, 1969.

Lotterhos, J. F., and Waldrop, J. H.: A historical perspective of employee alcoholism programs. *Investory, North Carolina Department of Mental Health, 22*:14-18, 1972.

Maddox, G. L.: *The Nature of Social Problems: The Case of Alcohol Use in the United States.* Athens, University of Georgia Press, 1968.

Maurer, H.: The beginnng of wisdom about alcoholism. *Fortune,* 1968.

Maxwell, M. A.: Early identification of problem drinkers in industry. *Quart J Stud Alcohol, 21*:655-678, 1960.

Moore, R. A.: Alcoholism in Japan. *Quart J Stud Alcohol, 25*:142-150, 1964.

Mulford, H.: *Meeting the Problems of Alcohol Abuse.* Cedar Rapids, Iowa Alcoholism Foundation, 1970.

Mulford, H., and Miller. D. E.: An index of alcoholic drinking behavior related to the meanings of alcohol. *J Health Human Behav, 2*:26-31, 1961.

National Institute of Alcohol Abuse and Alcoholism: *Occupational Alcoholism: Some Problems and Some Solutions.* NIAAA, 1972.

Orr, M.: Business and the compulsive drinker. *Addictions, 19*:39-43, 1972.

Pell, S., and Alonzo, C. A.: Sickness and absenteeism of alcoholics. *Journal of Occupational Medicine, 12*:192-210, 1970.

Presnell, G.: Folklore and fact about employees with alcoholism. *J Occup Med, 9*:87-94, 1967.

Pritchit, S. T.: *A Study of Some Measurable Consequences of the Problem Drinker.* Virginia Polytechnic Institute, 1967.

Reader, D. H.: Alcoholism and excessive drinking: A sociological review. *Psychologia Africana Monographs, 3*:1-69, 1967.

Reinert, R. E.: Alcoholism: Disease or habit. *Federal Probation, 32*:12-15, 1968.

Roman, P. M., and Trice, H. M.: The sick role, Labelling theory, and the deviant drinker. *International J Soc Psychiatry, 14*:249-251, 1968.

————: *Spirits and Demons at Work: Alcohol and Other Drugs on the Job.* Ithaca, New York State School of Industrial and Labor Relations, 1972.

Rubington, T.: Failure as a heavy drinker: The case of the chronic drunkness offender on Skid Row. In Pittman, D. J., and Snyder, C. R. (Eds.): *Society, Culture and Drinking Patterns.* New York, Wiley, 1962.

Saint, E. G.: Alcohol and society, *Med J Aust,* 2:69-76, 1969.

Schur, E. M.: *Labelling Deviant Behavior: Its Sociological Consequences.* New York, Harper & Row, 1971.

Seeley, J. R.: Alcoholism is a disease: Implications for social policy. In Pittman, D. J., and Snyder, C. R. (Eds.): *Society, Culture and Drinking Patterns.* New York, Wiley, 1962.

Shilo, B. F.: Olechenii limonnym sokom khronicheskikh alkogobikov. (On the treatment of chronic alcoholics with lemon juice). *Z dravookr Belorurss,* 7:54-55, 1961.

Simmons, O. G.: The sociocultural integration of alcohol use: A Peruvian study. *Quart J Stud Alcohol,* 29:152-171, 1968.

Snyder, C. R.: Studies of drinking in Jewish culture. *Quart J Stud Alcohol,* 17:124-143, 1956.

Steiner, C. M.: The alcoholic game. *Quart J Stud Alcohol,* 30:920-938, 1969.

Strachon, J. G.: *Practical Alcoholism Programming.* Vancouver, Mitchell Press, 1971.

Trice, H. M., and Belasco, J. A.: Supervisory training about alcoholics and other problem employees: A controlled evaluation. *Quart J Stud Alcohol,* 29:382-398, 1968.

Ward, R. F., and Faillace, L. R.: The alcoholic and his helpers: A system view. *Quart J Stud Alcohol,* 31:684-691, 1970.

Williams, R. M.: *American Society.* New York, Alfred Knopf, 1970.

Winslow, W. W.; Hayes, K.; Prentice, L.; Powles, W. E.; Seeman, W., and Ross, W. D.: Some economic estimates of job disruption. *Arch Environ Health,* 13:213-219, 1966.

Warkov, S.; Bacon, S. D., and Hawkins, A. C.: Social correlates of industrial problem drinking. *Quart J Stud Alcohol,* 26:58-71, 1965.

Chapter 2

THE EVALUATION OF TROUBLED-EMPLOYEE AND OCCUPATIONAL ALCOHOLISM PROGRAMS

Daniel W. Edwards, MP.H., Ph.D.

This chapter was written with an eye to many different groups who have an interest in Occupational Alcoholism Programs. It is hoped that this chapter will be useful for executives in industry and labor responsible for the development of occupational alcoholism or troubled-employee programs, for those who implement and have direct responsibility for the day-to-day operations of programs, for the outside or state consultant trying to encourage employers to develop programs (especially the Thunderin' Hundred), for the consumers and general public who ultimately pay for and receive the benefits of programs, and for the researcher charged with developing an evaluation of a program.

Certain beliefs are held by the author and are partially supported by material in this chapter. They are derived from the literature cited here and from several years' experience in the area of program evaluation and applied clinical research in the mental health area. An effort will be made to substantiate or offer evidence for each of these in the following sections:

1. *If your program is doing some people some good, it is probably doing other people some harm.*
2. *Evaluation efforts and data collection can and should be an integral part of any treatment or referral program.*
3. *Rigorous and controlled evaluations are required but usually have to evolve as program personnel first become used to descriptive data, then pre-post comparisons, and finally controlled evaluative studies.*
4. *Evaluation efforts serve many purposes and both explicit and implicit goals of evaluation should be considered by all parties concerned with programs.*

5. *Models do exist for the evaluation of applied programs.*
6. *Measures do exist which can be systematically utilized to gain indications of program outcome.*
7. *Employers may have to require the evaluation of treatment programs to insure that employees are getting the assistance contracted for.*
8. *Much more stress can and should be placed on preventive programs by employers.*
9. *Good information is needed on the numbers of employees with a drinking problem who improve solely through supervisory confrontation.*
10. *More information is needed on the casualties of existing treatment and referral programs.*

BROADBRUSH, TROUBLED-EMPLOYEE AND OCCUPATIONAL ALCOHOLISM PROGRAMS

T HIS PAPER IS emphasizing Broadbrush or troubled-employee programs over defined occupational alcoholism programs for several reasons. First, a broad-scale attack on "human problems" in the work force appeals to the author's biases in favor of comprehensive community mental health. It makes more sense to try and attack all related problems rather than to focus on one. Just as the schools are viewed as an ideal location for primary prevention of mental health problems for children and adolescents, the workplace is an ideal location for establishing primary prevention programs for adults. A large portion of the adult population is in the workforce and spends a considerable amount of time in the work place. Secondly, the National Institute on Alcohol Abuse and Alcoholism (NIAAA, 1972) notes that they are emphasizing a Broadbrush approach since it does not have the stigma which often accompanies a labeled alcoholism program. They maintain that up to 50 percent of problem employees referred to a Broadbrush program have a drinking problem. NIAAA feels that a Broadbrush approach will yield the highest penetration into the population of those with alcohol problems. Thirdly, while the etiology of various types of drinking problems is not clear, it is known that many types of problems and pressures can lead to problem drinking. Problem drinking may begin as a way of handling job stress, marital problems, etc., then become habitual and maladaptive. In cases such as these a Broadbrush approach instructs one to focus not just on cessation of damaging drinking patterns, but also on other life problems which may be playing a causative role in the deviant drinking behavior. Lastly, a Broadbrush approach should result in a more efficient use of resources and a coordinated attack on human problems even if the major emphasis, as with NIAAA, is alcoholism. There is evidence that a substantial number of other types of problems may be resolved with a Broadbrush approach.

Some data is available on the types of referrals a Broadbrush program might receive. The writer had the opportunity to help evaluate a training program for U.A.W. Community Service Workers from one county in Michigan in 1972. While the basic training was on referral practices, counseling techniques and referral sources, data was collected to ascertain the volume of contacts with employees and number of referrals being handled by these persons. Twenty-three community service workers were asked to indicate how many individuals they had seen in the last month in each of seven problem categories. They were asked to count each individual only once in the area of major concern. Table 2-I shows the tabulated responses for this group. These workers average over twenty contacts per month in the

TABLE 2-I

WORKER CONTACTS BY UAW COMMUNITY
SERVICE WORKERS (SPRING 1972)

Problem Category	Month Before Training*		Last Month of Training*	
	N	%	N	%
1. Personal (Psychological Problems)	83	20	96	18
2. Marital Problems	34	8	39	7
3. Problems with Children	41	10	44	8
4. Drug and Alcohol Problems	77	19	90	17
5. Medical and Health Problems	76	19	118	22
6. Consumer Problems	53	13	47	9
7. Welfare or Social Security Problems	44	11	112	21
Totals	408	100	546	100
Number of Referrals (outside agency)	93	23	124	23

* 23 Community Service Workers

seven categories listed. The reader will note that drug and alcohol problems (they were listed together in this study) accounted for 19 percent and 17 percent of the major problem areas reported. If persons with problems in any area who also had a drinking problem had been counted then the percentage for alcohol and drug problems may have equaled or exceeded the 66 percent figure reported by Chandler (1972) for the Hughes Aircraft program.

In addition to the immediate counseling provided employees by the Community Service Workers, in both months 23 percent were referred to outside agencies for specialized help. When the Community Service Workers were asked which problem area they felt they needed the most information in (both at the beginning and end of training), the drug and alcohol area was listed most frequently.

NIAAA has promoted the Broadbrush concept because of indications that penetration rates may be much greater than with more traditional occupational alcoholism programs. The experience of Hughes Aircraft (Chandler, 1972) and Kennecott Copper (Jones, 1972) would seem to support this view although there is a lack of hard data at this time. Two points seem important here and in support of a Broadbrush approach over a more traditional "constructive confrontation" program. First, Kennecott Copper reports a large number of voluntary referrals to its program. This may mean that more problem drinkers can be reached and helped before the problem drinking becomes habitual and of a job-threatening nature. Trice (1962) reports that a survey of Alcoholic Anonymous (AA) members reported a history of ten years of problem drinking before they sought help or found sobriety. An approach which gets help to people sooner is to be preferred.

Secondly, a Broadbrush program approach provides help to employees for any type of personal problem. This means that many who would not receive help from an occupational alcoholism program could be helped to resolve the personal problems they face. If problem drinking which interferes with job performance is symptomatic of other unresolved problems for a proportion of the work force, then a Broadbrush approach, if it delivers effective help, would truly be a preventive program for problem drinking.

Thus, the major arguments in favor of a Broadbrush approach are its ability to give help to more troubled persons in the work force, its potential for earlier detection and arrest of problem drinking, and finally, its preventive potential in helping employees resolve problems before they adopt continual inebriation as a solution of their difficulties.

THE NATURE OF THE PROBLEM

Alcoholism and problem drinking are regarded by some as a progressive addictive disease which can only be arrested by attaining and maintaining a state of sobriety. The experience of AA and the testimonials by many members of this fellowship would seem to support this view for a certain proportion of the population. Others see alcoholism as a symptomatic response which represents the maladaptive resolution of other problems. Another view would argue that problem drinking is a learned response and is best handled by teaching the individual to better discriminate stages of inebriation and build internal controls. There are other views and all probably have some truth in them for some group or proportion of the problem drinking population.

Perhaps the one certain fact about the nature of alcoholism is that the causes are not yet known or understood. It is known that alcoholism is treatable in many cases and can be arrested and in some instances (Gottheil, 1973; Pattison, Headley, Glesser and Gottschalk, 1965) the individual can return to "normal" drinking.

Another area of agreement between individuals concerned with alcoholism is that the problem is large, involving perhaps 5 percent of the population of the United States (NIAAA, 1971). NIAAA estimates that there are probably nine million problem drinkers in the nation and that six million are in the work force or dependents of workers. A solid basis for arriving at these estimates and concise and well-defined criteria for what constitutes problem drinking are issues which are still not resolved.

Perhaps the best source of information on the drinking practices and problems of Americans is a series of surveys by Cahalan and his associates. A recent article (Cahalan and Room, 1972) summarizes the results of these surveys in terms of "Problem Drinking Among American Men Aged 21-59." The results of this informative and provocative summary of three nationwide surveys are reviewed here.

Cahalan and his colleages used an inclusive definition of problem drinking. The repetitive use of alcohol which results in physical, psychological or social harm to the drinker or others is the definition taken from Plaut (1967) and others as a starting point. In the survey, thirteen indices are used to assess potential severity of the problem if it exists. These indices include "Heavy Intake," "Binge Drinking," "Problems on the Job," "Policy Problem," "Finances," etc.

In their survey they developed scores for each individual which indicate whether he had no problem, a problem of minimal severity, or a problem of "higher severity" for each of the thirteen indices. The investigators also tried to differentiate current problems (in the last three years) from whether or not the person had ever had a problem in this area. This look at both current and historical events provide one of the most interesting findings of the study.

For example, for the index of heavy intake, 24 percent are rated to have a problem of at least "minimal severity" and 13 percent of these people fall into the "higher severity" category. When asked if this was ever a problem, the investigators found that 41 percent had had at least a minimally severe problem and 26 percent fell into the "higher severity" category.

The item concerned with problems on the job showed similar but lower percentages. The current problem category showed 10 percent judged to have a problem of minimal severity while 6 percent had a problem of higher severity. The historical question (if ever a problem) showed 21 percent had a minimally severe problem while 13 percent had the problem at a higher level of severity. Note that twice as many people report having had the problem at some time as compared to those who currently have the problem. The major conclusion is that a large proportion of people move into and out of the problem drinking population in a three-year period.

A second finding which has implications for this chapter is that problem drinking was consistently found to be the highest in the younger age group (twenty-one to twenty-four years) and to decrease over time. This finding does not agree with the occupational literature where the majority of the problem drinkers are typically found in the forty to sixty age bracket. A look at the percentages provided by Cahalan and Room (1972) for the index "Problem on the Job" in part explains this contradictory finding. While 10 percent of the twenty-one to twenty-four-year-old group are judged to have higher severity problems, the percentage drops considerably for the next two age groups (twenty-five to twenty-nine, 4%; thirty to thirty-four, 3%). However, the percentages again rise for the next four groups with a sharp drop for the fifty-five to fifty-nine age group (age thirty-five to thirty-nine, 5%; forty to forty-four, 5%; forty-five to forty-nine, 5%; fifty to fifty-four, 6%; fifty-five to fifty-nine, 2%). The uniform trend for decreasing problems with age seems in part due to generally higher scores for the twenty-five to thirty-nine year-old groups on "belligerence" and "problems with wife." It is very interesting that the proportions (excluding the twenty-one to twenty-four age group) run between 3 and 6 percent for severe problems on the job (average of 4.3%) which is in the mid-range of estimates from different occupational alcoholism programs.

What are the implications of Cahalan and Room's (1972) report? First, if it is true that large numbers of persons move into and out of the severe problem drinking category every three years, then industrial alcoholism programs cannot take credit for all improvement observed. This is especially true for those three, four and five-year follow-up studies. The "success" of occupational programs is going to have to be based on the fact that more workers moved out of the problem drinking category quicker than they would have otherwise, and that those who might have become addicted (when and if they can be identified) were helped to achieve controlled drinking or sobriety. A treatment program cannot take credit for improvement which was not a result of its efforts. Obviously, much more information is required on natural successes and failures of problem drinkers and on the time it takes various types of people in varied situations to move out of the problem drinking category.

The second implication is that, at least to date, the group with the highest proportion of severe problem drinkers (age twenty-one to twenty-four) is the group least reached by the traditional occupational alcoholism program. Perhaps this must be, given the low company investment, the high job mobility, and perhaps a certain cultural sanction for youth "kicking up its heels." But perhaps some modifications can be made in programs to reach this group which has the highest health and injuries problems from drinking and probably the highest fatal accident rate (NIAAA, 1971).

Another relevant paper is "Alcoholism as a Self-Limiting Disease" (Drew, 1968). This paper looks at data from Victoria, Australia and examines epidemiological data cited in eighteen other studies from various nations (including the U.S.). Data on inpatients and outpatients, on acute complications (i.e. alcoholic psychoses), on drunken driving, and on "Official Action" (i.e. public intoxication) leads Drew to conclude that alcoholism is not a progressive irreversible condition. The author concludes that in all instances, the absolute number of alcoholics reached a maximum before fifty and then rapidly tapers off. He admits that the higher mortality of alcoholics probably account for part of the decline, but feels that "spontaneous recovery" probably accounts for a significant proportion of the observed decrease.

Again, the major implication of this article is that a certain proportion of individuals may move out of the problem drinking population without the benefit of treatment. If this is true, then a treatment program must consider this fact in evaluating the impact of its methods. It will require looking at how quickly the person in a program recovers instead of only whether or not he recovers. It certainly requires that more data be gathered on the problem drinker who does not receive treatment and his outcome.

THE NATURE OF THE INDUSTRIAL PROBLEM

Several general articles exist on Alcoholism in Industry (Norris, 1968; Presnall, 1967; Raleigh, 1968; Sadler and Horst, 1972; Smith, 1957). These articles are of a general nature and discuss approaches, types of treatment, basic facts and fallacies, and provide a general overview of problem drinking in industry and how the problem is being attacked. Perhaps the best single reference on occupational alcoholism programs is a report of a study done by The National Industrial Conference Board called *Company Controls for Drinking Problems* (Habbe, 1969). This report summarizes information provided by several hundred companies and is filled with illustrations of different programs and solutions which have been developed. The National Council on Alcoholism is also a good source of up-to-date information and currently produces a *Labor-Management Alcoholism Newsletter* on a bimonthly basis. The National Council on Alcoholism (1970) estimates that in 1968 the national prevalence of alcoholism was 5.3 percent. In five industries which have relatively good statistics the estimated prevalence ranges from 4 to 10 percent of the work force.

Different companies have varying figures for estimating the size of the problem drinking population in the work force. Eastman Kodak uses a 3 percent figure in an information brochure for employees as did Franco (1957) when analyzing data from the Consolidated Edison Company. Jones (1972) reports a 5 to 10 percent estimate for a heavy industry like Kennecott Copper. The Burlington Northern uses a 10 percent figure (Vaughan, 1973). It is generally agreed that the estimates apply across the board to both labor and management although most operational programs have been oriented more towards helping the blue-collar worker.

Seven papers were found which present salient information on various facets of alcohol abuse in industry. These studies range from looking at sickness-absenteeism, to behavior on the job, to estimating the cost of problem drinking to the company, to early identification, and a theoretical paper on "risk factors" which seem to contribute to or increase the risk of developing a problem-drinking pattern. In examining these studies the data are interpreted in terms of measures of effectiveness and efficiency, findings of the study, and implications for the evaluation of troubled employee programs.

The Costs of Industrial Problem Drinking
(Pell and D'Alonzo (1970)

Pell and D'Alonzo (1970) look at the "costs" of problem drinking by examining sickness-absenteeism and other indices. They report on a study of 764 alcoholic persons and 863 "normal" controls employed by DuPont. The study was started in 1964 and while a variety of health problems are examined, the major contribution may be the measures which were developed and applied to the study group. A wide variety of measures of sickness-absenteeism are used in the available literature and there seem to be no common definitions. One of the major problems in comparing various studies is this lack of common definitions. Pell and D'Alonzo provide three measures which could be adopted as standard measures of sickness-absenteeism. They use rates which can be computed for any given standard period (a month, a year, etc.). The first is called Frequency Rate. It is defined as: Frequency Rate = Number of sickness absences/ Number of persons. This rate allows one to compute the relative number of absences per person in a given group and different groups can then be compared (i.e. an alcoholic group versus the total plant population).

The second rate is called the Disability Rate. This rate is defined as: Disability Rate = Number of days of disability/ Number of persons. This rate goes beyond number of incidents to look at the average number of days of disability for a given group. Groups can then be compared on a before-after basis or with other groups to get a picture of the effects of a treatment program or the differences between varied groups.

The third rate is called Severity Rate. This is defined as:

Severity Rate = Number of days of disability/Number of sickness-absences. This rate yields the average number of days per absence for a given group. The average severity per person in a group can be obtained by dividing the Severity Rate by the number of persons in the group.

FINDINGS. Four groups were looked at in this study. The alcoholic group was divided into the known alcoholics, suspected alcoholics and recovered alcoholics. For each person admitted to the study a matched control person was selected (matching was done by age, sex, payroll class and geographic area). Three measures of sickness absenteeism are developed; Frequency Rate, Disability Rate and Severity Rate. Age distributions showed the majority of the "alcoholic" sample to fall in the forty to fifty-nine age group (79%). While it is noted that absenteeism is higher for all alcoholic groups, a significant number have no problem here. Out of 764 alcoholics in the sample, 37.8 percent had no sickness-absenteeism, and a total of 422 (55%) had reasonably good attendance for the year of the study. Average number of days of disability per person was 19.4 days for the "known, uncontrolled" alcoholics, 10.8 days for the "suspected" group, 11.7 days for the "recovered" group and 5.8 among the controls.

No cost figures are cited though it is pointed out that the "known, uncontrolled" alcoholic, on the average, has fourteen more days of disability or sickness-absenteeism than the control group.

IMPLICATIONS. Three major contributions may be found in this article. The most important is that sickness-absenteeism may be represented by three separate rates which isolate different elements of absenteeism. If these measures were adopted across the country, it would allow comparison in different situations and increase the comparability of different studies.

The second contribution is the provision of actual figures on absenteeism for the different normative groups. The various "alcoholic" groups have absenteeism rates which are two, three and four times as great as the normal population depending on which group is examined.

The third contribution is the reporting on the numbers and percentages of those in the "alcoholic" group who do not show an absenteeism problem. That 55 percent of the sample had reasonably good attendance shows the weakness of this variable and highlights the fact that other measures are needed to assess program outcome or the extent of the problem.

Job Behavior of Problem Drinkers
(Trice, 1967)

This second report combines the results from questionnaire surveys and interviews in two studies. Over 750 male members of AA were surveyed. The major goal of the studies was to gain some concrete information about the effects of excessive drinking on job performance.

Five areas were queried: work efficiency, absenteeism, coverup of drinking, job turnover and work accidents. These are important areas to assess for any occupational alcoholism or troubled employee program. In addition, the type of occupation, the amount of job freedom, and off-the-job drinking practices with fellow employees were also assessed. Unfortunately, the outcome measures are not detailed in this article.

FINDINGS. The author reports a consensus on the fact that work efficiency declined. However, lower status job occupants tended to be absent while in higher status positions the men came to work in poor condition and functioned as "half-men." Coverup of drinking was associated with a high degree of job freedom while in highly supervised positions absenteeism seemed the rule. A major surprise was the low reporting of work accidents.

IMPLICATIONS. The results of this study suggest that type of occupation and different social forces effect the course of development of alcoholism and the types of problems the problem drinker encounters. The author calls for further study of the different roles job factors, organizational factors and peer group factors have in the development of occupational alcoholism.

This study also highlights the importance of work performance ratings. It may be that only the individual with the problem is available to rate the quality and quantity of his work performance. It does seem clear that work performance ratings would be a valuable aspect in assessing the outcome of any troubled employee program. In many structured situations the immediate supervisor may be able to provide an independent assessment of work performance.

Alcoholic, Psychotic, Neurotic and "Normal" Employees (Trice, 1965)

This third report compares alcoholic, psychotic, neurotic and "normal" personnel on a number of variables. The study is based on archival data (plant records) and looks at subjects before, during and after diagnosis. A major contribution of this study is its Broadbrush approach and the attempt to uncover the similarities and differences between "types" of problem employees as contrasted with a 1 percent "normal" sample.

This study is a general fact-finding effort to determine the nature, extent and correlates of various problem conditions. For example, in this company of approximately 20,000 employees (estimated from the 1% sample of 204 "normals") there were 388 diagnosed cases of alcoholism, neurosis, or psychosis recorded by the plant's medical department over a four-year period. A 50 percent sample was studied (72 alcoholic, 83 neurotic and 39 psychotic individuals) which indicates that 144 alcoholic, 166 neurotic and 78 psychotic conditions occurred in this 4-year period. Thus in a four-year period the medical department diagnosed about .74 percent of its employees as alcoholic, .83 percent as neurotic, and about .39 percent as psychotic (assuming a work force of 20,000). These figures are much lower than would be expected given other estimates of the prevalence of problem drinking (3 to 10% of the work force at any one time (Presnall, 1967), or the prevalence of psychosis (1 to 2% of the population at any one time (Dohrenwend and Dohrenwend, 1966). The figures do provide an estimate of the treatment load and formal diagnosis that might be expected in the medical department of a large company.

Certain indices used are appropriate for studies of program effectiveness, and the percentages given provide baselines for the four groups under study which might be utilized in other investigations. Absenteeism is looked at in terms of number of days and number of separate incidents. Data is also provided for on-the-job accidents (four types). In terms of serious absenteeism (ten days or more) two years prior to diagnosis, 5 percent of the "normals," 17 percent of the neurotics, 16 percent of the psychotics and 29 percent of the alcoholics were in the serious absenteeism category. During the year before diagnosis, percentages rose with 6 percent of the "normals," 31 percent of the neurotics, 34 percent of the psychotics, and 30 percent of the alcoholics showing absences of ten or more days. In the year of the diagnosis a larger rise was noted for neurotic and psychotic categories: 6 percent for "normals," 83 percent for neurotics, 74 percent for psychotics, and 37 percent for alcoholics. After therapy was recommended or instituted there is a dramatic drop: 7 percent of "normals," 12 percent of neurotics, 13 percent of psychotics, and 15 percent of the alcoholics in the ten days plus absent category.

OUTCOME MEASURES. Incidence of absences, the number of absolute days absent per year, lost time accidents vs. nonlost time accidents, the number of accidents during a five-year period, and data on responsibility and presumed cause of the accident are discussed. In addition, demographic or descriptive data such as age, sex, marital status, type of job, and length of time with the company are reported for the various groups.

IMPLICATIONS. Perhaps the most general implication is that all three types of problem employees are very costly to business, especially at the peak of their illness (i.e. when job performance deteriorates to the point where the medical department is called in). While the lack of a control group makes it impossible to say diagnosis and treatment definitely helped, there are strong implications that it did. The alcoholic group, for example, shows 17 percent of this group moving out of the high absenteeism category.

Another implication lies in the high absenteeism of the "alcoholic" group over the three years prior to diagnosis. The other groups show a rather sudden upsurge in absenteeism shortly before diagnosis. The alcoholic group has high absenteeism in all three years prior to diagnosis. This probably indicates the existence of a long-standing problem. One of the goals of a Broad-brush program approach would be to get help to these individuals earlier in their careers.

A Four-Year Follow-up of Psychiatric Patients in Industry
(Cole and Shupe, 1970)

This is a follow-up study which is not concerned with problem drinkers but does provide some interesting data on other problem employees. An earlier study (four years before) had shown no difference in job performance or the earning of "merit awards" for former psychiatric patients and their matched "normal" controls (a comparison group). Separate breakdowns into psychoneurotic and schizophrenic subgroups showed lower work scores for the schizophrenic group while the psychoneurotic group did not differ from its matched comparison group. This study reports on a four-year follow-up of these same individuals.

OUTCOME MEASURES. A major contribution of this study may be the Work Performance Inventory (WPI) which is discussed. It is said to assess quality and quantity of work, initiative, cooperativeness, and other aspects of job-related behavior. Sickness-absenteeism, on-the-job accidents, visits to the medical clinic, and promotions and demotions are also examined for the four groups.

FINDINGS. This study of different groups does not include any objectives or treatment which would allow estimates of effectiveness. Baselines are provided from a four-year follow-up of neurotic, psychotic and "normal" groups matched for age, education, vocational status and verbal IQ. Both the neurotic and schizophrenic group are found to have a lower proportion of promotions and more medical retirements than the control groups. Both groups are found to have more days of sickness-absenteeism in the four-year period than the controls but for the schizophrenic group, one person accounts for 45 percent of the days lost. When he was removed from the sample (n=32) the schizophrenic group had fewer days absent than their control group. Work performance ratings (6-point scales) continued to show significantly lower ratings for the schizophrenic group while there were no differences for neurotics and their controls. This finding is moderated by the fact that the performance of the schizophrenic group was adequate to the extent of allowing them to maintain their jobs over the four-year period. On-the-job accidents were rare for all groups and neither the schizophrenic nor neurotic groups appeared different than their controls.

Baseline measures can be obtained from promotions and medical retirements. By the end of the four-year period, 29 percent of the schizophrenic group and 47 percent of its comparison group had been promoted. Medical retirements were granted to 16 percent of the schizophrenic and none of the control group in the same period. In the neurotic group, 39 percent had been promoted as compared to 47 percent of their controls. Medical retirements here were 9.8 percent and 1.1 percent respectively.

Job adequacy ratings in three categories (inadequate, average, and superior) showed 22 percent of the schizophrenics and 20 percent of the neurotic group rated inadequate as opposed to 12 percent and 13 percent in respective control groups. Average performance was almost identical (72%, 72%, 72% and 75%) for the four groups.

IMPLICATIONS. This study has shown that while there are some differences between psychiatric groups and matched controls in general, these differences are not as great as popular beliefs might lead one to think. The majority of each group (72 to 75%) perform adequately, there are no differences in on-the-job accidents, and a sizable proportion of each group (minimum of 29%) are promoted over a four-year period. The psychiatric groups do have higher absenteeism and more medical retirements. If the Work Performance Inventory is a reliable rating instrument, it might serve as a valuable outcome measure for the evaluation of many troubled employee programs. This study also shows that one "chronic" individual can make a group's performance, in terms of averages, look much worse than it actually is. As shall be seen later, mean score comparisons between groups can be helpful, but at times can also be misleading. In this instance, the deterioration of one individual makes the group look much worse than the one it was compared to. This is similar to the finding cited earlier (Pell and D'Alonzo, 1970) where, while the alcoholic sample had absenteeism rates two, three or four times that of the "normal" group, examination showed these high levels to be due to only 45 percent of the group. Approximately 55 percent of the group had reasonably good attendance while 38 percent had no sickness-absenteeism.

Economic Estimates of Job Disruption
(Winslow, Hayes, Prentice, Powles, Seeman and Ross, 1966) ✓

This paper focuses on ways of systematically estimating the costs to a company for various procedures (compensation, grievances, disciplinary actions, hospital-medical claims, absenteeism, etc.). In the paper the costs of a "suspected problem drinking" group is contrasted with a "miscellaneous problems" group, and a "problem-free" group. Cost figures do indicate that "suspected drinking" and "miscellaneous problems" groups cost the company, the employees and the insurers between two and three times as much as a "problem-free" group.

Two working populations employing a total of 3,600 were the focus of the study. Matched samples were used and no information is given on the actual size of the problem groups or of the capacity of the companies' programs.

OUTCOME MEASURES. This paper provides a formula for computing; 1) the cost of impaired productivity, 2) the cost of interpersonal frictions as shown in grievance and discipline proceedings, 3) the cost of absenteeism, and 4) the cost of health and accident problems. One of the authors also developed a supervisor's efficiency scale (eight 5-point rating scales) to assess the cost of impaired productivity (e.g. "What percent of an employee's potential is actually being realized?").

FINDINGS. Groups which followed recommendations of the medical department were found to have lower costs to the company than those which did not follow recommendations. However, in the twenty-seven month follow-up the mean differences in cost for the two groups were not significant.

While savings or cost of treatment were not the focus of this study, the base for systematically computing cost figures is laid down. Yearly costs to the company per person for the two problem groups were estimated at $1,652 and $1,622 compared to $867 for the problem-free group. Yearly costs to the employees were estimated at $433 and $213 for the "suspected drinking" and "miscellaneous problems" group respectively, compared with a low of $28 for the problem-free group. Cost to insurers were similar with $373 and $248 for the two problems groups compared to $162 for the problem-free group.

IMPLICATIONS. This paper should be in the hands of every program administrator. While there are many ways to calculate "costs" this paper provides a systematic method which could be applied to all programs. Comparisons of different industries, different programs and types of treatment will require that programs to be compared use equivalent measures. Since it will probably not be possible for any one company to experiment to a great extent, the comparisons will have to be made across companies. This will reqiure the use of equivalent measures such as those developed in the paper reported here.

The fact that the large cost differences were not significant indicates that at least one group had a large range of costs for its members. It is suspected that some in the problem group had no costs to the company while others cost a great deal. Again the averages do not reveal this important variation.

The Early Identification of Problem Drinkers
(Maxwell, 1960)

This is a report of a fact-finding survey which obtained information about the signs of problem drinking. A four-page questionnaire was developed from information obtained from alcoholics, supervisors and other industry personnel who had contact with problem drinkers. This questionnaire was then sent out to "alcoholics" who were recovered or in treatment. In addition to background information, respondents were asked to indicate the time between the onset of problem drinking and the time of first seeking help. They were also asked to rate forty-four behavioral signs of problem drinking in terms of their occurrence (never, rarely, mild, frequently).

Maxwell notes that over half of his respondent sample had a drinking problem on the job for four or more years before seeking help. The maximum was twenty years for one individual.

The percentages are listed for each of the forty-four signs which were reported as being among the first five signs of drinking on the job. The signs are:

1. Hangovers on the job (66%)
2. Morning drinking before work (36%)
3. Increased nervousness/irritability (25%)
4. Absenteeism—half day or whole day (27%)
5. Drinking at lunch (24%)
6. Hand tremors (21%)
7. Drinking during work (19%)
8. Late to work (18%)
9. More unusual excuses for absences (16%)
10. Leaving work early (16%)

Maxwell concludes that using the behavioral patterns he develops on the basis of these signs, 72 percent of his sample would have been identified as possible problem drinkers. He notes that other factors could be responsible for these signs occurring in an employee but that these patterns give one cues which can then be followed up. This should result in earlier identification of problem drinkers on the job. He also gathers evidence that problem drinking conditions existed for a long time in many of these people before they sought help.

Perhaps the most important implication of Maxwell's study is that not enough is yet known about problem drinking. While he notes that based on his patterns of signs, 72 percent of the problem drinkers could have been successfully identified, he also points out that other people might be included. How useful his patterns are has not yet been determined (to the writer's knowledge). However, false positives are a problem that any screening instrument must be evaluated for. Maxwell's correctly selected group (the 72%) might only be a very small fraction of those tentatively identified as problem drinkers.

The Development of Deviant Drinking Behavior:
Occupational Risk Factors
(Roman and Trice, 1970)

Roman and Trice (1970) discuss nine factors which seem to be related to a higher risk of developing problem drinking. These nine factors fall into two general categories; 1) an absence of supervision and 2) low visibility of job performance. While both of these can be viewed as lack of accountability to others or a lack of awareness of others about what the individual is doing, Roman and Trice point out that in terms of organizational structure there are other implications. The person with a lack of supervision or low visibility of performance may also find himself in a situation where he cannot perform or where there is no positive feedback for good performance. Such a job role may also lack structural definition and clarity about where the individual fits in the organization and this may be a stress which leads to the use of alcohol.

The nine factors which were examined are:

1. Being in a job role where production goals are not well-defined.
2. Being in a job role where hours of work are up to the individual's discretion.
3. Being in a job role where the work requirements keep one separated from one's supervisor and associates.
4. Work addiction.
5. Occupational obsolescence.
6. Occupying a novel work role in the organization.
7. Occupying a work role where drinking is seen as part of the job.
8. Occupying a work role where pathological drinking is beneficial to others in the organization.
9. Moving from a heavy drinking job status where there are strong social controls on drinking to a job role where the social controls are absent.

Examples of the operation of each factor are discussed. For example, the factor of being in a job role where pathological drinking is beneficial to others in the company is illustrated by situations where the chief executive officer is chronically inebriated and his decision-making power has been taken over by a small clique of his former assistants. As long as the chief executive is protected and remains intoxicated the assistants can keep their decision-making power. Should he recover or his condition become generally known, they stand to lose their power.

IMPLICATIONS. The authors note that job roles which possess the factors mentioned above have in common a stress producing element. In this article the authors examine aspects of the environment, aspects of the peer group, and aspects of the person which can increase the risk of problem drinking. While it is a theoretical article, it is based on the extensive experience of the authors. It is one of the few articles which tries to examine the role of the job environment in contributing to problem drinking.

Mental Health-Related Activities of Companies and Unions (Slotkin, Levy, Wetmore and Runk, 1971)

This is the report of a survey of companies and unions in the greater Chicago area. Alcohol programs were covered along with a variety of other mental health related issues in a questionnaire. In reporting the major findings of the survey, it is pointed out that approximately two thirds of both companies and unions provide some program to prepare their workers for retirement. In contrast, while alcoholism was considered to be a problem by 72 percent of the companies and 61 percent of the unions, only 22 percent of the companies and slightly over 55 percent of the unions had any sort of a program for alcoholic employees. Referral to AA seemed to be the most favored treatment resource. Only 5 percent of the unions had any sort of a counseling program for alcohol problems.

The three counseling programs most reported by companies were centered around work problems (80%), retirement (69%), and financial problems (68%). Unions provided similar programs in some instances. The top three programs reported by unions were work problems (78%), personal and family problems (67%), and retirement (61%). This survey does reveal a high proportion of counseling programs offered by both companies and unions. It is limited in that it is wholly dependent on responses to the questionnaire and no data was gathered on the actual ongoing operation of programs.

IMPLICATIONS. This survey does indicate that alcohol programs have a relatively low priority in relation to other types of employee programs for both companies and unions. Later, programs will be discussed in terms of "appropriateness." Appropriateness is defined as the priority of an alcohol program in relation to other employee programs. A paper by Roman (1972) based on a survey of executives, suggests that the alcoholism problem is of low priority for most executives. The survey reported here on companies and unions in the Chicago area essentially confirms the low priority of alcoholism programs on an empirical basis (within the limitations of the survey method). However, a Broadbrush approach which had an alcoholism aspect as one component would seem to mesh well with the Chicago area counseling programs. It should be noted that 80 percent of the companies and 78 percent of the unions provide counseling programs on "work problems." If an alcoholism component is lacking, it would seem to be a natural addition.

Summary

The following points seem to sum up the findings in this section on the nature of the problem.

1. Problem drinking has been found to have the highest prevalence in the youngest age group (twenty to twenty-four) and to decrease with age.
2. Problems on the job (excluding the youngest age group) peak in the forty to fifty-five age groups.
3. Large numbers of persons move into and out of the problem drinking population in a three-year period, probably without the benefit of formal treatment.
4. Industrial problem drinking involves 3 to 10 percent of the work force with the average percentage around 5 percent.
5. While problem drinking groups may cost two, three or four times as much "on the average" in sickness absenteeism when compared to a "normal" population, evidence is available in one study that 35 percent of the problem drinkers have no absenteeism problem and that up to 55 percent show reasonably good attendance.
6. Several studies show that "problem drinking" and accompanying absenteeism exist for a long time (four to ten years on the average) before being diagnosed or treatment is offered. More clearly defined psychiatric conditions of neurosis and psychosis were indicated to have been found earlier in terms of absenteeism data. These findings indicate the need for earlier intervention in the work force for problem drinking.
7. Definitions for various rates of sickness-absenteeism are available which, if used nationwide, would increase the comparability of different studies and program evaluations.
8. Analysis of groups solely in terms of mean scores may have obscured differences and smilarities in the groups studied and

important program achievements. The indications are that more than mean scores need to be examined. Groups assumed to be homogeneous often are not.

9. Work performance measures of quality and quantity of work will be required to examine the nature and extent of problem drinking in more detail. Such ratings should also be utilized (where possible) in the evaluations of programs.

10. Standardized ways of defining costs have been presented in at least one study and should contribute much to the assessment of efficiency in future studies.

11. Behavioral signs of problem drinking have been studied but much work remains to be done before solid behavioral criteria are available.

12. Factors which increase the risk of problem drinking have been examined in at least one paper and are conceptualized in three categories. Most important perhaps is the often overlooked factor of aspects of the job environment.

13. A survey of companies and unions in the Chicago area indicates that a low priority exists for labeled occupational alcoholism programs.

A MODEL FOR PROGRAM PLANNING AND EVALUATION

The model presented here has been developed by a group of researchers at the University of Michigan School of Public Health. It was developed out of the need for a systematic and well-defined set of definitions of program attributes and the need for a conceptual model which would facilitate the planning, implementation and evaluation of health programs. Deniston, Rosenstock and Getting's model (1968) consists of nine basic terms and their definitions.

Programs

"An organized response to reduce or eliminate one or more problems. This response includes; 1) specification of one or more objectives, 2) selection and performance of one or more activities and 3) acquisition and use of resources."

Note the implied linkage between objectives, activities and resources. Perhaps most important is the priority of objectives in this definition. In most human service organizations the objectives are implicit, assumed or so general as to be unquantifiable.

Deniston, et al. (1968) offers a method for defining "program objectives."

Objective

"A situation or condition of people or of the environment which responsible program personnel consider desirable to attain. To permit subsequent evaluation, the statement of an objective must specify: 1) what—the nature of the situation or condition to be attained; 2) extent—the quantity or amount of the situation or condition to be attained; 3) who—the particular group of people or portion of the environment in which attainment is desired; 4) where—the geographic area of the program; and 5) when—the time at or by which the desired situation or condition is intended to exist.

Within this framework they define three types of objectives: 1) ultimate objectives which are desirable in and of themselves and with which no one would argue (i.e. eliminating problem drinking in the population of concern; 2) a program objective represents the outcome of implementation of the program (i.e. identification and rehabilitation of 90 percent of the problem drinkers in the work force in a given year); 3) sub-objectives are those objectives which are necessary to attain before the overall program objective(s) can be realized. Acquiring sufficient resources, training supervisors, conducting referral or treatment activities, or administering evaluation instruments can all be considered as sub-objectives of a troubled employee program.

Activity

"Work performed by program personnel and equipment in the service of an objective. Activity as we use it does not imply any fixed amount or scope of work; it may be applied with equal validity to such diverse efforts as writing a letter or providing comprehensive health care."

Resource

"Personnel, funds, materials and facilities available to support the performance of activity. Resources, like activities, may be described with varying levels of specificity."

A program then can be seen schematically as:

resources ———→ activities ———→ sub-objectives ———→ objectives

Certain assumptions underlie this model and, if they are not valid, will make it impossible to realize the program objectives. The first major assumption is that the expenditure of resources will result in the performance of the planned activities. If the resources are utilized but the activities do not occur, the objectives will not be reached.

The second assumption is that performance of the planned activities will lead to the attainment of sub-objectives and thus the program objective(s) will be attained. Again, if the activities are not conducted, the sub-objectives would not be expected to be attained.

The third assumption is that the sub-objectives must be attained to achieve the program objectives and that attainment of sub-objectives necessarily implies attainment of program objectives.

Most human service programs are not currently planned as to include specification of measurable program objectives. Thus, the first order of business for any evaluator is to work with program personnel to define the objectives in a measurable fashion. While this is never an easy task, it is almost always possible to come up with some measurable indices of program objectives. The beauty of Deniston, Rosenstock and Getting's model is in its specificity and guidelines for evaluation. Looking at the model, it becomes apparent that some assessment of resources and their utilization must be made. Actual activities must be documented and sub-objectives assessed. If this is done, weaknesses in the program, trouble spots and strengths are readily apparent. In fully half of the evaluation efforts the author has been connected with, it has been discovered that activities were not actually being conducted as planned. There are varying reasons for this but in all cases where this has occurred, the specific program objectives have not been achieved.

The final four concepts and definitions provided by Deniston, Rosenstock and Getting concern the types of evaluative questions asked by concerned groups. These four concepts—appropriateness, adequacy, effectiveness and efficiency—can be defined separately, and each is directed toward different types of issues. Many times in discussions of programs the conversation will slide from one of these types to another without the participants being aware that the major focus of the discussion has changed. These concepts and distinctions are especially relevant to program administrators who must make policy decisions about the programs they are responsible for. Data can usually be obtained for each conceptual area, but the types of data and the issues involved are radically different. Rational planning and decision-making requires that the distinctions between these four concepts and their related evaluative questions be kept separate.

Appropriateness

"Questions on appropriateness concern the importance of the specific problems selected for programming and the relative emphasis or priority accorded to each. Program directors are concerned with appropriateness when they ask, 'Are our program objectives worthwhile and do they have a higher priority than other possible objectives of this or other programs?' "

Adequacy

"Ideally, objectives are oriented toward elimination of the problem which gave rise to the program, but various constraints may necessitate reducing the scope of an objective from focus on complete solution of a problem to the more modest scope of reducing a problem by a specific amount or limiting an objective to a portion of the population experiencing the problem rather than trying to reach all those at risk. Questions concerning how much of the entire problem the program is directed toward overcoming refer to the adequacy of the program objectives."

Effectiveness

"Programs may differ in their effectiveness; that is, in the extent to which preestablished objectives are attained as a result of activity. Effectiveness in attaining objectives is distinct from program appropriateness and adequacy."

Efficiency

"Program efficiency is defined as the cost in resources of attaining objectives. The efficiency of a program may be unrelated to its effectiveness, adequacy and appropriateness."

Deniston, Rosenstock and Getting (1968) point out that these questions may be asked before a program is started and thus constitute part of the planning process. When they are asked about an ongoing program, they represent an evaluation of program performance. The four major questions which will be answered by this process are: 1) Is the program focused on' important problems? 2) Is the program directed at all or only part of the problems? 3) How much of the predetermined objectives have been attained? 4) How much did it cost to get the degree of attainment observed?

In the following sections, this model and the four major concepts—appropriateness, adequacy, effectiveness and efficiency—are used to evaluate the literature on occupational alcoholism or troubled employee programs.

DESIGNS FOR EVALUATING PROGRAM EFFECTIVENESS

Designs for evaluation are generally concerned with answering the question, "What happened?" The basic question can be made more specific, can be elaborated, and can become quite complex, but the general question is always "What happened?" Those who would like to pursue the types of designs which have been developed for applied research could read Isaac (1971), Suchman (1967), or Campbell and Stanley (1966).

Table 2-II shows the four basic types of designs which will be discussed here. It is hoped that this discussion will enable the reader to better understand and criticize the program evaluations which will be discussed later. Good applied research has to evolve over time and its evaluation in a setting will probably follow successively more rigorous attempts similar to the ascending complexity of the five designs in Table 2-II. While shortcuts can be taken based on what others have done in the past, it is not always possible to start evaluations at a highly complex level.

One of the major factors which has prevented many applied evaluation efforts is the feeling that a study has to be rigorously controlled or it is not worth doing. It will later be demonstrated that this is not the case. In a sense you have to walk before you can run, run before you fly, and you must surely be able to fly before you can get into orbit when you are on top of the problem.

In looking at the evaluations of troubled employee programs, the evidence indicates that most efforts are still at the walking stage. A few evaluations seem to have reached the running stage, although many still seem to get tripped up.

Four questions of increasing specificity can be discerned in the logic of the designs in Table 2-II

1. "What happened "
2. "How much happened?"
3. "How much happened compared to doing something else?"
4. "How much happened compared to doing nothing?"

Each of these four questions and designs are looked at in detail.

What Happened? (Or What Is Happening?)

This question, in the simplest case, is commonly answered in two ways. The first way looks at individual cases, either for a testimonial or assertion that something occurred, or in a more systematic case study method. Testimonials can be very descriptive and informative, but have the drawback of being suggestive and possibly influenced by many diverse factors.

Case studies are a highly respected clinical method for

Note

TABLE 2-II

SOME DESIGNS COMMONLY USED FOR EVALUATION

"WHAT HAPPENED?"

row 1				O		
row 2			X	O		

"HOW MUCH HAPPENED?"

row 3			O	X	O	
row 4	O	O	O	X	O	O	O

"HOW MUCH HAPPENED COMPARED TO DOING SOMETHING ELSE (OR NOTHING)?"

row 5		O	X	O (the treatment group)
row 6		O		O (the no-treatment group)

describing what happened. Vaschak (1969) presents three case studies of alcoholic employees. A wealth of information is presented on the progression of the drinking problem and the resolution which is or is not achieved. Case studies are usually done at the level of row 1 or row 2 of Table 2-II. As with testimonials or expert opinions, the first instance would be observation of individuals and a detailed write-up of "what happened" from the observer's view. In the second instance, the X O of row 2, some treatment (X) is administered such as visits to the medical department and for each case a write-up is made describing "What happened." The testimonial or case study is hampered by its focus on individual cases and by the wealth of material—some relevant and some irrelevant—which is presented. One cannot get a good overall picture of the effectiveness of a program by this method.

The second way of answering the "what happened" question can be at either row 1 or row 2 of the table. In row 1—observation (O) only—one might want to look at the population of a plant during a specified period and determine how many persons had drinking problems and of these how many kept or lost their jobs. Most of the studies examined earlier on the nature of the problem were of this type.

If there is an alcoholism program or troubled employee program, we then have the situation in row 2 where there is some treatment offered or applied. Many evaluations of occupational programs fit at this level. The following statement is illustrative of the summary provided by this type of study design: "Of the 110 employees referred to the program, 88 (80%) retained their jobs and returned to satisfactory work performance."

An example of this type of "after only" design is provided by an item from an evaluation battery used by the author in evaluation of the effectiveness of a program conducted by the National Occupational Alcoholism Training Institute of East Carolina University. This program was attended by 112 new Occupational Program Consultants.

At the end of a three-week training program, the trainees were asked to indicate how much they had been helped to increase their knowledge by the training. For the item "How much were you helped to increase your knowledge of the various roles of industry in generating solutions for problem drinking?" the mean score for the group of 107 respondents was 3.4. This 5-point scale revealed that on the average the respondents felt that their knowledge was increased between "some" (3) and "quite a bit" (4). No one said the program was of no help. While this example also gives some information on "How much happened?" it is fairly weak information. For example, 12 percent said the program was of "very little" help, 39 percent said the program was of "some" help, 43 percent said the program was "quite a bit" of help, and 4 percent rated the program as "a lot" of help.

How Much Happened?

This question not only asks "What happened" but tries to quantify the degree of accomplishment or change. The designs in rows 3 and 4 of Table 2-II are most commonly used to evaluate this question. Note that these designs indicate that observations (O) are made before the treatment (X) and after the treatment. The design in row 4 is called the extended time-series design and the multiple observations allow one to show the stability or trends in the behavior both before and after treatment.

Often with this design, statistics are brought into play. The use of statistics allows the evaluator to say to what degree the change could be the result of "chance" factors. If the results are statistically significant it is unlikely that the change is due only to chance factors.

An example of this type of pre-post design is also obtained from the evaluation of East Carolina University's National Occupational Alcoholism Training Institute. At the beginning and end of the three-week training program the trainees were asked to indicate how much they felt they knew about "the various roles of industry in generating solutions for problem drinking." This item used the same 5-point scale as was used to evaluate the question of how much they felt the program increased their knowledge. The mean score for the 101 trainees who answered was 2.8 at the beginning of training and 3.3 at the end of training. This difference was statistically significant (t=5.381, p < .00005).

Note that while the mean at the end of training is almost identical to the mean discussed previously on how much participants felt they were helped to increase their knowledge, the conclusion is much stronger. In this latter case, with a pre-test and a posttest it can be concluded that the change is probably not a chance result and represents a real change in perceived knowledge.

The "how much of a change" question is answered by showing a non-chance change of .5 point in the mean score of the group and by noting that on the pretest 35 percent of the respondents said they had "none" or "very little" knowledge in this area while on the posttest only 12 percent fall into these two bottom categories of the 5-point scale.

How Much Was Accomplished Compared To Doing Something Else (Or Nothing)

The designs in rows 5 and 6 add the new element of a group that gets a different treatment or a group that receives no treatment. Here scores in row 5 are compared to scores in row 6. These are called the pretest—posttest comparison group design and the pretest—posttest control group design. The last uses a no-treatment control group which is identical to the treatment group. This is considered the epitome of empirical research and is a basic design for experimental studies. It allows the evaluator not only to answer the questions of what happened and how much happened, but also the question of how much happened compared to doing nothing. Unfortunately, even with this design, only changes in mean scores are usually looked at. As will be pointed out in the discussion of psychotherapy research, a number of people show changes in the absence of treatment. This pretest—posttest control group design allows the researcher to say whether or not the change is greater than would have occurred without treatment in addition to saying whether or not the change observed was large enough to be a non-chance finding. The control group design is still seldom found in applied research.

The "comparison" group design is found more often and is used when there is a group which does not get the treatment or which gets a different treatment, but there is no way to say that the two groups are identical. This design is not as strong as the "control" group design since differences on measures may be due to differences in the two groups. The National Occupational Alcoholism Training Institute again provides an example of a type of comparison group design, although it is not a pretest–posttest design. Five months after the three-week training program, a follow-up workshop was held. Ninety-one of the original participants attended, along with nineteen new persons who had not attended the three week training program. At the beginning of the workshop, the participants were again asked how much they felt they knew about "the various roles of industry in developing solutions to problem drinking." This comparison group design could be diagrammed as shown in Table 2-III. Comparison between the means of the treatment and comparison group showed the mean scores to be significantly different ($F=5.563$, df=1, 108, $p<.05$).

In this case, if we can assume that the two groups are basically the same, we can conclude that something about the training experience led to significantly greater perceived knowledge than no training experience. This assumption is risky since many uncontrolled factors could be responsible for the observed difference. It is not possible to conclude that the three-week training program was responsible for the difference, but the evidence is suggestive. If a control group had been used initially, a stronger conclusion would be possible.

The major points made in this section are that evaluation questions generally are concerned with answering the question of "What happened?" Evaluation efforts may have to start at a fairly

TABLE 2-III

AN EXAMPLE OF THE USE OF A MODIFIED
COMPARISON GROUP DESIGN

	Before Training	Training	After Training	Five Months Later
The Design				
Treatment Group	O	X	O	O
Comparison Group				O
The Mean Scores at Each Observation Point				
Treatment Group	2.8	X	3.3	3.4
Comparison Group	——		——	3.0

basic observational level and evolve toward the more refined questions of "How much happened?" and "How much happened compared to doing something else?"

It was pointed out that a major stumbling block to starting evaluation efforts is the feeling that one must begin at the highest possible level using a no-treatment control group. It should be recognized, especially in applied situations, that this is not usually possible and that a successive evolution toward more complex evaluations must occur. It is suggested that instead of trying to get into orbit before learning how to walk, it is more advantageous and less frustrating to first learn how to walk (identify "What happened"), then to run ("How much happened"), then to fly without crashing (using comparison groups), and finally to achieve escape velocity and get on top of the problem.

SOURCES OF BIAS IN ALCOHOLISM TREATMENT RESEARCH

Miller, Pokorny, Valles and Cleveland (1970) have reviewed the research on alcoholism treatment and identified eleven sources of bias which frequently occur. Each of these eleven types of bias may invalidate conclusions of a study. They are discussed here since the literature on occupational alcoholism programs often contains these sources of bias.

Different Definitions of Alcoholism

This problem prevents the direct comparison of studies and is still a major problem area for occupational and troubled-employee programs. The varied penetration rates and prevalence rates noted by different programs may be due solely to the use of different definitions of problem drinking and alcoholism. While it is unrealistic to expect common definitions to be arrived at quickly given the changing nature of the field, each investigator could spell out the specific definition used in his program. Often the definition used in a specific study is not reported.

Case Selection from Special Populations

Some attempt has been made to note the influence of this

factor in occupational programs. The estimate of a 3 percent problem drinking prevalence in the textile industry as compared to a 5 to 10 percent for heavy industry, indicates the awareness of special populations. Many company programs, however, have not attempted to survey the prevalence of the problem within their own population. The results of a program may vary widely because of the characteristics of the population served.

Reputation of the Treatment Program

Treatment programs often gain a reputation for being especially good with certain types of clients and poor with others. This can result in selective referral to the program which means that the clients of a program are selected from and not necessarily representative of the total population. Those company programs which serve only blue-collar employees could be an example of this type of selection.

Refusal of Referral

This is an especially important category for occupational programs. Often some (or possibly many) clients refuse treatment and this is often overlooked in evaluations of programs. The characteristics of clients who refuse treatment and their eventual outcome have major implications for programming. In addition, if a large number of referrals refuse treatment, the success of a program cannot be generalized to the total population.

Rejection of Applicants

This is a source of bias similar to clients refusing treatment. If the program rejects a certain type of client, its results are applicable only to a portion of the problem population.

Dropouts

Two types of dropouts exist. Those who drop out after being accepted for the program before treatment and those who drop out in the middle of treatment. Again, these groups may differ systematically from each other and from those who complete treatment. Often the dropouts are ignored and the proportion is not even reported.

Exclusion from the Study

Clients in treatment are sometimes excluded from a study because of complicating factors; this is not always reported. An example is a study of an occupational program where persons with other mental health problems are excluded (e.g. a person suffering from problem drinking and psychosis who is excluded from the study). If this type of exclusion is not reported, the results could be erroneously assumed to apply to the total work force.

Living or Moving Beyond Follow-up Distance

Miller, et al. (1970) note that follow-up studies often cannot reach all those who went through the treatment program. This type of exclusion from a follow-up study is often a source of bias, but is seldom reported. The proportion or number of clients who could not be found should always be reported.

Deaths

Clients who die during the follow-up period often cannot be rated in terms of improvement at follow-up. This group of clients may differ substantially from others involved in the treatment program, especially in terms of a higher incidence of physical problems. The proportion of clients who died before follow-up should always be reported if possible.

Refusal to Participate in Follow-up

Those who refuse to participate in a follow-up study may be very different from those who cooperate. Thirty-four outcome studies of alcoholism treatment are reviewed by Miller, et al. (1970) and they note that less than half of the studies took the above factors into account when reporting their results. The authors note that the studies covered may be based on a selected 5 percent of all alcoholics in the general population. If this is true, the treatment literature being accumulated may be good only for this 5 percent. Thus, principles emerging from studies of treatment which are thought to be generally applicable, may in fact be relevant only for a very small segment of the population of interest. Failure to report on sources of bias can have very serious implications for the occupational alcoholism field.

The Effect of Testing

Trice and Belasco (1968) and Belasco and Trice (1969) report on a controlled evaluation of supervisory training in a large organization in upstate New York. This article is presented here since it provides some relatively clear-cut information on the effects of pretesting. Those wishing to conduct evaluations of programs will find many arguments arising against evaluation and one will be focused on the effects of testing. In human performance and achievement areas, testing effects have been found. Usually this means that the practice gained on the pretest leads to a gain on the posttest without any treatment being given. In IQ testing, for example, there is an average one- or two-point increase on the second testing.

In working with therapists and counselors, one will often be told that testing will destroy the therapeutic relationship. There may be some truth in this argument and it must be weighed carefully. Testing is used routinely in many programs and testing, as with doing anything else, may have positive or negative consequences. It will depend in part on how it is handled and in part on a large number of unknown factors. However, the only way to improve programs is by finding out where they are successful and unsuccessful and using this information in an attempt to improve practice. At the present time there exists enough information on the negative effects of treatment or on treatment failures to justify a continuing search for improved methods. The following study sheds some light on the effects of testing in a training program. Similar studies are needed in therapeutic programs.

The study by Trice and Belasco (1968) had as a major objective the assessment of the effects of training so that training programs could be improved. They used 222 supervisors or 86 percent of the total supervisor population of the company in the study.

The design used by Trice and Belasco (1968) is called the Solomon four group design. It is the pretest-posttest control group design discussed earlier with two additional groups which allow the investigator to determine the effects of testing. This design can be diagrammed as:

Group 1	O	X	O
Group 2	O		O
Group 3		X	O
Group 4			O

Three major objectives are stated: 1) the development of a more favorable attitude toward alcoholism; 2) increased knowledge of alcoholism; and 3) changes in supervisory behavior which result in constructive action toward the alcoholic employee. Knowledge was assessed by a thirty-item multiple choice scale, attitudes by a set of semantic differential type scales, and behavior by a self-report "action scale." Small but significant increases are reported for training.

The group which received a pretest and training had the largest increase in scores. The group which received training without the pretest showed an increase over its control group, but slightly lower scores than the pretest and training group. Most significantly, the group which received the pretest but no training showed a decrease in its scores. Thus, there is an interaction between pretesting and training where pretesting has a facilitative effect with training and a negative effect without training.

The authors conclude with four implications for practical applications: 1) concentrating on the illness aspects of alcoholism may foster increased tolerance rather than constructive confrontation. It is suggested that attention be focused on the plight of the alcoholic and the continuing problems he causes for his supervisor, fellow workers, and family; 2) it is suggested that pretesting can play a strong functional role in training programs, enhancing the training effects by calling the trainees' attention to relevant questions; 3) the trainers and the participants should be matched on relevant characteristics for best outcome; 4) the Broadbrush approach is an advantageous way of attacking the problem of alcoholism in industry. Training in the broader "problem-employee" approach produced more favorable attitudes, in the authors' judgment, than comparable approaches which emphasize the uniqueness of alcoholism.

IMPLICATIONS. While the implications have been mentioned above, two are important enough to restate here. First, pretesting can be a powerful tool in increasing the effects of a training program, provided that the training program concentrates on, or offers material in those areas covered on the pretest. If the training does not cover those areas tested, a strong negative effect can be expected. Secondly, although based mainly on the authors' judgment, support is offered for a Broadbrush or human problems approach to alcoholism in industry.

Summary

In this section the basic logic behind evaluations has been examined. Four basic questions of increasing detail are seen to guide evolving evaluation efforts. The basic designs are looked at and provide the necessary background for a scrutiny of existing evaluation efforts in the occupational field.

Eleven sources of bias which commonly threaten the validity of evaluations are examined and discussed. While many of these sources of bias can be controlled and all can be reported, this is often overlooked in the literature on occupational alcoholism programs.

Finally, a paper which examines the effects of testing is reviewed. While it is admitted that testing may have negative effects, the study examined shows that asking questions of participants can also have a facilitative effect which is beneficial. It is suggested that testing can have a similar facilitative effect in treatment programs.

A LESSON FROM PSYCHOTHERAPY RESEARCH

In 1952 an English researcher by the name of H. J. Eysenck published an article which asked "Is psychotherapy effective?" He collected data from earlier studies which, in his opinion, showed recovery rate without psychotherapy to equal about 70 percent and recovery rate with psychotherapy to equal about 70 percent. He concluded that he could find no evidence that psychotherapy worked and thus started a heated controversy which still rages in many places.

Bergin (1971) offers an excellent and rigorous evaluation of the literature on verbal psychotherapy with basically neurotic individuals and effectively counters Eysenck's original and continuing criticisms. Part of Bergin's analysis is presented here since it illustrates four problems that will have to be faced by even the most crusading spirit for occupational alcoholism or troubled-employee programs. The four issues are "spontaneous recovery" (recovery without formal treatment), "regression effects," "effectiveness," and harm or "deterioration" caused by treatment.

Spontaneous Recovery

Bergin's (1971) search of the psychotherapy literature reveals fourteen studies which yield estimates on the number or percentage of persons who recover without formal treatment. The percentages range from 0 to 52 percent with an average percentage of around 30 percent in a given time period (usually a year). For the purposes of this paper, this question can be translated as: "What proportion of occupational problem drinkers will recover in a given time period without treatment?" Studies reviewed later give some clues but no "hard" answers.

Investigations into this spontaneous recovery phenomenon indicate that some of it may be self-generated and some of it may be due to informal treatment sources in the community (doctors, clergy, the neighbors) to whom the person turns for help in a time of stress and trouble. One follow-up study of persons in psychotherapy (Stone, Frank, Nash and Imber, 1961) showed that all of these individuals sought out at least one helping person each year over a four-year period. Over half of the incidents of help seeking seemed to be related to emotional problems.

Psychotherapy and troubled-employee programs can be justified on the basis of helping more people get better faster as easily or perhaps easier than by claiming "miracles," dramatic personality changes, or permanent sobriety. For example, the demonstration could be that an occupational alcoholism program can help 80 percent of those identified get better a year quicker than they would have without the program. There will still be large savings to the company, the individual and his family.

It should be remembered that, as with psychotherapy, a certain proportion of those who improve during the course of a program would have gotten better anyway. The program cannot legitimately take credit for these individuals in computing its effectiveness.

Regression Effects

This issue is related to the spontaneous recovery issue, but is a serious enough threat to evaluative research to be considered separately. In many physical and behavioral problem areas, a person does not seek help until he is really desperate. At this point, many of them are at the height of pain or despair and a look at them a week or two later will show them better regardless of treatment. A recent study with an arthritis treatment program (Deniston and Rosenstock, 1973) shows how a simple before-after design overestimates the effect of treatment. They were able to obtain this data because they incorporated a no-treatment control group in their study. In the same vein, the use of a comparison group (a group similar to the experimentals) underestimated the effects of treatment.

The important point is that regression effects do occur. Any program dealing with desperate persons, or persons in an extreme state, will have its before-after estimates of the effects of treatment contaminated by regression effects. Thus, absenteeism will drop for a group placed in a treatment program, but it will also drop for an identical group not getting treatment. The proof of the effectiveness of treatment lies in the differential success of the treatment group.

Effectiveness

Perhaps this has already been covered enough. In the psychotherapy research Bergin (1971) found estimates of proportions of successful outcomes to range from 20 to 90 percent with an average value around 70 percent. The problem in assessing effectiveness, recognizing spontaneous recovery and regression effects, has been faced in only one of the papers cited in this chapter. Partly the data is not yet available, partly investigators have not thought through their evaluation designs to make the necessary distinctions, and partly because it is more "political" to claim the highest possible rates of success.

Deterioration Effects

This will perhaps stand out as Bergin's (1971) most valuable contribution to psychotherapy and human problems programs. Many controlled outcome studies of psychotherapy, well-conducted studies, show no significant differences between those who received treatment and those who did not. Similar reports may be found in Winslow, Hayes, Prentice, Powles, Seeman and Ross (1966) and Cole and Shup (1970) for job performance measures.

Puzzled by this lack of treatment effect (or lack of mean differences in the groups), Bergin examined the data in the studies to determine "How much happened?" He found a greater variation in the treatment group than in the controls. That is, he found that a sizeable number in the treatment group did improve and that a lesser but considerable number got worse. The variation within the control groups did not change greatly. In global averages, across studies that differ considerably in their rates, Bergin estimates that about 70 percent get better, 20 percent show no change and about 10 percent get worse because of the treatment.

Since occupational alcoholism and "troubled-employee" programs deal with similar behavior disorders, we could expect to find similar phenomena although the averages may be different and the rates may vary by type of industry, geographical location, guiding philosophy, or other factors.

The major point is that if you have a treatment which is powerful enough to help some people, you will most likely be hurting a certain proportion of the persons who get the treatment. This is especially true in our present state of ignorance about the effects of different treatments on different types of people with different problems in different settings.

EXISTING EVALUATIONS OF OCCUPATIONAL ALCOHOLISM AND BROADBRUSH PROGRAMS

In this section actual program evaluations are examined. The studies range from reporting on a few cases to highly sophisticated articles which provide information on appropriateness, adequacy, effectiveness and efficiency. The material in this section was gathered by two major methods. The literature was searched for all relevant studies using the bibliographies in known studies, NIAAA's Clearinghouse for Alcohol Information and random searches through relevant journals. Undoubtedly some good reports have been missed. Business journals were not searched and many popular and professional publications were not available to the author.

The second approach used was to personally write to nineteen of twenty-two companies which have strong alcoholism programs. Many of these companies replied within a short period and most regretted that they did not have information available on appropriateness, adequacy, effectiveness or efficiency.

Hopefully, the sampling presented here will be sufficient to illustrate what has been accomplished to date in the evaluation of occupational alcoholism programs. Seven factors are looked for and evaluated in each program which is examined here. These seven factors are:

1. Appropriateness—any data on priority of the problem or program in relation to other "necessary" employee services.
2. Adequacy—the capacity of the program given the size of the problem.
3. Effectiveness—the "cure rate" or proportion of objectives achieved over what would have occurred without the program.
4. Efficiency—the cost per successful case in relation to the cost without the program or the cost of alternative solutions.
5. Outcome Measures—the indices used by program personnel to assess the above points.
6. Treatment Methods—the types of treatment or referral sources utilized.
7. The Design—the conceptual framework utilized by program personnel to assess its performance.

The definitions for effectiveness and efficiency have been discussed at length. In the following discussion of programs the relative effectiveness is not examined. None of the evaluations have information on the percentage of persons who would have improved in the absence of the program. Most programs claim credit for all who improve. Data on actual efficiency or costs are also lacking. In the following write-ups any information which is available on costs was reported. Often this is the change in absenteeism for those who go through the program. In one instance the cost of the program and the estimated savings in sick pay are reported. At the present time this is the best information available on program efficiency.

It should be noted that the company programs which are examined here are a highly selected group of pioneers who have programs for their employees. They are even more select in that they have had the courage to publish evaluative reports on their programs. While the following discussion is often critical, this is done with the intent of improving future evaluations, not with the idea of belittling the evaluation efforts which exist at present.

The National Council on Alcoholism estimates that fewer than three hundred companies in this country have operating occupational alcoholism programs for their employees. Of the possible three hundred company programs, fewer than twenty had the courage, dedication and resources to attempt an evaluative effort and publish the results. Any weakness in these evaluations is more an indication of the early stage of development of this area than of an oversight on the part of the evaluation staff.

The Case Study Method

As the reader will recall, the case study method looks at individuals, either through testimonial or through the eyes of an observer. This method provides a wealth of data about each case and is usually either based solely on observation (O) or an observation during and after some treatment (X O).

Vaschak (1969) reports three case studies observed in a New Jersey company. A "failure," a "success" and an "early" case are provided to illustrate the behavior, life problems and job performance of problem drinkers. The article's conclusion stresses the need for a program which has the support of company management and emphasizes the need for and benefits which result from early detection. In this instance, a balanced presentation is attempted in which both successes and failures are discussed. Usually the case study method is used to stress the successful aspects of a company program.

A publication by the National Industrial Conference Board (1970) titled *"Company Controls for Drinking Problems"* contains a wealth of information about occupational alcoholism programs. Five companies provide a total of thirteen case studies (Weyerhauser Company, 2; Corning Glass Works, 3; Great Northern Railway Co., 5; Gulf Oil, 1; and North American Rockwell, 2). These cases illustrate the types of drinking problems—and solutions—found by individuals at all levels of the work force.

Case studies can be invaluable for teaching about problem drinking, for selling a program, or for trying to identify similar elements in different individuals or programs. This method is not very useful in evaluating the effectiveness or efficiency of a program, however. Imagine a small program which sees only one hundred cases a year. One hundred case studies would be difficult to use in estimating effectiveness until they were classified together in some countable fashion. For example, one could look at the number who maintained their jobs as the proportion of successful outcomes, or cases could be classed as to degree of improvement (i.e. marked, slight, none, got worse). While the case study method has its particular uses, it is not an efficient method for evaluating the performance of a program.

Systematic Evaluations of Programs

As has been noted earlier, estimates of the prevalence of problem drinking in the work force range from 3 to 10 percent. Secondary sources typically cite estimates of program effectiveness from 50 to 80 percent for employees who accept help from an occupational alcoholism or troubled-employee program. Reports were found for sixteen company programs which have some bearing on the questions of appropriateness, adequacy, effectiveness and efficiency. Table 2-IV contains a summary of the estimates of effectiveness and efficiency and the measures used in these sixteen programs. A few of these programs were in the start-up phase and their data is tentative. Other reports did not indicate how the estimates were arrived at or are "professional estimates" of cures due to the program activity.

None of these company programs had a "control group" which did not receive the treatment program. In two of the sixteen program evaluations, the proportion of persons who refused participation in the program but maintained their job is reported. A total of three reports contained information on the absolute number of persons refusing participation in the program. Franco (1957) reports that 18 percent of those referred to the program refused help; Davis (1970) reports that 13 percent

TABLE 2-IV

SOME EVALUATIVE DATA ON OCCUPATIONAL PROGRAMS

Program and Reference	Proportion Improved in the Program	Measures	Savings
Consolidated Edison (Franco, et al., 1957)	72%	Maintained job Improved job Performance	67% reduction in days absent
Esso Standard Oil (Thorpe & Perret, 1959)	65%	Controlled Drinking	41% reduction in days absent
Oil Refinery in the Caribbean (Turfboer, 1959)	82%	Maintained Job	33% reduction in days absent
American Cynamid Co. (Clyne, 1965)	——	Job Maintenance	——
Eastman Kodak (Raleigh, 1968)	65%	Satisfactory Employment	——
New York Telephone (Kamner & Dupong, 1969)	80%	Maintained Job	Large savings mentioned
A Large Prime Airframe Producer (Davis, 1970)	87%	Maintained Job	84.4% reduction in days absent
New York State Employee Programs (Ashby, 1971)	65%	Not Defined	——
Illinois Bell (Asma, 1971)	72%	Maintained Job	46% reduction in days absent
Hughes Aircraft (Chandler, 1972)	80%	Acceptable Job Performance	Large savings mentioned
Kennecott Copper (Jones, 1972)	——	Improved Attendance	50% reduction in days absent
New York City Transit Authority (Warren, 1973, personal communication)	80%*	Maintained Job	1 to 2 million dollars per year in sick pay
Hoffman-LaRoche (Calabrese, 1973, personal communication)	80%*	——	——
Union Carbide (Welsh, 1973, personal communication)	70%*	Maintained Job	——
DuPont (Lawlor, 1973, personal communication)	80%*	Rehabilitation Rate	——
Burlington Northern (Vaughan, 1973, personal communication)	75%*	Controlled Drinking	——

* Estimated proportion improved

of the referrals refused to participate; and Asma, Eggert and Hilker (1971) report that 5 percent of their referrals refused to participate. Two companies report data which allowed computation of the proportion of those who refuse the program but maintain their jobs: Clyne (1965), 35 percent, and Franco (1957), 61 percent.

Thus, there are estimates that between 5 and 18 percent of employees referred to an occupational program will refuse to participate and that in terms of maintaining their job, between 35 and 61 percent of those refusing participation will improve job performance enough to maintain employment.

Estimates of effectiveness reported in Table 2-IV range from a low of 65 percent to a high of 80 percent for several programs. Efficiency estimates are usually provided in terms of decreases in absenteeism and accidents. Fifteen of the sixteen programs will be looked at in some detail.

Consolidated Edison
(Franco, 1957)

This evaluation of one of the earlier occupational programs is one of the better articles found by the writer. An attempt is made to be comprehensive and to develop new assessment methods.

APPROPRIATENESS. In this early paper, the prevalence of problem drinking in the work force is estimated at 2 percent. Approximately forty new cases were being found each year or about two cases per one thousand employees. No data is provided on the relative priority of the alcoholism program in relation to other employee services. It is implied that the program has fairly high priority and that management was concerned about problem drinking and its detrimental effects.

ADEQUACY Nothing is stated about the adequacy of the program. Given the above estimates of a 2 percent prevalence rate with a 0.2 percent penetration rate, it could be concluded that although the program might be adequate to handle the problem, improvements were needed in the case finding area.

EFFECTIVENESS. Franco reports that 72 percent of those who stay in treatment for one year maintain their jobs. Those who refuse treatment have a high level of job maintenance (61%), while those who drop out of treatment before a year is up have the lowest survival rate (45%). Franco also presents interesting data showing improvement in the effectiveness of the program over time. He notes that the proportion who maintain their jobs has increased from 42 percent to 53 percent to 72 percent. While it is often said that it takes time to develop an effective program, here is some data on the actual trends:

A recovery scale was used by Franco to evaluate improvement over time. Use of the scale (unimproved to recovered) requires a four-year follow-up of clients. Of those who maintained their jobs over the four-year follow-up, they found 60 percent to be rehabilitated or socially recovered and 30 percent much improved, with only 3 percent unimproved (of those in treatment a year). Those who refused treatment had much lower ratings on the Recovery scale with 31.2 percent in the unimproved category and only 25 percent considered to be rehabilitated or socially recovered.

Efficiency. Savings are reported only for those who stayed in treatment. In the three-year period before identification, sickness-absenteeism averaged 13.5 days for this group. This was reduced to less than four days per year after treatment. This is a 70 percent reduction in average days absent.

Design. The basic design used here is a time series design without a control. It can be diagrammed as:

O   O   O   X   O   O   O   O

While an attempt is made to develop comparison groups from those refusing treatment and those who drop out of treatment, this attempt is at a descriptive level and no tests of statistical significance are made.

Outcome Measures. Four measures of outcome are recorded in this study: job maintenance, the Recovery Scale, supervisor's ratings of work performance and sickness-absenteeism. The Recovery Scale has five steps: 1) recovered, 2) socially recovered, 3) much improved, 4) somewhat improved, and 5) unimproved. The scale is tied to the years of follow-up in that a person cannot be assigned to categories 2 or 3 until the end of the first year. Attainment of the recovered category requires two to four years of abstinence. These requirements limit the usefulness of the rating scale without modifications.

TYPES OF TREATMENT. The company used the "Consultation Clinic for Alcoholism" (Pfeffer, Feldman, Feibel, Frank, Cohen, Berger, Fleetwood and Greenberg, 1956) which was developed specifically for industry. Psychiatric help and referral to AA are utilized in treatment.

Esso Standard Oil Company
(Thorpe and Perret, 1959)

This report is based on the experience of a company with employees in eighteen states. The company's program for problem drinkers, partially disabled employees and chronic absentees was started in the early 1950's.

APPROPRIATENESS. The authors report a prevalence rate of 0.7 percent for identified problem drinkers in their work force. They state that this is most likely an underestimate and cite the 3 percent figure as a more likely indication of the actual number of employed problem drinkers. They state that 90 percent of their problem drinkers are over 40 years of age. No data is given on relative priority of the alcoholism program, although the authors note that the company's program is oriented toward many problems and not just drinking.

ADEQUACY. The authors note that treatment varies from location to location based on the community resources available. In a sense this report is an overview of a number of different programs. Adequacy cannot be assessed here until the individual units are examined.

EFFECTIVENESS. Of the total 278 problem drinking cases, 18.3 percent had been abstinent for a year on follow-up, 28.5 percent were considered to be improved and 19.7 percent were unimproved (34% were retired, terminated or died). These figures include those who refused treatment in addition to those who were helped. The authors provide a table showing the percentages improved by four treatment methods and no treatment: 59.7 percent improved with medical treatment only, 64.3 percent improved with psychiatric treatment only, 59.6 percent improved with AA experience, 58.2 percent improved with some combination of the three treatments, and 37 percent who refused treatment improved. The AA treatment group had the largest proportion of abstinent persons (48.1%).

EFFICIENCY. A separate study of problem drinkers in one refinery showed absenteeism in the problem drinking population to drop from 29.9 days to 17.6 days over a four-year period. Figures for the total employee population went from 10.5 days to 8.9 days in this same period. While this represents a 41 percent reduction in absenteeism, the authors note that it was probably due in part to changed company procedures and not just the alcoholism program.

DESIGN. The design of this study is retrospective using the medical records of the medical records of the various company units. A total of 278 problem drinking cases were identified over a nine-year period (1948-1956). At the time of follow-up, all cases were assigned to one of six categories (abstinent, improved, unimproved, retired, terminated or died). This design might be diagrammed as:

X   O

The approach is basically historical.

OUTCOME MEASURES. The major outcome measure is composed of the six status categories at outcome and is based on material drawn from company files or talks with various medical officers.

TREATMENT TYPES. Medical, psychiatric treatment and referral to AA are the three major treatment modalities mentioned. The treatment available was dependent to a large part on the location of the particular plant. An interesting comparison is made between treatment methods, showing AA to have the highest proportion of abstinent clients, but all three modalities had similar proportions of unimproved cases (35% to 42%).

An Oil Refinery in the Caribbean
(Turfboer, 1959)

This report describes the efforts of primarily one individual in setting up a company program. This required developing community resources on an island with a major alcoholism problem and limited treatment resources.

APPROPRIATENESS. Appropriateness is discussed at length in this paper. It is noted that the company was the major employer on the island. Alcoholism and alcohol abuse are documented as a major problem for the island and the company. For example, each year one out of every sixty islanders was listed in a police report in connection with alcohol abuse. Since the island government had not yet taken steps to solve the problem (prior to 1955), the company was reluctant to make the first move. This was resolved by setting up an Island Foundation on Alcoholism, with joint government and company support. The foundation carried out educational programs, started a clinic for alcoholics, and supported the establishment of an AA group.

ADEQUACY. It was estimated that about 6 percent or approximately four hundred of the company employees were problem drinkers. Over a one and one-half year period, 160 men were seen and given some form of treatment in the clinic. Adequacy is not discussed in terms of the capacity of the clinic given the size of the problem. Over the year and a half, a penetration rate of 40 percent is reported, or approximately 27 percent penetration per year into the problem drinking population.

EFFECTIVENESS. A group of seventy-six referrals is evaluated to assess program effectiveness. Forty-five men or 59 percent were still active cases and were considered to be partially or completely rehabilitated. Another 17 or 23 percent had lost interest in the treatment program, but were still employed. Thus, 82 percent of those referred to the program maintained their jobs.

EFFICIENCY. Data was sought on absenteeism for forty-five of the workers who had participated in the treatment program for a year. Data was obtained for thirty-one cases. On the basis of this limited and possibly biased sample, a reduction in the number of days absent was found. Data is presented for 1953, 1954, 1955 and 1956 (the year of the program). Absenteeism increases from an average of 11.3 days in 1953 to a high of 22.0 days in 1955. This then decreases to 14.7 in 1956. The comparison between 1955 (22 days average absenteeism) and 1956 shows a 33 percent decrease in absenteeism for the thirty-one persons in the sample.

DESIGN. This design again is basically a historical approach to evaluating outcome with records of absenteeism as the major outcome variable. This retrospective design can be diagrammed as:

$$O \quad O \quad O \quad X \quad O$$

The lack of available information on all cases of interest illustrates the major weakness of the historical approach. Since the design was not planned ahead of time and data was not systematically recorded, much information was not available at follow-up. The problem is so severe in this report that the author's findings are only suggestive of a positive impact on the program.

OUTCOME MEASURES. In addition to the partially successful effort to gather information on absenteeism, the author describes at length his attempts to construct a recovery scale for use by observers. He provides a good description of the problems he ran into in this effort. A case study of one individual is also presented to give the reader an idea of the types of problem drinkers the company program worked with.

TREATMENT TYPES. Referral to AA, counseling and disulfiram were major treatment modalities. AA was seen as the most useful.

American Cynamid Company
(Clyne, 1965)

This report describes the initiation of a company alcoholism program. The discussion of the supervisory training program is extremely detailed and may be of use to others initiating programs. The data which are presented on outcome are based on the first three years of operation and the authors are reluctant to draw conclusions from it. They are still in a period of development and are trying to obtain increased support for the program. This report is discussed here since they do provide some information on the effectiveness of a new program in its early stages.

APPROPRIATENESS. The authors cite the 3 percent estimate of prevalence of problem drinkers in the work force to show that the problem is sizable. They also point out that alcoholism is fourth among major health problems facing citizens in this country. They go on to cite survey findings which show problem drinkers cost employers three times as much as the normal employee in terms of sickness benefits, absenteeism, accidents and inefficiency.

ADEQUACY. Adequacy of the program is not discussed, although it is noted that universal acceptance of the program has not been attained and there is a perceived need for continuing education. Information on the size of the work force is not presented and prevents the computation of a penetration rate.

EFFECTIVENESS. The authors note that of the 107 employees seen in the first three years of operation, forty-six (43%) are actively employed and undergoing rehabilitation. Another thirty-eight (35%) refused rehabilitation but are still employed. Of the remainder, fifteen were terminated, four retired, two died and two are currently hospitalized. Data are not provided on the number who received treatment and improved or did not improve. In short, it can be concluded that the program is in operation, but no estimates of effectiveness can be made on the basis of the data presented.

EFFICIENCY. No data are provided on the question of efficiency.

DESIGN. This approach appears to be another example of a historical design:

$$X \qquad O$$

Data may have been systematically collected before and after treatment but it is not apparent in this report.

OUTCOME MEASURES. The authors merely report the current job status of the 107 problem drinkers seen by the program over a three-year period. Absenteeism, accidents, medical costs and work performance are referred to in the introduction but no data is presented in these areas.

TREATMENT TYPES. Evaluation by the medical department and referral to AA, consultation clinics for alcoholism, the medical profession, religious groups, and the National Council on Alcoholism are all mentioned. A weekly follow-up is conducted by the medical department.

Eastman Kodak
(Raleigh, 1968)

This chapter on alcoholism in industry briefly describes the Eastman Kodak program as one approach to helping problem drinkers. A case study is presented with a four-year follow-up demonstrating how this program was successful with one employee. At the end of the article it is noted that the Eastman Kodak program has treated 450 employees and that 65 percent were rehabilitated and returned to satisfactory employment.

The introduction to the chapter lays the groundwork for a discussion of appropriateness of alcoholism programs in industry. However, the discussion is not specifically related to the Eastman Kodak program. No information is presented on adequacy, efficiency or outcome measures.

TYPES OF TREATMENT. The plant medical department was the major treatment resource. Referrals were made to AA and to available community facilities.

New York Telephone Company
(Kamner and Dupong, 1969)

This article is a fairly straightforward attempt to describe and evaluate the occupational alcoholism program of the New York Telephone Company from 1961 through 1968.

APPROPRIATENESS. The authors note that in 1961 they were confronted with several employees who were referred to the medical department for problem drinking. This forced the medical department to confront this problem area and realize the need for a program. In this situation it appears that the work force demanded a solution by the medical department which required that a program be developed to deal with problem drinking.

ADEQUACY. Data are not given on adequacy of the program nor on the size of the work force. While it is noted that three hundred employees have been seen for problem drinking from 1961 through 1968, penetration rates cannot be estimated.

EFFECTIVENESS. Job maintenance is the major outcome criterion used. Eighty percent of the three hundred employees seen either kept their jobs or left employment for reasons unrelated to alcohol. One interesting finding is presented in terms of the age of employees when first seen by the program. The numbers increase with age up to the sixty-plus group with the majority of identified problem drinkers belonging to the forty to fifty-nine age bracket (64%).

EFFICENCY. No data are provided on efficiency.

DESIGN. Again a historical design is presented:

$$X \qquad O$$

OUTCOME MEASURES. The major measure was "status at follow-up" with two categories: 1) terminated because of alcoholism and 2) employed or terminated for a reason other than alcoholism. No job performance ratings or information on absenteeism is presented.

TYPES OF TREATMENT. The authors note that their program used a wide variety of referral sources. AA, psychiatric aid, and the alcoholism units of four hospitals had been utilized at various times.

A Large Prime Airframe Producer
(Davis, 1970)

This brief report tantalizes the reader with details and statistics but leaves many questions unanswered.

APPROPRIATENESS. The author states that 6 percent of the work force is adversely affected by alcohol. He stated that alcoholism steals profits and destroys the men who make the profits. No data are reported on the relative priority of the alcohol program in relation to other programs.

ADEQUACY. The work force of the organization is stated to average around ten thousand. No data are presented on the capacity of the program, the 6 percent estimate would indicate that approximately six hundred persons have an alcohol problem at any one time. Davis reports that 340 individuals have been seen in seven years of operation. This would be an average of forty-nine cases per year and might indicate a penetration rate of 12 percent a year. Since this seven-year period probably includes the start up of the program, accurate figures on penetration rate cannot be computed on the data available.

EFFECTIVENESS. Of the 340 cases seen over the seven-year period, 220 are considered to be controlled or recovered (65%). Another 75 had had relapses of varying degrees but are still employable. This would yield a total of 295 (87%) who have maintained their jobs. The author notes that 45 persons (13%) refused help and in many instances are no longer employable. Exact figures are not given on those who refused help, but maintained their jobs.

EFFICIENCY. Comparing the before-after absenteeism of "a large group" who had gone through the program, the average lost time in the year before the program was three days per month. One year after the program this figure was down to an average of 3.75 hours per month. The author notes that this is an 84.4 percent reduction in absenteeism.

DESIGN. Again a historical design with job maintenance as the outcome criterion is utilized for evaluation. Some information is provided on the question of efficiency but the group is not specified. There is no way of telling how many of the treatment group were included or excluded. Unfortunately, this report does not allow one to say much about the adequacy, effectiveness, or efficiency of the program. The design could be diagrammed:

X   O

OUTCOME MEASURES. Job maintenance and absenteeism are used.

TYPES OF TREATMENT. AA, disulfiram, hospitalization, financial clinics, religious support and psychiatric clinics are reported to be utilized.

The New York State Employee Program
(Asby, 1971)

This is a general article describing the New York State Employees' program three years after its inception. Hard data are lacking throughout the paper and there is not enough information presented to be analyzed in terms of the seven categories. Impetus for the program seems to have come from the Federal government (i.e. Public Law 91-616 and a Federal grant). Thus, appropriateness was justified to some extent by the Federal emphasis. Adequacy of the program is not discussed, though the scope of the program is to include all state employees.

Effectiveness is referred to in citing the results from projects around the Albany area. It is stated that more than one hundred state employees have been seen and the results of referral have been markedly successful in 50 percent of the cases. It is further reported that an additional 15 percent of the referrals have shown a lesser degree of improvement. The basis for concluding improvement is not reported, although indications of 65 percent improvement are noted.

Efficiency, design, outcome measures and types of treatment are not reported on.

The Illinois Bell Telephone Company
(Asma, et al., 1971)

This is one of the better evaluations to be found in the existing literature. Findings are reported for 402 employees for whom data was available for five years before and five years after the referral to the program.

APPROPRIATENESS. The program was started in 1951 when it was decided that the alcohol problem was significant in terms of human loss, loss of business efficiency, increased sickness disability, and in increased on- and off-the-job accidents. No data are given comparing the priority of this program to other areas.

ADEQUACY. The company has 42,000 employees. No company estimates of the prevalence of alcohol problems are provided, though other estimates are referred to. It is noted that no survey has been conducted within the company. While no data is presented on adequacy of the program, it is reported that the alcoholism program has evolved into a more general "Health Evaluation Program" for any type of job performance problem which cannot be handled by usual management procedures. Thus, it seems that this program has evolved toward a troubled-employee or Broadbrush program.

EFFECTIVENESS. The outcome is examined for a total of 402 employees, on whom records are available for five years before and after referral to the program. A total of 230 or 57 percent of the employees were judged to be rehabilitated. Rehabilitated meant that they stopped drinking completely for at least one year. Another 60 or 15 percent were judged improved which meant their job performance was satisfactory even though their drinking was not "controlled." Five percent or 20 employees were considered to be failures and outcome was uncertain for the remaining 23 percent. Thus, for the 402 employees, 290 or 72 percent were judged to be improved.

Job efficiency was estimated by the employing department for each of the 402 employees. Overall ratings of good, fair or poor were assigned for the five years before the program and for the five-year period after referral to the program. The estimates are given separately for men and women. In the five years before referral to the program, 54 percent of the women were rated as showing "fair" or "good" work efficiency. This rose to 78 percent for the five-year period after referral to the program. Similar results are reported for men where 78 percent were seen as "fair" or "good" before the program and 90 percent fell into these categories in the five-year period after the program.

EFFICIENCY. Sickness disability is examined by counting the number of incidents. The number of days absent are not examined. In the five year period before the program, there were 662 cases of sickness disability for the group while in the five-year period after referral this dropped to 356 cases. This is a 46 percent reduction in the number of incidents of sickness-absenteeism. On-the-job accidents decreased from fifty-seven for the five-year period before referral to eleven for the five-year period after referral. This is an 81 percent decrease in on-the-job accidents. Off-the-job accidents (where disability lasted more than seven days) went from seventy-five to twenty-eight in the two five-year periods. This is a 63 percent reduction in off-the-job accidents.

DESIGN. The design here is again historical, but data are systematically recovered from medical records for a five-year period prior to referral to the program. It could be diagrammed as:

O   O   O   O   O   X   O   O   O   O   O

Since the data for the five-year periods before and after treatment are collapsed together it is essentially an historical before-after design with no control or comparison groups.

OUTCOME MEASURES. Ratings of improvement (recovered, sobriety for at least one year; improved, satisfactory work performance; accepted help, as an uncertain category; and not controlled, failures) are used to retrospectively assess the impact of the program. Supervisors were also asked to rate job efficiency in terms of good, fair or poor for all 402 employees. Incidents of sickness-absenteeism, lost time for off-the-job accidents, and number of on-the-job accidents are also examined.

TYPES OF TREATMENT. The facilities of the plant medical department include a full-time alcoholic rehabilitation counselor in addition to the usual medical staff. Referrals are made to AA, to hospitals, or to community facilities when needed. Asma et al. report that 87 percent of those referred accept the company program and that 55 percent accept referral to AA.

Hughes Aircraft Company
(Chandler, 1972)

This speech covered the nature of problem drinking in industry on a national basis and then gives some results of a pilot program at one Hughes Aircraft facility.

APPROPRIATENESS. The company employs 30,000 people in forty-four different units. A 6 percent estimate of prevalence is used to arrive at an estimate of 1,800 alcoholics in the work force employed by the company. Conservative calculations by the company estimate a cost of $6,000 per problem employee per year due to absences, group insurance claims, and low job performance. This means that the 1,800 problem drinkers cost the company in excess of $10 million per year.

In addition to this dollar loss, it is pointed out that by ignoring the problem, management was helping the problem drinker commit occupational, if not actual, suicide. No data are given on the relative priority of the alcoholism program compared to other programs.

ADEQUACY. The program was started in one of the company's largest divisions which has approximately 6,000 employees. The program is designed to handle all types of employee problems and is a Broadbrush or troubled-employee program not restricted solely to alcoholism problems. Results are presented for roughly the first four years of the program. During this period 572 employees were seen. Alcohol problems were predominant in 66 percent of the referrals and marital, financial, drugs, employee relations and a miscellaneous category accounted for the balance of the problem employees. Penetration rate per year cannot be estimated from the data presented, although the 6 percent figure yields an estimate of 360 problem drinkers at any one time for this work force. A total of 389 problem drinkers were seen in the report period.

EFFECTIVENESS. Effectiveness is not reported separately for each problem category. An 80 percent figure is reported for the number attaining acceptable job performance.

EFFICIENCY. No data are reported which estimate savings to the company. The 80 percent figure cannot be combined with the estimated cost of $6,000 per employee since it is known that a group of problem employees costs more than a non-problem group even after work performance has returned to an adequate level (Franco, 1957; Pell and D'Alonzo, 1970). It is pointed out that this problem group referred to the program had an average of twelve years of service to the company and that two thirds of the alcoholic group were salary or white-collar employees with an average income of almost $18,000 per year.

DESIGN. This is essentially a loose descriptive, historical design. Only those employees referred to the program since its inception are reported on. The design can be diagrammed:

X   O

OUTCOME MEASURES. The only outcome measure reported in this paper is a rating of acceptable versus unacceptable job performance. It is not stated how this rating is arrived at.

TYPES OF TREATMENT. The company counseling department represents a referral source for the problem employee. The problem is discussed and referral may be made to a marriage counselor, the credit union, a psychiatrist, an M.D., AA, or other sources. This Broadbrush approach recognizes and utilizes a broad spectrum of helping agents.

Kennecott Copper Corporation
(Jones, 1972)

This paper was the basis for a talk which describes a program started in 1970. As with the preceding description of the Hughes program, the critical theme is a description of the program although some evaluative data is presented.

APPROPRIATENESS. This presentation discusses the extent of the problem and estimates that between 5 and 10 percent of the work force is in the problem drinking category. No data are presented on the relative importance of the alcohol problem in relation to other problems. The fact that this is a Broadbrush or troubled-employee program which seeks to help employees resolve any problem which results in impaired job performance, reduces the need for establishing the priority of the alcohol problem.

Data are reported on a thirty-seven-man alcoholic sample which shows this group to have five times as much absenteeism as the total work force. It is also pointed out that sickness and accident costs are five times as high and health maintenance costs are three times the cost for the rest of the work force.

ADEQUACY. The capacity of the program is not discussed. The company employs 8,000 persons in the Salt Lake area and there are approximately 24,000 dependents of workers who are also offered the facilities and referral sources (220 community service agencies are reported) of the company.

Perhaps adequate capacity can be assumed from the report of 2,407 persons who solicited help from the program in the first twenty months of operation. This represents 1,053 employees and 1,180 dependents. It is noted that for employees, the greatest single problem has been alcohol abuse (269 cases) followed by family, legal, marital, financial and drug abuse cases. The problems of dependents fall into a different order with family problems followed by marital, legal, financial, drug and alcohol.

While it is stated that penetration rates are vastly superior to any other company, exact figures are not reported. The large volume of problem employees and dependents seen in such a short time period would seem to support this assertion.

EFFECTIVENESS. No effectiveness data are reported for the

total program. Some figures are given for a thirty-seven-man alcoholic sample, twelve of whom enrolled in the program and for an eighty-seven-man "chronically absent" employee group. The 12 (32%) alcoholic employees who enrolled in the program were seen to reduce absences, sickness and accident costs, and health costs.

Sixty-seven (77%) of the eighty-seven chronically absent employees improved their attendance. Overall improvement is cited to be 44 percent, but it is not clear what this figure refers to.

EFFICIENCY. The twelve-man alcoholic group which enrolled in the program reduced absences 50 percent, reduced sickness and accident costs 67 percent, and reduced health costs by 50 percent. No other efficiency data are given and the data reported must be viewed as suggestive of the potential of the program until a more systematic evaluation is conducted.

DESIGN. It is difficult to talk about a design here. Essentially two groups are looked at in retrospect. The paper does not report how systematically these observations were carried out or the outcome for all of those in the samples. The design might be diagrammed as:

$$X \quad O$$

OUTCOME MEASURES. Absenteeism, sickness and accident costs, and health costs are referred to in this paper.

TYPES OF TREATMENT. The program can make referrals to any one of 220 community service agencies in the area. This indicates that many diverse services must be drawn upon by the program.

New York City Transit Authority
(Warren, 1973, personal communication)

The write-up presented here is based on data found in the National Council on Alcoholism's *Labor-Management Alcoholism Newsletter* (Vol. 1, Number 9). This bulletin was proved by Mr. Joseph Warren.

APPROPRIATENESS. Appropriateness is discussed in terms of the strict rules of the company and the necessity of having sober employees operating the Transit Authority's equipment. No data are provided on the priority of the alcoholism program in relation to other company services.

ADEQUACY. No data are provided on the adequacy of the program, although the immediate referral of any employee suspected of drinking would indicate adequate capacity to handle the extent of the problem. The program is said to handle an average of 251 cases a year.

EFFECTIVENESS. It is pointed out that the program does not like to talk in terms of numbers for it is felt that none really capture what is accomplished by the program. Several quasi-studies have been carried out over the years which provide some information. A review of 200 cases picked at random from the 1958 to 1963 period showed that less than forty had left the company (an 80% estimate of success based on job maintenance). It is also pointed out that some of these individuals who left employment did so for reasons not connected with alcohol.

EFFICIENCY. The program costs approximately $100,000 per year to operate. In the early years a study was made of the savings which resulted from the program. At this time it was estimated that more than $1 million a year was saved in sick pay alone. It is felt that savings in this area are currently more than $2 million a year.

DESIGN. There is no formal design in this paper. It is basically a descriptive article. The study of the 200 employees was of a historical nature.

OUTCOME MEASURES. Job maintenance and sick pay or the cost of sickness-absenteeism are mentioned.

TYPES OF TREATMENT. Individual counseling by a seven-man in-house staff, referral to AA, and hospitalization are utilized when appropriate.

Union Carbide Corporation
(Welsh, 1973, personal communication)

This write-up is based on answers provided by Dr. Welsh in response to a letter asking about the appropriateness, adequacy, effectiveness and efficiency of the program.

APPROPRIATENESS. It is felt that a high priority is given to the alcohol program throughout the corporation, although it is noted that the emphasis may vary from division to division.

ADEQUACY. It is felt that the program currently sees about half of the problem drinkers in the work force. In any given sample examined by the company, about 2 percent of the work force has been involved in the alcoholism program.

EFFECTIVENESS. Hard data were not available on this question. Estimates of the percentage of employees who make a satisfactory work adjustment and maintain their jobs range from 65 to 70 percent.

EFFICIENCY. No data were available on costs or savings at this time. Unfortunately, questions were not asked about the types of treatment used by the program.

DuPont
(Lawlor, 1973, personal communication)

Mr. Lawlor provided a copy of testimony by Dr. C. A. D'Alonzo before the Senate subcommittee on Alcoholism and Narcotics in 1969. The testimony describes the need for occupational alcoholism programs and outlines the DuPont approach to helping employees with drinking problems.

APPROPRIATENESS. The DuPont program has been in operation since 1942. The company employs between 90,000 and 115,000 persons. In this paper it is estimated that there are 6.5 million alcoholics in the country, with three million of these individuals employed in business, industry or the government. It is pointed out that one out of every thirteen men who drink have a drinking problem and that the problem drinker on the average loses twenty-two working days a year more than the average employee. No other data are presented on the relative priority of the alcoholism program in the company.

ADEQUACY. No data are given on the adequacy of the program or on the penetration rate.

EFFECTIVENESS. It is pointed out that DuPont's rehabilitation rate had been about 65 percent but had improved to 81 percent in the previous two years.

EFFICIENCY. No data are given on efficiency, costs or savings.

DESIGN AND OUTCOME MEASURES. These were not discussed in this presentation.

TYPES OF TREATMENT. Referral to AA, counseling and hospitalization are mentioned as forms of treatment.

The Burlington Northern
(Vaughan, 1973, personal communication)

Again this write-up is based on information provided by the program director in response to a letter asking about appropriateness, adequacy, effectiveness and efficiency.

APPROPRIATENESS. It is stated that the program was originally started for the Great Northern Railway Company because of a recognition of the extent of the problem and the need to deal with it. The program is strongly supported by management.

ADEQUACY. The program is available to all personnel, blue-collar and managerial. Previously the program had served 1,726 persons out of a work force of 16,000. The recent merger with three other railroads, none of which had alcohol programs, has increased the total work force to 45,000 and the caseload to 2,625. It is felt that the present staff will be adequate to handle all problem employees for the next four to five years.

EFFECTIVENESS. It is estimated that 75 percent of the cases seen have satisfactory solutions with respect to job performance and drinking behavior. Mr. Vaughan notes that attention to the problem drinker has had a positive influence in changing the drinking patterns of nonalcoholic employees. He points out that absenteeism has dropped, that drink-related accidents have decreased, and that morale has improved.

EFFICIENCY. It is noted that while the cost of running the program is known, the company currently has no way of comparing these costs to savings to the company. The major problem is that there is currently no way to estimate the company's investment in the employee. It is felt that the company realizes large savings by being able to keep trained and experienced personnel who otherwise might be lost. It is also pointed out that the program has positive value by creating goodwill, not only with the employees, but also with the people in the communities served.

DESIGN. No data are given.

OUTCOME MEASURES. None were used systematically, but satisfactory job performance, controlled drinking, absenteeism, accidents and medical costs are mentioned.

TYPES OF TREATMENT. The program basically uses AA-oriented treatment approaches, although other methods, including hospitalization, are available when required.

This review of existing evaluations has shown most designs to be of a simple historical nature. There are widely varying estimates of the size of the problem-drinking population, although this may be related more to the time period of the article than to the characteristics of the working population. Many of these evaluations showed evidence of the types of bias discussed earlier and a high proportion rely on job maintenance as an outcome measure.

Although many of the papers report absenteeism data, the varied definitions make it difficult to compare the programs. A few studies attempted to assess social recovery or job performance, but none utilized the client or working person as a source of evaluative data. While none of these studies used control groups, one did attempt to compare different forms of treatment.

SOME EVALUATIONS OF TREATMENT PROGRAMS

Only a few of the many evaluations are looked at in this section. The evaluations which exist are typically follow-up studies which use a variety of outcome criteria. Many of the evaluations surveyed did not report the percentage or number of cases which improved. Instead, mean pre-post differences are looked at for the total groups. While this methodology lets the reader know whether or not there was a significant gain, it does not allow assessment of the numbers of successes and failures. Another curious feature of the alcoholism treatment literature is that appropriateness and adequacy are almost never discussed. Appropriateness of the treatment program seems to be a given, substantiated by the existence of the program. Efficiency, or cost figures, are rarely reported. The attempt to evaluate the treatment literature in terms of appropriateness, adequacy, effectiveness and efficiency was not successful. Table 2-V summarizes the results from this look at thirteen treatment programs. As can be seen from Table 2-V, the percentages with successful outcome range from 15 to 80 percent. Measures of outcome range from "not being rehospitalized" to improvement in "drinking status" scales. This variation in outcome measures prevents direct comparison of the studies. Also, different groups of alcoholic persons are used and different follow-up periods are reported.

In addition to affiliation with Alcoholics Anonymous, various types of counseling or psychotherapy are the most common form of treatment.

Psychotherapy and Problem Drinking

Hill and Blane (1967) review forty-nine studies of psychotherapy with alcoholics which were published between 1952 and

TABLE 2-V

SOME DATA FROM EVALUATIONS OF TREATMENT PROGRAMS

Study and Reference	Percent Improving	Comparison Group	Measure
Inpatient Programs			
Fitzgerald, Pasework & Clark (1971)	44	No	7 Category Sobriety Scale
Kish & Henmann (1971)	64	No	6 Category Drinking Adjustment Scale
Knox (1972)	15	No	Not Rehospitalized
Pokorny, Miller & Cleveland (1968)	51	No	Degree of Sobriety
Wolff & Holland (1964)	75	No	Attendance & Job Status
Belasco & Trice (1969)	49	Yes	Adjustment Ratings
Gottheil (1973)	68	No	Drinking Frequency
Outpatient Studies			
Mayer & Myerson (1971)	*	No	Reduced Drinking
Goldfried (1969)	*	No	7 Category Improvement Scale
Pattison, Headley, Gleser & Gottschalk (1968)	68	No	Abstinence/ Normal Drinking
Robson, Paulus & Clark (1965)	60	Yes	12 Scales
Pfeffer & Berger (1957)	80	No	Sobriety (?)
Bill (1965)	43	No	Sobriety 1 Year

* Trends reported.

1963. Their major conclusion is that the published literature does not offer conclusive evidence for the value of psychotherapy in treating alcoholic persons. Five factors or methodological problems were seen as responsible for this lack of conclusive data. The majority of studies used inadequate designs, had severely biased samples, used questionable outcome measures, used possibly unreliable measures, and were mainly of a historical nature without actual data collection before treatment. Hill and Blane (1967) offer suggestions to remedy these problems, both for experimental and general evaluative studies. The reader will note that the evaluations of occupational programs discussed earlier suffer from some of the problems noted by Hill and Blane (1967).

The Consultation Clinic for Alcoholism
(Pfeffer, et al., 1956; Pfeffer and Berger, 1957)

Pfeffer and Berger (1957) describe a follow-up study of 160 patients seen by the Consultation Clinic between 1952 and 1955. The majority of the workers were referred to the program by Consolidated Edison. Thirty-nine came from fourteen other companies. Thirty-three of the workers were seen in an initial interview but declined the treatment offered. They are included in the follow-up study. Five areas were examined in the follow-up:

1. Physical health
2. Psychiatric conditions
3. Drinking pattern
4. Social status
5. Vocational status

Data could be obtained for only 60 of the 160 patients (38%). However, Consolidated Edison did provide supervisors' ratings of work performance on 127 patients. The ratings were a simple classification of satisfactory, fair or unsatisfactory.

The sixty patients were divided into three groups on the basis of the drinking pattern they reported in the interview. The largest group was abstinent (n=48), followed by "changed pattern" alcoholics (n=7) and "drinking" alcoholics (n=5). Of those on whom follow-up data is available, 80 percent are abstinent. The implications of this percentage and of other findings in the study are not clear since 62 percent of the clients did not participate in the follow-up.

However, 65 percent of all patients referred to the program had maintained their jobs. Absenteeism for those at Consolidated Edison was reduced from fifteen days per year before the program to an average of five days per year in each of three years after starting treatment.

IMPLICATIONS. This study highlights one of the most crucial problems of follow-up studies: being unable to contact a high proportion of participants. One suggestion made to increase the number of patients in follow-up studies is to contract with the person for follow-up at intake.

Abstinence and Normal Drinking
(Pattison, Headley, Gleser and Gottschalk, 1968)

In this study, thirty-two male patients of an alcoholism clinic are followed up at least a year after termination of treatment. Each man had to have had at least ten treatment sessions to be included in the sample. A total of forty-six men were eligible for the study, but eight were either dead or could not be located, three were in distant cities, and two refused to participate.

Five major outcome criteria were looked at in this study. Since none of the measures had been collected at the time treatment began, the study relies on ratings based on clinical records and the recall of the patients about their former drinking status. An assessment battery developed by Gerard and Saenger (1966) was used to record status on indices of physical health, interpersonal health and vocational health. The Spitzer Mental Status Schedule (Spitzer, Fleiss, Burdock and Hardesty, 1964) and a Drinking Status Scale developed by Pattison's group were also used. The Drinking Status Scale has a range from 0 to 15, with 0 being abstinence, 1 to 6 being normal drinking, and 7 to 15 being pathological drinking. The scale considers the frequency, intensity, compulsivity, social pattern and handicapping sequels of drinking behavior. This scale may prove useful in other studies since it defines "normal" drinking as well as abstinence and pathological drinking.

FINDINGS. On the basis of follow-up ratings by the thirty-two patients, three groups emerged. These are the abstinent drinkers (n=11), normal drinkers (n=11), and pathological drinkers (n=10).

Interviewer evaluations were slightly more conservative with only eight persons in the drinking without difficulty (normal drinking) category. Thus, there was a favorable outcome for the drinking problem for twenty-two persons (69%) on the basis of patient ratings and for nineteen persons (59%) on the basis of interview ratings.

Results are reported separately for both patient and interviewer ratings on the four health scores. Patient ratings of physical health did not differ between groups, while the "pathological drinking" group had higher (less healthy) scores than the other groups. There were significant differences for the mean scores on the vocational health, interpersonal health, and mental health measures for both patient and interview ratings. Generally, the "abstinent" group had the healthiest scores and the pathological drinkers the most unhealthy scores. Differences between "abstainers" and "normal" drinkers were generally small.

In this study, a large number of descriptive variables were examined and found to have no significant relationship to outcome. Age, marital status, occupation, motivation at intake, and number of treatment sessions were found to be unrelated to type of outcome. These findings may, of course, be due to the highly selective nature of the sample.

INDICATIONS. The major implications are twofold. First, a set of measures is provided which may prove useful in other studies. The fact that both patient and interviewer ratings are included is a unique feature. There was generally a high degree of agreement between the two ratings, although the interviewers were typically more conservative.

The second implication, and perhaps the most important, is the definition of "normal drinking" which is developed. The authors found that given their definition, a considerable number of "alcoholic people" do become normal drinkers. Thus, abstinence need no longer be the sole criterion of outcome or program effectiveness.

Clinic Evaluation with Comparisons
(Robson, Paulus and Clarke, 1965)

This study is an attempted follow-up of 200 clients of the Alcoholism Foundation of British Columbia. A comparison group of 100 clients was composed of individuals who had been seen for less than five sessions and then dropped out of treatment. The authors note that it is impossible to have a random no-treatment control group since the Foundation must give treatment to all who request it. The experimental group received more than five sessions (average of sixteen sessions). The two groups were matched on age, marital status, occupation, employment status and elapsed time since intake.

The follow-up required the equivalent of one person's time for an eight-month period. The three interviewers traveled over 7,000 miles within the province in an attempt to contact former patients. Interviews were completed with 155 persons or 72 percent of the sample at an estimated cost of $28 per interview (circa 1963). Nine persons were located who refused to be interviewed.

Patient and interviewer ratings were obtained in six areas: drinking, physical health, work, family relations, social functioning and insight. Interviewer ratings were also combined to give a summary score of overall adjustment. Some of the six areas contained one or two scores so that a total of thirteen indices were available for comparison between the experimental and comparison groups.

FINDINGS. Percentages are reported for the experimental and control groups in terms of those judged improved, showing no change and showing deterioration. Only four of the thirteen comparisons showed significant differences between the experimental and comparison groups. There were significant differences for the patients' rating of physical health and the interviewers' ratings of drinking problems, of insight into reasons for drinking, and the overall interviewer score.

The overall score shows 60 percent of the experimental as compared to 42 percent of the comparison group to have improved. Sixteen percent of the experimental group and 33 percent of the comparison group are rated as showing no change, while 23 percent of the experimental and 25 percent of the comparison groups are rated as deteriorated.

On almost all ratings, the interviewers are more conservative than the patients. On the drinking problem index, the patients reported improvement for 72 percent in the experimental group and 61 percent in the control group, while interviewers rated 58 percent and 39 percent improved (a 6-point improvement scale is used for this rating).

IMPLICATIONS. This study shows no deterioration effects due to treatment as might be expected given the previous discussion of controlled outcome studies of psychotherapy. The study does document the fact that deterioration does occur in both groups and that improvement does occur in both groups.

The authors point out that in many evaluative studies the programs attribute all improvement to program efforts. They very clearly point out the error and show that, based on their overall index, their progam can only claim credit for improvement in 18 percent of the clients since 42 percent of their comparison group improved with minimal treatment.

They do not discuss the issue of facilitating improvement and it may be that their program facilitated improvement so that it occurred quicker than in the comparison group. As has been suggested earlier, justification of treatment programs may have to take into account the time required for improvement. This area awaits further study.

This is a landmark study in that within the limitations of an applied setting the authors are able to set up a fairly rigorous comparison group design and carry it through to completion. The fact that they were able to follow-up 72 percent of their client sample should encourage others contemplating such follow-up studies.

Alcoholism Treatment Centers
(Patterson, 1973, personal communication)

The National Institute on Alcohol Abuse and Alcoholism (NIAAA) has established a number of Alcoholism Treatment Centers across the country. The Institute is attempting to go beyond the usual body-count required by Federal grants in an attempt to obtain data on the effectiveness of these treatment centers. NIAAA has contracted with Stanford Research Institute to develop an information system which will deliver routine monthly and quarterly reports on these treatment centers.

The actual data collection instruments are still in the development and pilot testing stage, but they are operational in centers at the present time. While major revisions may occur before the final information system is in operation, several unique features require that this effort be discussed here.

The information system routinely collects background information about the clients and about staff activities. The most exciting development is the Client Progress and Follow-up Form. It is planned to administer this form at intake and then at 30 days, 90 days, 180 days and every six months after, for as long as the client remains active. It is not known if planned follow-up after termination is scheduled, but it would be easy to incorporate this feature in the design.

The Client Progress and Follow-up Form contains four indices and depends heavily on the patient's response to items. Thus, the client will be relied on as a major source of evaluative information. This source has previously been underutilized in studies of occupational programs. The four indices which will probably be used routinely are: 1) a quantity/frequency index of drinking behavior, 2) an alcohol impairment index which quantifies impairment due to excessive alcohol intake, 3) a self-concept index which quantifies self-perception, and 4) a worry index which quantifies concern about drinking behavior.

This information system is devised to be systematically applied to every client who enters the program, it is prospective or future-oriented as opposed to trying to collect information after the fact, and it is designed to use the patient as a major source of the evaluative data.

SOME GUIDELINES FOR EVALUATING OCCUPATIONAL PROGRAMS

Many evaluative efforts have been reviewed in this paper. All try to answer the question "What happened?" Many tried to go beyond this and answer the question "How much happened?"

One or two tried to determine "How much happened compared to doing something else?" Four major weaknesses were noted in the majority of these efforts. Most evaluations are of a historical, retrospective or "after the fact" nature. Information is not collected at the beginning of treatment. This requires program personnel to make judgments about (or assumptions about) the status of the employees when they began treatment. In addition, these evaluations are dependent on existing record systems which often are not set up with evaluation specifically in mind. Much of the incomplete reporting in the reports may be due to this factor. Most evaluations are not systematic. Part of this is due to the fact that data are lacking because of the retrospective nature of the designs. However, the numbers of persons in the program, the numbers refusing treatment, and the numbers lost to follow-up should always be reported. Often it is unclear whether the evaluation applies to all those in the program or to some selected subgroup. Since there is a lack of systematic data collection, there is often incomplete reporting on outcome.

Many evaluations do not report on the specific definitions used for problem drinking or for the outcome measures. An example is the term abstinence, where in one paper it is not defined, in another it means not having a drink for a year, and another defines abstinence as no more than one "slip" in a year's time. Often when definitions are reported, they are unique to a particular study. This lack of common defintions makes it difficult and at times impossible to compare the various studies.

In almost all cases the worker's definition of the problem and his assessment of outcome is ignored. While it is agreed that there are many problems with self-reports on the effects of treatment, it is also agreed that the person directly involved in the treatment has the most information on its process and outcome. Evaluations by the patients in a program will complement staff reports and give a more complete picture of treatment outcome. Asking the patient to participate in the problem definition and outcome ratings might, in and of itself, serve as an additional motivating force which could improve the proportion of successful outcomes.

The major focus of this section is to raise and define the questions which any interested person should be able to ask about an occupational alcoholism program. It is expected that most of the readers of this chapter will not be evaluators in the strict sense. However, evaluations can be facilitated by having all interested parties know what questions to ask. If you can ask the right questions the answers can usually be obtained.

Later in this section a possible evaluation system is discussed. This example is provided for illustrative purposes with the goal of offering guidelines for the evaluation of occupational programs. There are always many ways to answer a specific question and providing one example may be helpful.

QUESTION 1. How Big Is the Problem? This question asks how many people in a given work force have a drinking problem. While national statistics have been cited showing that 3 to 10 percent of any given work force may be problem drinkers, this question should always be answered for the specific work force of concern. Many programs do rely on the national estimates and these may be the only data it is possible to obtain. However, these national estimates can be misleading and may underestimate or overestimate the true size of the problem for a given work force.

QUESTION 2. What Is the Priority of the Alcohol Problem Given the Other Problems Which Must Be Solved? This is a question of appropriateness. It may be more important for occupational alcoholism programs than for troubled-employee programs. The relative priority of a problem should determine the amount of resources devoted to the solution of the problem. While this is not always the case, if one has information about the size of the problem and its relative priority, then the question of resource allocation can be argued. If one does not have this information, it is difficult to argue for the program on a rational basis. Examination of this question may show that a program should receive more or less resources.

QUESTION 3. What Are the Specific Objectives and Sub-objectives of the Program and Do Measures Exist for Each? This is a crucial question which is often overlooked by program personnel. If objectives are not stated, then there can be no evaluation. If they are not stated, one cannot check program activities to ascertain the linkages between activities and objectives. If there are no measures of the objectives and sub-objectives, then they will have to be developed to allow evaluation. The occupational programs which have been reviewed rather consistently looked at job maintenance, sickness-absenteeism, accident and health cost information. Each of these variables is somewhat lacking for evaluating a rehabilitation program. It is known that a large proportion of alcoholic individuals manage to maintain both their drinking and their jobs for long periods of time. Similarly, it was shown that large numbers had no absenteeism problem. These measures continue to be used because they are available and they have been related to program outcome in a number of studies. Specification of program objectives will allow the development of more specific program-related measures of outcome.

QUESTION 4. WHAT IS THE MAXIMUM CAPACITY OF THE PROGRAM? This is the question of adequacy. If one has an estimate of the size of the problem, then solutions can be planned on the basis of the available resources. It seems to be a fact of existence that the available resources are always less than what is deemed necessary. In part this is due to the continual redefinition and expansion of the problem, at least in the human problems area. If one can define the extent of the problem and the resources available, then the actual operating program can be examined to determine how adequate it will be. Knowing these items of information may lead to a reconceptualization of the program so that the capacity can be enlarged by using the resources in a different fashion. A switch from individual to group counseling is one way that resources have been reallocated for a larger capacity in some treatment programs. There is nothing wrong with setting goals for adequacy at a lower level than 100 percent, in fact it is a common-sense procedure. The capacity of the program must be known for the establishment of program objectives on the number of people to be helped.

QUESTION 5. WHAT IS THE PENETRATION RATE OF THE PROGRAM IN TERMS OF THE SIZE OF THE PROBLEM? This question can only be answered when, for a given period, both the size of the problem and the number of persons reached are known. The question could be rephrased as, how many of the known (or estimated) problem drinkers have been contacted by the program in the past year. This question is independent of how many persons have actually been helped. A program which can only handle 10 percent of those with the problem can, at maximum, only have a penetration rate of 10 percent, but theoretically it could be 100 percent effective in that all those seen were helped. Penetration rate is especially important in determining such things as the need for more supervisory training, the need for educational programs for workers, the need for earlier detection models, or the need for a different approach to the problem.

If one has a high priority program which is adequate to handle the problem and the program has a high penetration rate, then attention can be turned to the real question of effectiveness.

QUESTION 6. OF THOSE WITH THE PROBLEM WHO ARE SEEN BY THE PROGRAM, HOW MANY ARE HELPED, HOW MANY DO NOT CHANGE, AND HOW MANY ARE HURT BY THE PROGRAM? This ques- is the most crucial for any program, but cannot be answered definitely until the preceding five questions have been answered. A pure measure of effectiveness depends on knowing the amount (percentage) of people that the program is designed to help and comparing this with the number who actually are helped by the program. The situation becomes more complicated when it is realized that program efforts can hurt some individuals. A statement of program objectives should indicate the maximum percentage planned to be helped and the maximum percentage it is estimated will be hurt. Drawing upon the literature on psychotherapy, the limits of 80 percent helped and less than 10 percent hurt would seem to be sensible goals for a program given present knowledge.

Answers to the question of effectiveness will always be somewhat tentative, but should become better as programs and measuring instruments evolve. If the above percentages were adopted as program goals, then a program which helped 70 percent of those seen would have an effectiveness of 88 percent (70/80). This assumes that all of those helped would not have changed if there had been no program. Thus, it is an absolute, rather than relative statement of effectiveness. Absolute effectiveness is discussed here since obtaining it for all existing programs would be a large step forward. Relative effectiveness takes into account those who were helped or changed, but who would have changed anyway in the absence of the program. One check on this problem is discussed next.

✓ QUESTION 7. HOW MANY PERSONS WHO REFUSE TREATMENT IMPROVE WITHOUT THE HELP OF THE PROGRAM? It is much more desirable to look at a group which is the same as those who receive treatment, but who are not offered the treatment program. This is always difficult and often impossible. The next best estimate which is available for any program is the number who refuse treatment but seem to improve. An extreme example is used to illustrate the importance of having this information.

It is not hard to imagine a program where 50 percent of those referred refuse treatment. Now imagine an evaluation of those receiving treatment and those refusing treatment. The findings might show that 90 percent of those who refused treatment showed improvement, while only 40 percent of those who accept treatment improved. While it is unlikely that such programs exist, it is a possibility. The findings in this example indicate that the treatment program is either destructive or that those who refuse treatment are a very special group. If there were no differences between the two groups, one would have to conclude that the treatment program was worse than doing nothing. This extreme example is used to highlight the importance of comparison and control groups. As was seen in the paper by Robson, Paulus and Clarke (1965) on the Alcoholism Foundation of British Columbia, 60 percent of those accepting treatment improved, while 42 percent of those who received less than five sessions improved. In this comparison their program could only claim credit for 18 percent of those who improved.

QUESTION 8. WHAT IS THE COST OF EACH UNIT OF PROGRAM ACHIEVEMENT? While evaluations of efficiency of treatment programs are always done, they are often intuitive and unsystematic. Accurate assessment of efficiency depends on knowing the relative effectiveness of the program. In the British Columbia example above, the total cost of the program would have to be charged against the 18 percent which the program was credited with helping. Assessment of efficiency will play its most important role in deciding between different forms of treatment or in determining the utility of assigning different groups of people to different types of treatment.

As the examination of the literature has shown, the occupational alcoholism field is in a relative state of ignorance about the merits of various approaches, the effectiveness and costs. If this current state of ignorance is acknowledged and evaluation efforts move forward, there should be an evolution of better methods and increased knowledge about these interventions and their impact.

The eight questions presented here should be asked about every program. The program which can answer Question 1 through 6 at the present time is one of the leaders in the field. Answers to each of the 8 questions will most likely raise other questions about the program which can then be focused on. For example, when it is known how many people are hurt by a program, one can ask about their characteristics (can they be identified before treatment) and search for alternative treatment strategies for this group.

Additional Guidelines for the Evaluation of Programs

The following pages offer some additional guidelines for the evaluation of programs. These pages will probably be most helpful for program administrators or program evaluators.

When evaluation is to be set up for a particular program, four points should be kept in mind.

1. KEEP IT SIMPLE. Many evaluation efforts literally stop before they begin because too much data collection is desired. Outcome measures should be limited to less than ten indices, preferably around five at the most. Remember that program staff and clients have a lot of things to do besides fill out forms. No matter how short the forms are, there will be resistance and grumbling on the part of the staff about completing them. However, the simpler and more obviously valuable the ratings, the easier it will be to obtain high-quality information.

2. MAKE IT SYSTEMATIC. A system should be set up so that

information is routinely collected from all necessary sources. Checks should be built into the system so that missing information and lost data can be detected quickly and the problem rectified. Nothing is as frustrating as putting months of effort in data collection, only to find that much information is missing when the analysis is started. For example, absenteeism data should be collected routinely and it should not be supposed that the information can always be retrieved in a year from the company archives. Another feature of routine data collection is that a little is collected continuously and one is not faced with the enormous task of trying to go through records at the end of a year searching out relevant factors. A systematic information system can be large, expensive and computerized or it can consist of a box of 5" x 7" cards and the appropriate forms for data-gathering. The type of system which is set up will depend on the resources available and the amount of information which must be processed. A program with a large number of referrals such as that described by ones at Kennecott Copper, might require computer facilities or a large number of clerks. Most of the programs examined in this paper were not that large and can use less complex and costly programs such as that described by Warren of the New York Transit Authority.

3. EVALUATIVE EFFORTS USUALLY HAVE TO EVOLVE. Remember that most evaluative efforts will have to evolve over time. Maintaining an evolutionary perspective will allow one to escape the paralyzing frustrations which accompany the failure to implement a highly sophisticated design in a short period of time. The acceptance by management and program personnel that evaluation is desirable and possible may take considerable time. Moving toward systematic collection of relevant data on clients may represent a second stumbling block which requires time to implement. In many cases a retrospective study of former clients may be a useful way to highlight the need for prospective data collection and to create active interest in evaluation on an ongoing basis. Complex evaluations can easily be created on the drawing board but it may take considerable time and effort to get to the point where the evaluation is in fact operational.

4. DISTINGUISH BETWEEN CLINICAL AND PROGRAM PERSPEC-

TIVES. Most program staff and therapists will be oriented toward helping individual persons and will insist on the uniqueness of each case. This position can be called the clinical perspective. It is often put in opposition to a program perspective, but it should be made clear that these two perspectives need not be opposed, but can be complementary.

The focus of the clinical perspective is on the individual and the major interest is in maximizing the gains for each person. The focus of the program perspective is on the total client population and the major interest is in maximizing the gain for all clients as a group or for different groups of clients.

Most treatment personnel will be trained in the use of the clinical perspective and will use it continually in their work. Most personnel will not have been trained in the program perspective and will often object to its use. The important point here is that treatment personnel can be trained in the appropriate use of both perspectives. Clarification of the two perspectives and illustration of their various uses may do much to facilitate evaluative efforts. For example, the use of the case study method has been described as a good way of summarizing a wealth of data about an individual and illustrating principles of case management. It was also pointed out that a collection of case studies is an awkward way of collecting information to evaluate the success of a program. These two perspectives provide different vantage points for viewing individuals in a program and enable one to answer different types of questions. If one wants to help an individual or to illustrate some particular individual dynamics, then the clinical perspective is most appropriate. If one wants an overview of the successes and failures of the program, or seeks to determine costs, then the program perspective is the most appropriate.

An Example

In the following pages a plan for the evaluation of an occupational alcoholism or Broadbrush program is outlined. This plan may be inappropriate or impossible to implement in some situations. Questions which are crucial for a particular program may not be answered by this design. In addition, the design in the following pages is the best which could be done at this point in time. Six months from now a very different plan would be proposed, although the essential features would remain. It is hoped that this design will serve as an example. Its purpose is to provide a model which will stimulate and facilitate improved evaluations of occupational programs. It should be clear that this plan is not *the* answer for any program or situation. It is a source of ideas about program evaluation, not a definitive answer for evaluative questions.

Table 2-VI contains a checklist which may prove useful to those developing evaluations.

The first item on the checklist has to do with developing a specific definition of problem drinking which all staff will use. A possible definition is: "Any situation where consumption of alcohol periodically is interfering with work performance, social relations, or physical health." This definition is not very specific, but it does provide a starting point from which more precise definitions might evolve. Each program should define the nature of problem drinking as specifically as possible and then classify

TABLE 2-VI

A CHECKLIST OF SOME IMPORTANT TASKS

( ) 1. Has a specific written definition of "problem drinking" been established for use by program personnel? (For Broadbrush programs definitions should be available for the ten or twelve most frequent categories of problems.)

( ) 2. Has the issue of confidentiality been resolved?

( ) 3. Has a list of measurable program objectives been drawn up?

( ) 4. Is a consultant available for help on establishing indices, developing methodology, and assisting in the analysis?

( ) 5. Has the information system for program evaluation been created?

( ) a. Is there a basic fact sheet for descriptive information?

( ) b. Is there an easily accessible central collection system which compiles data from the various sources?

( ) c. Have procedures become operational for the routine collection of client and staff ratings of status for each client periodically?

( ) d. Is follow-up after treatment contracted for at intake, and is the follow-up procedure routine?

( ) e. Have procedures become operational for the routine collection of absenteeism, accident and health costs?

( ) f. Have procedures become operational for the routine collection of grievance costs (where applicable)?

( ) g. Have procedures become operational for the routine collection of job performance ratings from supervisors (where applicable)?

all referrals as to their major problem area. The use of the drinking status indices discussed earlier is one way to define problem drinking operationally and precisely. The Pattison, et al. (1968) Drinking Status Scale or the NIAAA quantity/frequency index could be used to define problem drinking. These scales have the limitation of not being developed specifically for the work situation.

The second issue is that of confidentiality. This may or may not be a problem depending on the specific company situation. Where records cannot be kept secure, the techniques utilized by the New York Transit Authority may be useful. In this case all records are identified by a case number and the individual's name does not appear on them. The names which match the numbers exist only in a locked file. The program director and his assistants are the only persons with access to this file.

The third task is the defining of objectives and sub-objectives. It has been pointed out that this is a critical step in program planning and evaluation. Care should be taken to define objectives in terms of the target population, the expected results, the time period, and the activities which will lead to the accomplishment of the objectives. At this point measures or indices of the objectives must be obtained.

The fourth item on the list focuses on the availability of an evaluation consultant who can help with instrumentation, design and data analysis. If you know the questions for which you want answers, then an evaluation consultant can be invaluable. He can show you how to get definitive answers to those questions, or how the questions have to be reworded to be assessable. He can help you to develop scales which have mutually exclusive (non-overlapping) categories which will be suitable for analysis, and he can be of help in analyzing the data which are collected.

However, if you do not know the questions, an evaluation consultant has as much chance of being a hindrance as a help. This is especially true if the consultant is required to guess the content of the questions to be answered. It is possible that at the end of a time-consuming and possibly expensive evaluation you will find yourself saying, "But we were not interested in that!"

All of the points listed under Item 5 are concerned with

setting up systematic data collection procedures. They are listed in order of priority (in the writer's opinion). Demographic (descriptive) data, staff and client ratings of outcome, and a centralized system which records these items are considered most important. Information on absenteeism, accident and health costs, grievance costs, and job performance ratings are given a lower priority. However, all are important and every program should try to obtain these types of information. The next section provides an illustrative model. An easily accessible central data record is discussed along with a descriptive information sheet, ways to record information from company records, and client and staff ratings of outcome.

An Example of a Data System for Evaluation

A data system for evaluation has somewhat different requirements than a patient records system which contains the case notes and information on each client. While the two can be combined, the focus here will be on the system which is most appropriate for evaluation. The difference is the same as that discussed earlier on the difference between the clinical and program perspectives. A clinical records system is one which contains all information about a specific patient in one place where the treatment personnel have easy access to the data. The evaluation records system is one where all the information on all clients seen in a given time period is easily available to the evaluator or administrative staff. It should immediately provide answers to such questions as: did referrals fall off this month; was one section, or type of problem overrepresented in the new admissions this month; what percentage of clients seen for a six-month period had successful outcomes.

THE HEART OF A DATA SYSTEM: A 5" x 8" CARD. The simple 5" x 8" card is used as an example here since it is relatively inexpensive and could be put into operation in many of the programs reviewed in this paper Each card could contain complete coded information about a client. Figure 2-1 shows the possible layout of such a card. The cards would most likely be printed and the sections on the card would be filled out as information was collected over time. This example uses only

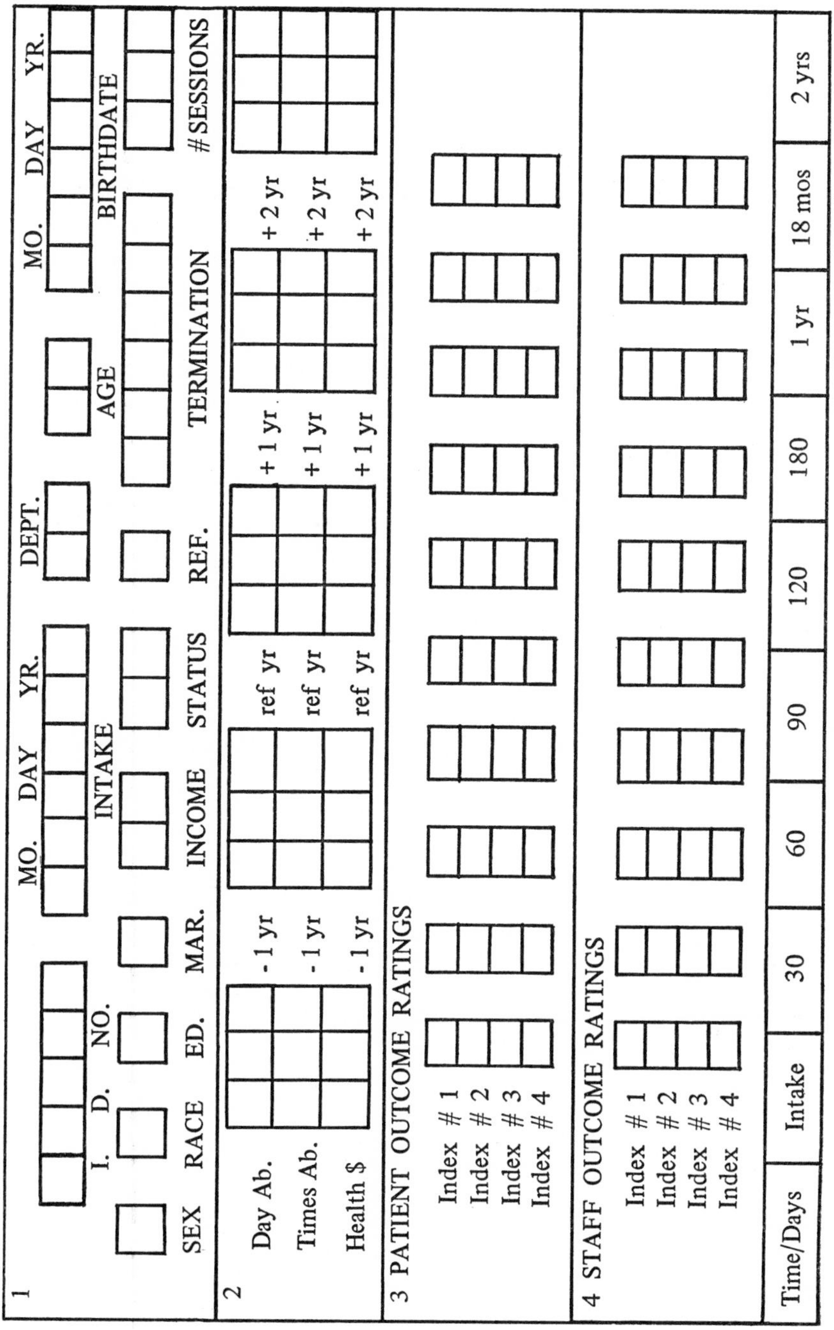

Figure 2-1. An example 5" x 8" data record.

the front of the card. Additional information could be recorded on the back.

This system gives one ease of access to information on all those in the program and allows quick tabulations. The card is divided into four parts which represent four types of data which might be collected. The first section contains the basic descriptive data which would be obtained upon referral to the program. This would include information like I.D. number, date of referral, type of referral, age, sex, education, marital status, income, type of problem, and occupational status. This descriptive information gives a picture of the types of employees using the program. This will be required for comparisons between different company programs. The information will also reveal the representativeness of the problem in the program compared to the total work force. The program might be underutilized by white-collar groups, by one racial group, by an age group, or by a certain division or department. This information will allow assessment of the effectiveness of supervisory training or education programs and may reveal problem areas where more work has to be done. A third purpose is served by these data as soon as outcome measures are available. It may be that different groups profit more by one treatment approach than another. This descriptive information may reveal these relationships and allow the program to become more effective through differential assignment to treatment. For example, single individuals may do best with individual counseling, while married and separated persons would do best in a conjoint or family-oriented approach, and widowed individuals would improve most in a widower's group which emphasized social activity and learning to live without the departed spouse.

The second section on the card contains data from company records. In this example, absenteeism (number of days per year and number of incidents per year) and health costs are recorded. Other items could be recorded here or on the back of the card. This information is collected over time and should reveal changes in "costs" as a result of treatment. This space is provided for recording for the data two years prior to referral, the year of referral, and two years after referral.

The ⟨third⟩ section in this example contains the scores for the individual on the status indices which are used to document outcome. This might be something like Gerard and Sanger's (1959) Physical Health, Interpersonal Health, and Vocational Health indices; it might be the goal attainment ratings which will be discussed in the following pages; it might be any of the various ratings discussed previously; or it might be a set of ratings constructed specifically for a program.

The ⟨fourth⟩ section contains staff ratings of similar outcome measures. These ratings might be done by the counselor or therapist or in a referral program, they might be done by the referral personnel on the basis of recurrent interviews.

It is not necessary to have a card system such as that described here. The card is merely a convenient way of pulling together all of the information in an easily accessible way. If the cards are filed by month of referral and by year, a program administrator can tell at a glance the number of referrals in a given period. Tabulation of descriptive information would provide a quick assessment of the characteristics of a given group. A survey of follow-up information could be quickly gained in the same way by taking the group first seen two years ago and tabulating their follow-up scores in the most recent period.

THE DESCRIPTIVE INFORMATION SHEET. The information on this document is filled out at the first visit. It will vary given the needs of a specific program. Some might want to have the referring department or division listed to assess where most of the referrals were coming from. This could provide a check on the effects of a supervisory training program. Other information on the personal characteristics of the individual should be constant for all programs.

The most difficult problem with designing this form is in keeping it simple. It should not exceed two pages and should not be "crammed" with questions. The questions should be "matter-of-fact" and to the point. A major failure with intake documents or basic data sheets is a frequent attempt to collect too much information. It is not uncommon to find eight, ten, and twelve-page intake documents devised by program personnel. These long forms are always self-defeating. Either they do not get filled out by busy program staff, or they are filled out haphazardly and the information collected is useless. Table 2-VII shows a sample Descriptive Information Sheet which would collect the essential information. It is limited to one page. Another page could be added to obtain other information a specific program might require.

INFORMATION FROM COMPANY RECORDS. Ideally, this would be provided on a monthly or quarterly basis by the appropriate company division. It should be provided on all company employees with access to the program. The list should contain the employee's name, the number of incidents of absenteeism and the length of each incident, in addition to any information on accidents or health insurance costs. This type of report would make it possible to compute the norms for the total work force, for those who refuse treatment, and for those who enroll in the program. Data for each referral could be immediately transferred to the worker's master card.

THE CLIENT AND STAFF RATINGS. The major question in this area is one of deciding which instruments should be used to assess outcome. This will depend to a great extent on the particular goals of a program. The most useful ratings for occupational programs have yet to be designed. A number of different ratings have been mentioned in this paper. Most of those mentioned were not examined in depth and often the article did not contain the complete instrument which was used. While no specific set of scales can be recommended at this point in time, the scales finally adopted should make sense and seem to assess important status elements for the program. The amount of time available, the goals of a specific program, and the needs of program staff are factors which should be taken into consideration when choosing instruments for assessing program outcome.

One of the most important features of client and staff ratings is that they be done periodically for each client. Ratings could be done on referral and every thirty days for the first six months. Then ratings could be collected every six months to obtain data on the earlier periods. As has been pointed out several times, the effectiveness of treatment or referral programs is going to have to be based on the differential rates of improvement due to

TABLE 2-VII

A DESCRIPTIVE INFORMATION SHEET

Name: ....   I.D. No. ....

Address: ....   Division/Dept. ....

Date: ....   *Occupational Status* (Check One)

Current Age: ....   (1) Laborer

Birthdate: ....   (2) Service worker (like cook, waiter, janitor)

Sex: M(1) F(2)

Race: (1)Black (2)White

(3)Oriental (4)Unknown

Education (Check One)

(3) Semi-skilled worker (like a garage worker, gas station attendant, bus, taxi, or truck driver; assembly line worker; drill press, lathe or grinding machine operator; welder

(1) Grade school (or less)
(2) Some high school
(3) High school diploma
(4) Some college
(5) College degree (4 yrs.)
(6) Some graduate work
(7) Masters degree or equiv.
(8) Doctoral degree (MD, Ph.D)

(4) Protective service worker (like a policeman, fireman)

(5) Skilled worker (like a carpenter, electrician, mechanic, baker, pressman, machinist)

Marital Status (Check One)

(6) Foreman or inspector

(1) Single
(2) Married
(3) Married-Separated
(4) Divorced
(5) Widowed

(7) Clerical or office worker (like a bank teller, bookkeeper, file clerk, secretary)

Current Income
(Nearest $1,000): $........................

(8) Salesman or sales clerk (like an insurance agent, stocks and bond salesman, shoe salesman, department store clerk)

Type of Referral (Check One)

(9) Manager or administrator (like an office manager, sales manager, department head)

(1) Self
(2) Supervisor
(3) Medical Department
(4) Co-worker
(5) Union
(6) Family
(7) Other

(10) Professional (like an accountant, doctor, nurse, lawyer, teacher, draftsman, engineer)

treatment instead of the absolute rates which are in common use today.

Jefferson Goal Scaling

This is a rating technique which is still in the experimental stages. It is under development by the Research and Evaluation

Service of Jefferson Community Mental Health/Mental Retardation Center in Philadelphia. The rating procedure has been utilized with the staff and patients of a day hospital, with the staff of an outpatient psychiatric clinic, and with staff and clients of various consultation and training programs. The results to date have been promising enough to report on. It should be remembered that the rating procedure is still under development. It should not be used alone as the sole index of program outcome.

One of the problems with standardized scales is that they are often inappropriate for some clients, but have to be used anyway. In addition, many scales are not linked specifically to the focus of the treatment or intervention effort. If one looks for change in areas where there are no change activities, it is unlikely that change will be recorded. For example, one rating scale on hallucinations is used as part of an assessment by a large project. However, most outpatients do not have hallucinations and thus never change their status on this scale.

The procedure described here has developed out of an attempt to apply the Goal Attainment Scaling Methodology which is under development by the Hennepin County Community Mental Health Center in Minnesota (Kiresuk and Sherman, 1968). Various problems with the Hennepin procedure made it difficult to implement and the method described here evolved as an answer to some of the problems.

The rating procedure involves defining goals by both the patient and the staff person or therapist. This goal definition procedure and subsequent ratings of attainment are seen as an integral part of the treatment. It provides a fairly concrete focus for both the client and counselor and thus should facilitate change along these lines. The scale used to assess attainment is of a self-anchoring nature. It is a 9-point scale with a Not Changed category in the center. There are four negative categories to record moving away from attainment of the goal and there are four positive categories to record attainment of various degrees. The extreme categories are: "Impossible to reach" and "Completely attained." Table 2-VIII is an example of Jefferson Goal Scaling used in a retrospective assessment. In a prospective program the goals would be defined separately by client and

TABLE 2-VIII

A JEFFERSON GOAL SCALING FORM

On this page we would like you to write out your two most important treatment goals. Please be as specific as possible.

After you have written out the goals, we would like you to rate each of them on the two scales below.

My most important treatment goal is:...

....

....

My second most important goal is:...

My goals, as compared to before treatment are now:

First Goal:	Second Goal:	
—4	—4	Impossible to reach
—3	—3	Quite a bit further away
—2	—2	Somewhat further away
—1	—1	A little further away
0	0	Not changed
+1	+1	A little attained
+2	+2	Somewhat attained
+3	+3	Quite a bit attained
+4	+4	Completely attained

counselor at intake. These defined goals would then be rated on the 9-point scale at various times in treatment and at follow-up.

Each goal is specific to the patient or therapist, but they are of common type in that each is the "Most Important" treatment goal as viewed by that person. Since they share this common feature and are rated on identical scales, the ratings can be combined and treated statistically. A reliable coding scheme for types of goals has been developed and is being tested for its predictive utility. These codes allow probabilities to be assigned to each type of goal in terms of successful and unsuccessful outcome. It is expected that different types of treatment will have varied probabilities for similar types of goals and that a systematic assignment to a treatment condition will be possible given the specific goals of an individual.

This section has offered some guidelines and concrete suggestions for evaluating programs. While general solutions for evaluation of occupational alcoholism or troubled employee programs are not yet possible, following the guidelines proposed here should lead to improvement in current practice. It is hoped that the material provided here will accelerate the evolution of evaluative efforts and allow more programs to know "What happened," "How much happened," and "How much happened compared to doing something else."

SUMMARY

There are five questions which have been raised which could be answered by programs now in operation. This summary consists of highlighting these areas where research information is needed and should be easily obtainable.

1. Good Information Is Needed of the Outcome for Those Individuals Who Refuse Treatment. There are indications that a sizeable number improve without exposure to the treatment program. For those who do not get treatment from other sources, information is needed on the proportions who improve in a given time period. Information is also needed on how quickly the improvement occurs. This will help to ascertain the extent to which a treatment program does facilitate improvement.

2. Good Information Is Needed on the Number Who Deteriorate While in Treatment. Is this deterioration due in part to the treatment? Can treatment programs be changed to prevent this deterioration? Can individuals who are likely to have a negative outcome be identified before the deterioration occurs?

3. Good Information Is Needed on the Effects of Supervisory Confrontation in the Absence of a Treatment Program. Do 50 percent of those confronted change their behavior and improve their job performance in the absence of treatment? This question could be answered relatively easily in a large company which is just implementing a program. Chandler's description of the Hughes Aircraft program pointed out that it was not possible to set up the program in all plants immediately. One department or division could have been used to obtain information of the effects of supervisory confrontation in the absence of treatment.

4. Good Information Is also Needed Comparing Broad-brush or Troubled-employee Programs with Occupational

PROGRAMS. Is penetration higher for a Broadbrush program? Are there more self-referrals with this approach? Do those referred seem to be reached earlier in their drinking careers? Again financial limitations might make it possible to get up a natural experiment in comparable divisions or departments of a large corporation to test out these questions.

5. GOOD INFORMATION IS NEEDED ON THE PROPORTION OF SELF-REFERRALS TO A PROGRAM. A program which is preventive or which results in early intervention should have an increasing number of self-referrals. This indicates that the problem will be recognized by the individual in trouble before job performance deteriorates and outside intervention is required. A Broadbrush or troubled-employee program should encourage self-referrals. Are they serving a preventive function? The answers should be fairly easy to get in terms of self-referrals to the program.

Answers to these five questions and application of the information in the preceding section on guidelines should be a step forward in the evaluation of troubled-employee programs. It is hoped that many programs will be able to graduate from the walking to the running stage. Some may even be able to fly. In a decade many programs may be in orbit—on top of the alcohol problem—knowing that they provide effective and efficient help to troubled employees.

REFERENCES

Ashby, F. H.: The New York State employee program. *J Drug Education,* 1:261-266, 1971.

Asma, F. E.; Eggert, R. L., and Hilker, R. R. J.: Long-term experience with rehabilitation of alcoholic employees. *J Occup Med,* 13:581-585, 1971.

Belasco, J. A., and Trice, H. M.: *The Assessment of Change in Training and Therapy.* New York, McGraw-Hill, 1969.

Bergin, A. E.: The evaluation of therapeutic outcomes. In Bergin, A. E., and Garfield, S. L. (Eds.): *Handbook of Psychotherapy and Behavior Change: An Empirical Analysis.* New York. Wiley, 1971.

Bill, C.: The growth and effectiveness of Alcoholics Anonymous in a southwestern city, 1945-1962. *Quart J Stud Alcohol,* 26:279-284, 1965.

Cahalan, D., and Room, R.: Problem drinking among American men aged 21-59. *Am J Public Health,* 62:1473-1482, 1972.

Campbell, D. T., and Stanley, J. C.: *Experimental and Quasi-Experimental Designs for Research.* Chicago, Rand McNally, 1968.

Chandler, W. G.: An effective program to combat alcoholism in industry. Paper presented at the National Occupational Alcoholism Training Institute, East Carolina University, Pinehurst, North Carolina, June, 1972.

Clyne, R. M.: Detection and rehabilitation of the problem drinker in industry. *J Occup Med, 9:*265-268, 1965.

Cole, J. J., and Shupe, D. R.: A four-year follow-up of former psychiatric patients in dustry. *Arch Gen Psychiatry, 22:*222-229, 1970.

Davis, W. W.: Practical experience with an alcoholism program in industry. *Ohio State Med J, 66:*814-816, 1970.

Deniston, O. L., and Rosenstock, I. M.: The validity of non-experimental designs for evaluating health services. *Health Serv Rep, 88:*153-164, 1973.

Deniston, O. L.; Rosenstock, I. M., and Getting, V. A.: Evaluation of program effectiveness. *Public Health Rep, 83:*323-335, 1968.

Dohrenwend, B. P., and Dohrenwend, B. S.: *Social Status and Psychological Disorder.* New York, Wiley, 1969.

Drew, L. R. H.: Alcoholism as a self-limiting disease. *Quart J Stud Alcohol, 29:*956-967, 1968.

Eysenck, H. J.: The effects of psychotherapy: An evaluation. *J Consult Psychol, 16:*319-324, 1952.

Fitzgerald, B. J.; Paseward, R. A., and Clark, R.: Four-year follow-up of alcoholics treated at a rural state hospital. *Quart J Stud Alcohol, 32:*636-642, 1971.

Franco, S. C.: Problem drinking in industry: Review of a company program. *Ind Med Surg, 26:*221-228, 1957.

Gerard, D. L., and Saenger, G.: Interval between intake and follow-up as a factor in the evaluation of patients with a drinking problem. *Quart J Stud Alcohol, 20:*620-630, 1959.

Goldfried, M. R.: Prediction of improvement in an alcoholism outpatient clinic. *Quart J Stud Alcohol, 30:*129-139, 1969.

Gottheil, E.: As reported in "Experiment at Coatesville." *Alcohol Health and Research World, 1:*14-17, 1973.

Habbe, S.: *Company Controls for Drinking Problems.* New York, National Industrial Conference Board, 1969.

Hill, M. J., and Blane, H. T.: Evaluation of psychotherapy with alcoholics: A critical review. *Quart J Stud Alcohol, 28:*76-104, 1967.

Isaac, S. (In collaboration with William B. Michael): *Handbook in Research and Evaluation.* San Diego, Knapp, 1971.

Jones, O.: Insight. Paper presented at National Occupational Alcoholism Training Institute, East Carolina University, Pinehurst, North Carolina, June, 1972.

Kamner, M. E., and Dupong, W. G.: Alcohol problems: Study by industrial medical department. *NY State J Med, 69:*3105-3110, 1969.

Kiresuk, T. J., and Sherman, R. E.: Goal attainment scaling: A general method for evaluating comprehensive community mental health programs. *Community Ment Health J, 4*:443-453, 1968.

Kish, G. B., and Hermann, H. T.: The Fort Meade alcoholism treatment program. *Quart J Stud Alcohol, 32*:628-635, 1971.

Knox, W. J.: Four-year follow-up of veterans treated on a small alcoholism treatment ward. *Quart J Stud Alcohol, 33*:105-110, 1972.

Maxwell, M.: Early identification of problem drinkers in industry. *Quart J Stud Alcohol, 21*:655-678, 1960.

Mayer, J., and Myerson, D. J.: Outpatient treatment of alcoholics: Effects of status, stability, and nature of treatment. *Quart J Stud Alcohol, 32*:620-627, 1971.

Miller, B. A.; Pokorny, A. D.; Valles, J., and Cleveland, S. E.: Biased sampling in alcoholism treatment research. *Quart J Stud Alcohol, 31*: 97-107, 1970.

National Institute on Alcohol Abuse and Alcoholism: *First special report to the U.S. Congress on alcohol and health.* Department of Health, Education, and Welfare Publication No. (HSM) 72-9099, 121 pages. U.S. Government Printing Office, 1971.

National Institute on Alcohol Abuse and Alcoholism: *Occupational alcoholism: Some problems and some solutions.* Department of Health, Education, & Welfare Publication No. (HSM) 73-9060. U.S. Government Printing Office, 1972.

Norris, J. L.: Alcoholism in industry. *Arch Environ Health, 17*:436-445, 1968.

Pattison, E. M.; Headley, E. B.; Glesser, G. C., and Gottschalk, L. A.: Abstinence and normal drinking: An assessment of changes in drinking patterns in alcoholics after treatment. *Quart J Stud Alcohol, 29*:610-633, 1968.

Pell, S., and D'Alonzo, C. A.: Sickness absenteeism of alcoholics. *J Occup Med, 12*:198-210, 1970.

Pfeffer, A. Z., and Berger, S.: A follow-up study of treated alcoholics. *Quart J Stud Alcohol, 18*:624-648, 1957.

Pfeffer, A. Z.; Feldman, D. J.; Feibel, C.; Frank, J. A.; Cohen, M.; Berger, S.; Fleetwood, M. F., and Greenberg, S. S.: A treatment program for the alcoholic in industry. *JAMA, 161*:827-836, 1956.

Plaut, T. F.: *Alcohol Problems: A Report to the Nation.* New York, Oxford University Press, 1967.

Pokorny, A. D.; Miller, B. A., and Cleveland, S. E.: Response to treatment of alcoholism: A follow-up study. *Quart J Stud Alcohol, 29*:364-381, 1968.

Presnall, L. F.: Folklore and facts about employees with alcoholism. *J Occup Med, 9*:187-192, 1967.

Raleigh, R. L.: Alcoholism in industry. In Cantanzare, R. J. (Ed.): *Alcoholism*. Springfield, Thomas, 1968.

Robson, R. A. H.; Paulus, I., and Clarke, G. G.: An evaluation of the effect of a clinic treatment program on the rehabilitation of alcoholic patients. *Quart J Stud Alcohol, 26*:264-278, 1965.

Roman, P. M.: Alcohol abuse, executives and the work world: A survey of attitudes and experiences. Paper presented at the National Occupational Alcoholism Training Institute, East Carolina University, San Francisco, November, 1972.

Homan, P. M., and Trice, H. M.: The development of deviant drinking behavior: Occupational risk factors. *Arch Environ Health, 20*:424-435, 1970.

Sadler, M., and Horst, J. F.: Company/union programs for alcoholics. *Harvard Business Review*, September-October, 1972.

Slotkin. E. J.; Levy, L.; Wetmore, E., and Runk, F. N.: *Mental Health-Related Activities of Companies and Unions*. New York, Behavioral Publications, 1971.

Smith, J. A.: Evaluation and management of the alcoholic employee. *Ind Med Surg, 26*:67-72, 1957.

Spitzer, R. L.; Fleiss, J. L.; Burdock, E. I., and Hardesty, A. S.: The mental status schedule: Rationale, reliability, and validity. *Compr Psychiatry, 5*:384-395, 1964.

Stone, A. R.; Frank J. D.; Nash, E. H., and Imber, S. D.: An intensive five year follow-up study of psychiatric outpatients. *J Nerv Ment Dis, 133*:410-422, 1961.

Suchman, E. A.: *Evaluative Research: Principles and Practices in Public Service and Social Action Programs*. New York, Russell Sage Foundation, 1967.

Thorpe, J. J., and Perrett, J. T.: Problem drinking: A follow-up study. *Arch Ind Health, 19*:24-32, 1959.

Trice, H. M.: The job behavior of problem drinkers. In Pittman, D. J., and Snyder, C. R. (Eds.): *Society, Culture, and Drinking Patterns*. New York, Wiley, 1962.

Trice, H. M.: Alcoholic employees: A comparison of psychotic, neurotic, and "normal" personnel. *J Occup Med, 7*:94-99, 1965.

Trice, H. M., and Belasco, J. A.: Supervisory training about alcoholics and other problem employees: A controlled evaluation. *Quart J Stud Alcohol, 29*:382-399, 1968.

Turfboer, R.: The effects of in-plant rehabilitation of alcoholics. *The Medical Bulletin*, Standard Oil of New Jersey, *19*:108-128, 1959.

Vaschak, M. R.: Alcoholism: The constructive view by industry; three case histories. *J Am Med Wom Assoc, 24*:393-397, 1969.

Vaughan, C. L.: Personal communication, 1973.

Winslow, W. W.; Hayes, K.; Prentice, L.; Powles, W. E.; Seeman, W., and Ross, W. D.: Some economic estimates of job disruption from an industrial mental health project. *Arch Environ Health,* 13:213-219, 1966.

Wolff, S., and Holland, L.: A questionnaire follow-up of alcoholic patients. *Quart J Stud Alcohol,* 25:108-118, 1964.

THREE CANADIAN INDUSTRIAL ALCOHOLISM PROGRAMS

Stuart H. Lindop

BELL CANADA

Initiation of Policy and Procedures

THE BELL TELEPHONE Company of Canada with its head office in Montreal, Quebec, employing some 45,000 people, is the second largest employer in Canada. Beginning in the late 1940's, a growing awareness of problem drinking in the ranks of Bell employees and the loss of several valued long-service employees as a direct result of problem drinking led to intensive investigation of the problem. D. W. Ferrier, then Vice-President, Personnel and Public Relations, in an address delivered at the Ontario Alcoholism Research Foundation, Ottawa, 1953, observed, "The evidence would seem to indicate that when you look for it, alcoholism is found in all industrial groups of any size. It is also found in the professions, in homes and on the farms. It is apparently found in all levels of society, in all racial groups and in both sexes.

"As has been found elsewhere," he continued, "and as I am sure has been brought out in your discussions, we in the Bell were impressed by the apparently widespread occurrence of alcoholism throughout the employee force. It was found among our craftsmen, our line crews, our foremen and our clerks. It occurred in our middle levels of management and occasionally in the higher management group."

Ferrier went on to state, ". . . over the years I am sure that in addition to the great inefficiency and high absence rates of alcoholics, we have lost men and women for this reason who today would be making a valuable contribution to the business. As an example of this one might cite the case of a foreman who some years ago was separated from the business because of his drinking problem. He was an able supervisor and because of his record, apart from drinking, was so good he was taken back as a craftsman after he had been an abstainer for many months. On return to the Company he again demonstrated his supervisory ability and was elevated to the rank of foreman within a short time. However, his drinking problem recurred and he was dismissed for keeps in March, 1949. This man, apart from his problem drinking, was a valuable employee who is now lost to the force. One could cite many examples of highly valuable employees who have been separated from the business over the years because of inability to control their drinking."

Unwritten Policy ∨

In the Bell as in many other businesses, industrial and labor organizations, employees with a drinking problem were handled under an unwritten policy which permitted drinking to continue to the point where the employee was of no use to the company and, depending upon status, he was retired early or terminated. Immediate superiors, shop stewards, friends and relatives all entered into a conspirarcy of concealment, coverup and protection. This practice allowed the alcoholic to continue drinking to the point where separation was inevitable and rehabilitation most difficult, if at all possible. While some supervisors contributed a fair amount of assistance to problem drinkers under their supervision and were instrumental in bringing some uncontrolled drinkers under control, treatment on the whole varied from no action at all to too much action.

There was no official policy. There was no training for supervisory personnel. The subject of alcoholism on the job was seldom talked about. Where many supervisors had a sense of responsibility toward individual problem drinkers on a purely personal basis, others felt that they would be personally criticized for the behavior problem drinkers in their group, if they tolerated them at all.

Health Problem Versus Moral Lapse

At about the time the aforementioned limitations were being noted, other things were happening which caused management at Bell to take a closer look at the problem of alcoholism and their methods of handling it. There was an awakening of public interest and concern. Alcoholism was beginning to receive a great deal more attention than it had had at any previous time. It was being heard of as a major health problem in the community, business, industry, labor and in the home. For the first time it was beginning to be brought out into the open. There was an increasing resistance on the part of management at Bell to separate or to take disciplinary action against long-service employees afflicted with alcoholism.

Management at Bell was beginning to appeciate the health implications involved. At the same time there was a growing feeling that alcoholism was not just a moral lapse; that is, a desire to escape responsibility or an expression of delinquent behavior. The Medical Department urged that some consideration be given to the problem of alcoholism as a behavioral-health problem and managed to have a few cases referred for counseling. Positive results were of a sufficient number for the Medical Department to demonstrate that, in early stages at least, drinking patterns could be altered.

Implementation and Dissemination of Policy

The Employee Benefit Committee responsible for the administration of employee benefit plans had been aware for some time that some employees were receiving sickness benefits while under treatment for alcoholism but which was conveniently classified as some other disorder. The Committee was also aware that there were cases where superannuation was being accelerated for employees due to their alcoholic deterioration.

Although aware of the situation, there had not as yet been discovered any means for overcoming this economic waste. Developing trends, increasing public awareness and acceptance of alcoholism as a major behavioral-health problem, realization of the economic and human waste inherent in not having a policy, plus the development of treatment facilities in many communities, focused attention on the need for decisive action.

Thus, the concern and interest of the Medical Director for the alcoholic employee, his meeting in 1949 with his Vice-President of Personnel, their presentation to senior management, concurrent interest and concern of the Employee Benefit Committee and union representatives culminated in the formulation of a policy for dealing with alcoholism in the work force which was adopted in January, 1951. The Policy adopted in 1951 is as follows:

1. That it be recognized that most cases of alcoholism or "problem drinking" present a health problem.
2. That each case of incipient or suspected alcoholism or "problem drinking" be encouraged to seek medical investigation and advice without delay.
3. That each case involving a health problem be considered eligible for Sickness Disability Benefits or Disability Pension under the Company plan for employee pensions and disability benefits, if the condition is sufficiently advanced to produce disablement from work.
4. That, where possible, final disciplinary action in cases of alcoholism be delayed until health factors have been adequately reviewed and treatment undertaken without success.

Ferrier, commenting on the policy statement and its proposed implementation, had this to say:

"In the development of a program directed toward prevention and control of a problem such as alcoholism in industry the writing of the policy or the expounding of a philosophy is comparatively simple. To live up to it is difficult and yet absolutely necessary if management and employees are to have confidence. To implement the program is the big job!"

The task of disseminating information concerning the recently adopted policy will be appreciated when it is realized that at the time there were thirty top officers and department heads plus some 6,000 line supervisors. These supervisors were responsible for imparting information concerning the new policy to some 42,000 employees. Distance between offices in some cases was 1,100 miles which did not simplify the task. Responsibility for implementation of the policy was assumed by the Medical Department comprising, at that time, seven Company Health Centers, each with a fully qualified doctor in charge plus thirty-six nurses. Commenting on the Medical Department's assumption of staff leadership and responsibility for the successful implementation of the policy, the Medical Director, W. H. Cruickshank, M.D., had this to say, "It seemed appropriate to consider alcoholism as just another activity in the total health program of the company." He further stated, "we had already had some experience with methods directed to the control of other employee health problems and there did not seem to be any reason why we should not apply those same general methods to the control of alcoholism.

"These methods were actually based on five main principles: education, early diagnosis, treatment, control of environmental factors, and rehabilitation."

Education

Fundamental to any successful industrial program for dealing with alcoholism is education directed to improving the skills of management in early case-finding and referral to the Medical Department for diagnosis. The Medical Department initiated educational programs directed toward improving the skills of all levels of management and supervisory personnel in the recognition of a developing problem. It also assisted with education, diagnosis and the development of treatment and rehabilitation programs for individual cases. General information sessions were held for all employees which pointed up the effects of alcohol and emphasizing the need for individual employee participation, if the program was to be successful in the rehabilitation of fellow workers afflicted with alcoholism.

Early Diagnosis

The thrust of the educational sessions was to improve the opportunities for early diagnosis which is so important in the control of any health problem, particularly the health problem of alcoholism. The criterion for a developing problem was deteriorating job performance. Interested and concerned supervisors equipped with a working knowledge of the problem and its progressive nature could, it was realized, be very effective in early case-finding and motivation to treatment.

Treatment and Rehabilitation

Not too impressed with the general treatment of alcoholism, Medical Director Cruickshank commented, "It has been characterized by poor results. It is only within recent years that any significant advances have been made." The Medical Department assumed the role of advising and to some extent coordinating those treatment services required in individual cases. These services varied from intensive psychiatric counseling and elaborate measures for restoration of physical health, to the individual who merely needed to recognize his problem and to seek the kind of interests that would effectively substitute for his habituation. Active treatment in the Medical Department was usually confined to advice and superficial counseling rather than to actual provision of prolonged or continued treatment services. Rehabilitation and successful rehabilitation is the goal at Bell which justifies all other efforts. Criteria for successful rehabilitation was originally considered to be a minimum of two years sobriety and complete return to accepted standards of job performance.

Sickness-Pension Benefits

In cases where employee alcoholism is sufficiently advanced so as to cause inability to work and the employee is under recognized treatment acceptable to the Medical Department and the Sick Benefit Committee, Sickness Benefits are paid as in any other illness. Pension Benefits are applicable under the terms and conditions pertinent to other illnesses. Financial assistance is available to any employee, not necessarily alcoholic, who may have gotten into financial straits. Applications for financial assistance are carefully reviewed by the individual's department prior to submission to the Employee Benefit Committee.

Relapses

At present there is no rigid policy with respect to employees who have a relapse and return to drinking. Relapses occur with other illnesses and therefore cases of alcoholics who relapse are handled on an individual basis. Final disposition results from consultation between the employee's Department Head, Personnel Department and the Medical Department. Decision to terminate an employee is predicated upon job performance. Absenteeism, accident rates and the individual employee's attitude toward acceptance of treatment are also factors which are taken into consideration prior to a final disposition being made.

Strengths-Weaknesses

Much has been achieved since the initiation and implementation of the Bell policy and procedures in January, 1951. Employees have been rehabilitated. Absenteeism, accidents and terminations have been reduced. Morale has improved. It will be agreed, it is believed, that the basic strength of the Bell Policy and Procedures is in the explicit recognition of alcoholism as a health problem, an illness amenable to treatment.

It seems reasonable to state that the dedicated leadership, interest and concern evidenced by Dr. Cruickshank at the time of implementation enhanced the acceptance of the illness conception of alcoholism. Additional strength was to be found in the concerned interest of top management, in general, implicit in the policy. The impetus provided by Vice-President, Personnel and Public Relations D. W. Ferrier greatly facilitated the implementation of policy and procedures. The existing relationship of the Medical Department with all other Departments and the Employee Benefit Committee with regard to matters pertaining to general health plus the habit already formed by employees of discussing personal health problems with members of the

Medical staff provided an obvious, seemingly logical, already functioning medium for prompt, efficient implementation of the policy and procedures. Acceptance by the Medical Department of its mandate to implement the Bell policy and the dedication with which they undertook the discharge of their responsibility resulted in the successful rehabilitation of many Bell employees.

However, the initial effectiveness of the policy and procedures as implemented by the Medical Department may, paradoxically, prove to be their weakness. To date, formal administrative procedures have not been implemented. This would seem to indicate that management throughout the Bell tends to perceive the Medical Department as having sole responsibility for the policy and procedures. Abnegation of responsibility by management could well result in all levels of supervisory personnel relegating their responsibilities to the Medical Department. Concern in this matter is evident from a comment by Bell Medical Director, D. C. Bews, M.D., "It is only the immediate supervisor who can evaluate a peson's job performance on a day-to-day basis. Unless the cases are brought to our attention we do not even know about them in many instances." Further evidence of management's present seeming lack of concern for the continued success of the program could be implied from the fact that there has been only one assessment or evaluation of the program since its inception in 1951, and that was in 1968.

Summary and Evaluation

The Bell Policy and Procedures for dealing with the behavioral-health problem of alcoholism was well-conceived and implemented. Certainly it was in keeping with everything the Company stood for in the area of human relations. The Bell is to be commended for endeavoring to do something constructive about a situation which many corporations at the time chose to ignore. Even today there are relatively few corporations which have seen fit to initiate a similar policy. There are today in the Bell many men and women who, had there not been such a policy implemented, perhaps would not be alive, let alone making a worthwhile contribution to the company, their families and their communities. From the positive standpoint it must be said that the Bell made a tremendous contribution to the efforts being made regarding the changing of public attitudes toward alcoholism and alcoholics, when they went on record as recognizing alcoholism as a health problem, an illness amendable to treatment.

Those responsible for the initiation of the policy, W. H. Cruickshank, M.D., Medical Director, D. W. Ferrier, Vice-President, Personnel and Public Relations, through their personal interest and concern for the alcoholic worker provided the initial impetus so necessary for the successful implementation of a policy and program for dealing with alcoholism and alcoholics in the work setting. As in so many instances, those employees first referred to medical treatment would tend to be the more obvious, blatant, late-phase alcoholics. This is not to detract from the value of the program, but to keep events in perspective. The newly enunciated policy and procedures provided an alternative to early retirements and terminations. All levels of management were able to discontinue or at least decrease the practice of concealment and coverup which resulted in premature deaths, early retirements and terminations. It was unfortunate that it was not deemed advisable for top management to accept responsibility for the implementation of the Bell policy and procedures rather than having the Medical Department assume that responsibility. Formal or organized management training has not been undertaken. To date, it has been considered sufficient that supervisory personnel have a knowledge of the behavior patterns of the employees under their jurisdiction. Supervisors have been expected to identify employees evincing a problem and to obtain whatever assistance they considered necessary.

A well-written policy and a dedicated Medical Department provide two elements vital to any program for dealing with alcoholism. The third element is a supervisory personnel who have been provided with the training, information and skills necessary to identify an employee early in the alcoholism process when treatment efforts are more likely to succeed. Human nature being what it is, and in the absence of formal administrative procedures being clearly enunciated, ambivalence on the part of supervisors will result in the tendency to use the policy as a last resort. Being a "good" supervisor, he will endeavor to understand and handle the problem employee himself. This course of action will result in alcoholism progressing to the point where response to treatment is marginal and prognosis for rehabilitation not too positive. If the objective of the policy was the rehabilitation of employees with the more obvious and advanced cases of alcoholism, then it is understandable for the Medical Department to have been assigned the responsibility for the program. However, if pretreatment, intervention and prevention were the objectives, then certainly a completely different organizational strategy was required. "Muscle" would be required to implement formal administrative procedures and this could only come from top management.

In 1968, there were some 200 cases of alcoholism known to the Medical Department. Using the conservative factor of 3 percent to estimate the incidence of alcoholism in the Bell, the Medical Director stated, "We should be working with some 1,000 cases and I see no reason for thinking that our group is much different from others in business."

Perhaps this is the basis for the concern expressed by Dr. Bews, present Medical Director, in his earlier comment, "Unless the cases are brought to our attention we do not even know about them in many instances." Formal administrative procedures and organized training sessions for all levels of management and supervisory personnel would ensure more uniformity in the handling of alcoholic employees. It would also aid in precluding the tolerance, coverup and concealment which stems from the ambivalence on the part of supervisory personnel presently required to make individual decisions as to how to handle alcoholic employees under their jurisdiction. This should result in earlier case identification, earlier intervention, and motivation to treatment with more positive prognosis for successful rehabilitation.

GULF OIL CANADA LIMITED

Initiation of Policy and Procedures

Gulf Oil, employing some 11,000 people through approximately 6,000 service stations extending across more than 4,000 miles, provides service to Canadian motorists in each of the ten provinces from British Columbia on the West coast to Nova Scotia in the East. Annual sales and operating revenues exceed $800 million. Like many of their associates, top management at Gulf Oil were aware of the problem drinker in industry. They were also aware of the fact that alcoholism was a growing problem, but like many other corporations, were doing very little about it. In 1965, at the invitation of an executive of another oil company, J. D. Lovering, M.D., Medical Director of Gulf and one of his associates, attended a luncheon during which the problem of alcoholism in industry was discussed, and what, if anything, could be done about it. Concern about the problem and a desire to do something constructive about it resulted in representatives from Gulf being sent to a workshop on alcoholism sponsored by the Addiction Research Foundation of Ontario. This was in the early part of 1967.

Prior to this employees at Gulf who were found to have a problem with alcohol, in particular, those under the influence of alcohol on the job, were usually suspended and sent home pending an investigation. This investigation could result in: 1) a reprimand, 2) suspension for a stipulated period of time, or 3) dismissal. As was the practice in too many corporations, immediate superiors at all levels of management responsibility covered up, tolerated and in various ways hid the employee with a drinking problem. This coverup continued to the point where it was no longer possible to hide, and the employee drinking at the stage where prognosis for rehabilitation was at its least positive was terminated or retired early.

C. D. Shepard, Chairman of the Board at Gulf, commenting on alcoholism in business said, "Information from the Addiction Research Foundation in Ontario indicated that problem drinkers in Canada cost their employers an estimated one million dollars every working day. This staggering sum includes the cost of slowed production, absenteeism, sickness, labor turnover, wasted materials, insulted customers, errors in executive decisions and poor plant morale. Yet, most Canadian firms not only do nothing to cure this annual multi-million dollar hangover, they don't even know it is there."

Continuing, Mr. Shepard stated, "A score of authoritative studies discussed at the workshop indicated that, in the average industry, at least 3 percent of persons on the payroll drink to the point where their efficiency is impaired. Many experts believe this proportion to be much higher. The Addiction Research Foundation, for example, discovered that 6 percent of the people in one typical county were problem drinkers . . .

"Closer to home," he continued, "using the conservative factor of 3 percent, there could be at least 300 problem drinkers in our company. These people are absent some twenty days a year, that is five times more than average. They make too many mistakes; and often others have to be trained to replace them.

"Further," Mr. Shepard went on, "direct and indirect costs for these people were estimated at $1,300 per year, per person. So you see, our cost could be $400,000. This is a lot of money and requires much effort on the part of others to make it up. It is felt that it takes $9 of sales to make $1 of profit. It therefore would take $3.5 million in sales to pay for the drinking habits of 300 employees. Equally, if not more important," he continued, "is the fact that problem drinkers include people with skill, experience and intelligence, and their rehabilitation has tremendous value to the company as well as to themselves, their families and the community."

In November, 1967, the president and officers of Gulf, recognizing the problems inherent in not having a policy and procedures for dealing with the behavioral-health problem of alcoholism, introduced Corporate Policy 013.

Implementation of Policy

Policy Zero Thirteen, as it is known, introduced in November, 1967, is as follows:

1. The Company recognizes that most cases of alcoholism or problem drinking present a health problem. As such, it will provide whatever help it can to any of its employees who become so afflicted.

2. The Company draws a clear distinction between social drinking and problems of alcohol which seriously or continuously affect an employee's work or health.
3. The Medical Director, the Employee Relations Department, field personnel offices and retained doctors are responsible for implementing this policy. In all cases, the anonymity of the individual will be preserved.
4. Each case of suspected alcoholism or problem drinking is encouraged to seek adequate medical investigation and advice:
(a) Any employee may contact the Medical Director or Company's retained doctor in the locality, for consultation leading to a recommended pattern of therapy.

OR

(b) In smaller areas, the local medical facilities should be utilized to ensure a proper diagnosis.
5. If the recommended therapy requires time away from work, provisions of Policy 145 will apply.
6. Should the problem persist after all reasonable help has been offered, whether through lack of cooperation on the part of the employee or an unsuccessful therapeutic program, appropriate measures will be recommended for the consideration and further direction of the Officer concerned.

The Medical Department was assigned the responsibility of implementing the policy. In commenting on the new policy, Dr. J. D. (Jack) Lovering, Medical Director at Gulf, had this to say: "This new approach could well mark a turning point in the battle to control alcoholism. Studies have indicated," he continued, "that, with the development of a corporate policy, which recognizes alcoholism as an illness rather than a weakness of an individual's will and moral fibre; plus the interest, concern and support of top management, rehabilitation rates approaching 80 percent are being realized. In the past," Dr. Lovering went on, "supervisors have often protected alcoholic employees under their jurisdiction by covering up for them and rationalizing, 'Bill's a good fellow, he just drinks a bit too much.'"

Aware that the immediate superior, properly instructed, could be a decisive factor in the early identification of the alcoholic employee, the Medical Department initiated a series of staff meetings and special supervisory training sessions. Each of the more than 200 special training sessions scheduled across Canada was opened by a videotaped address from C. D. Shepard, Chairman of the Board. Format for the sessions included a full reading of the policy and procedures and elaboration on its importance in the conservation of skilled, trained employees. Representatives from local community alcoholism centers outlined the services and facilities available in each area. Films on alcoholism in industry were shown followed by discussion. The company physician or nurse gave details on the role of the Medical Department.

Early Identification and Problem Criterion

Commenting on the matter of early identification, the Medical Director, Dr. Lovering observed, "Early identification of even well-established alcoholics is far from easy. The person with a drinking problem feels he must hide it, especially from his or her supervisor. The degree to which this can be accomplished successfully was pointed up dramatically in one company where 30 percent of those employees who voluntarily requested help from the Medical Department had not even been recognized as having a drinking problem." Realizing that alcoholism is an illness which adversely affects family relationships, Gulf made extensive use of the written word to advise its employees and their families about the existence and operation of the Company alcoholism policy and program. Apart from individually addressed letters, copies of the employee publication "Commentator" containing two feature articles on alcoholism were mailed to employee's homes.

Job performance is stressed as the key to the early indication of a developing problem with alcohol. It is pointed out that alcoholics also tend to be accident-prone, not only at work but in other situations as well. The alcoholic has trouble concentrating, often working in fits and starts, makes many mistakes and has lapses of memory. Another facet of alcoholic behavior which is brought to the attention of supervisory personnel is the alcoholic's moodiness and sensitivity to criticism. Using job performance, accidents and behavior as the criteria for recognizing a developing problem the supervisor is cautioned about making a diagnosis. Diagnosis is the prerogative of the Medical

Department. Supervisors are not required to diagnose suspected cases, but are advised to refer them to the Medical Department when certain signs or symptoms appear in addition to declining job performance. These symptoms include overtiredness, absenteeism, avoidance of supervisor or fellow workers, increasing irritability, nervousness, untruthfulness and distortion, odd or questionable rationalization of any of the foregoing behavior.

Treatment and Rehabilitation

The company doctor, or company-retained doctor, upon examining the employee and deciding that there is a problem with alcohol, refers the employee to this family doctor and/or appropriate community agency for treatment. The supervisor is then advised of the action taken. Gulf, while it doesn't expect an instant cure, knows what to expect in the way of progress. The Company is prepared to stand by any of its employees while they are following recommended treatment. Understanding and sympathy can be expected by afflicted employees so long as they cooperate in following recommended treatment. As the Medical Director, Dr. J. D. Lovering, puts it, "This approach has been the basis for the success other companies have had in dealing with alcoholics and problem drinkers. It is based on a carefully calculated combination of support and firmness. Along with the efforts of families, family doctors and community agencies, it has often been enough to turn the scales in favor of the employee."

C. D. Shepard, Chairman of the Board, in commenting on Gulf's Policy Zero Thirteen and the afflicted employee, had this to say: "Alcoholic employees who refuse to face their problem and start the uphill fight to complete sobriety cannot expect to last long at our company. But, those employees who want to help themselves will find a guiding hand in their supervisors, medical and personnel staffs. They may," he continued, "require treatment in a hospital or rest home. They certainly require the understanding of Alcoholics Anonymous. They will have the necessary security and stability of a job—if they recognize their problem and show signs of endeavoring to solve it."

Both top management and the Medical Director consider total abstinence or complete sobriety to be the only solution for the alcoholic employee. It is pointed out that experience indicates that once an alcoholic employee starts drinking, he cannot stop until he is irresponsible for his actions. The result, usually, is broken families, frequent absenteeism, poor work and often a danger to his fellow employees. Senior executives at Gulf, noting the increasing number of companies taking constructive attitudes toward alcoholism in the work force and effecting worthwhile programs to help afflicted employees recover, point to the ultimate goal of medicine prevention by education and earlier detection. It is in this area that we can and must do our part. "We must remember," said Shepard, "that whether we be manager, supervisor or staff member, we must each be prepared to do our part to make our policy effective by assisting those who need help towards diagnosis and treatment." In a similar vein, Dr. Lovering points to the dividend or bonus accruing to companies having similar policies and procedures for dealing with alcoholism as ". . . the saving of lives, conservation of skilled employees, preventing the breakdown of families, reduction of traffic accidents and the reaffirming of the role of business as an important social influence in the community."

Item Six of Gulf's Policy is pertinent to the question of relapses in that, "Should the problem persist after all reasonable help has been offered, whether through lack of cooperation on the part of the employee or an unsuccessful therapeutic program, appropriate measures will be recommended for the consideration and further direction of the Officer concerned." As in any other illness relapses do occur and alcoholism is no different. Dr. Lovering indicated that each case is considered separately and final decisions are predicated upon job performance, absenteeism and accident rate. As he states, "There have been relapses; however, the majority of recovering employees are getting along without alcohol."

Strengths and Weaknesses

The major strength of Gulf's Policy and Procedures lies in the recognition of alcoholism as a health problem, an illness to be treated as any other illness. Certainly the support of senior management serves to reinforce the policy statement which recognizes alcoholism as an illness. Implementation of the Policy by the Medical Department and the role played by representatives of senior management from the Chairman of the Board, on down to the lower echelons has done much to ensure awareness by the employees as a whole that the policy and program have the support of top management. This is considered a most vital factor in the implementation of any corporate policy. Further evidence of the importance of the Policy is obvious to the employees in the direct personal involvement of Dr. J. D. Lovering, Medical Director during the numerous meetings held across Canada to implement the policy. Implementation of the Policy has served to bring the drinking problem out into the open. An alternative to the "hide and ultimately fire" unwritten policy, the written policy makes it possible for employees with a problem to seek assistance without fear of termination. Supervisory personnel are able to offer an objective approach to a problem which had, prior to the policy, been a smoldering one without a constructive solution.

A weakness which is seemingly common to many corporate policies for dealing with alcoholism is the lack of statistical data. As a member of the Medical Department puts it, "Right from the start the whole aim of the program, was towards education of employees and supervisors, and not towards research and statistical data. As a result, we have very little data on 'success rates.' We consider it a success when someone comes and says he quit drinking because he read about the symptoms of incipient alcoholism in one of our educational booklets and did not like what he could be doing to himself. I do not think that that is very good statistical data, but, I prefer to think of it as a 'success story.'" It is pointed out by the Medical Department that it is not too hard to find out how someone is getting along on an industrial program once he has been put on the program; however, if a supervisor is not interested in the program, little or nothing is done in this area. The program would be more success-
ᵈl, it is believed, had it been implemented by management and
ᵉrvisory groups rather than by the Medical Department, which

should be more interested in diagnosis, treatment and follow-up. There is difficulty encountered in the ongoing educational process. As one representative of the Medical Department states, "The danger here is that people get turned off if they think we do nothing except talk about alcoholism. In fact, it is hard to keep thinking of different ways to approach the same subject time and time again." A corporate policy for dealing with alcoholism which has as its objective prevention as well as treatment must be implemented by management. A corporate policy which focuses on the preventative aspect has as its primary concern the pretreatment phase of alcoholism in the work force.

This pretreatment phase is the responsibility of all levels of management in that the early indications of a developing problem are observable in job performance, absenteeism and accident rates. Although the initial strength of a policy and program would appear to reside in its implementation by the Medical Department, there is an increasing conviction throughout the corporate structure that the Policy is the responsibility of the Medical Department.

Lack of comprehensive statistical data indicative of the effectiveness of the policy in each area across Canada in reaching the estimated total number of alcoholic employees in each area would seem to confirm the growing conviction that management has, or is gradually relegating its responsibility for the policy and procedures to the Medical Department.

Summary and Evaluation

Despite the vast amount of information being disseminated through business journals and periodicals indicating the cost inherent in not having a corporate policy and program for dealing with the behavioral health problem of alcoholism in the work force, Gulf is one of a relatively small number of business organizations which have seen fit to take constructive action toward alleviating the problem. It is obvious that considerable thought, time and effort went into the drafting of Gulf's Policy Zero Thirteen and the initial implementation. Certainly, Gulf is to be commended for taking a constructive approach toward solving a problem which, as research studies and surveys indicate, has proven to be very expensive, through direct and indirect factors; i.e. accidents, lowered productivity, poor morale, absenteeism, terminations and early retirements.

Unexpected dividends are being realized. As Dr. Lovering, Medical Director puts it, "Apart from those employees seeking help, who have a problem with alcohol, there are those individuals with personal and emotional problems who have been assisted and are now back on their feet. Employees whose spouse has exhibited symptoms of alcoholism have attended lectures to gain further information and knowledge about the nature of alcoholism. This information and knowledge enables these employees to cooperate in the treatment program." The comment made by a representative of the Medical Department that ". . . any program might be more successful if it were implemented by a supervisory group rather than by the Medical Department who should be more interested in diagnosis, treatment and follow-up" is a reflection, it is believed, of astute observation concerning Policy Zero Thirteen and its implementation.

There are two distinct phases in any corporate policy designed to deal with alcoholism in the work force; 1) treatment and 2) pretreatment. Often overlooked in the initial enthusiasm of a new policy is the fact that those employees first directed to the Medical Department for diagnosis are middle and early-late phase alcoholics, whose blatant, overt behavior is clearly indicative of a drinking problem. On the average, this behavior appears some fourteen to sixteen years after the initial onset of the illness.

In the pretreatment phase the indications of a developing problem are much more subtle; i.e. gradual decline in efficiency, change in interpersonal relationship with fellow employees, moodiness, erratic work pace, lowered, irregular, sudden higher, productivity. These are all within the prerogative and jurisdiction of supervisory personnel at all levels of management.

It is in the pretreatment phase that the greatest contribution can be made towards prevention. It is in this area that management's "muscle" is required to ensure uniform application of the policy throughout the corporate structure. With job performance, accidents and absenteeism, clearly within the jurisdiction of immediate superiors, should a "problem" exist with the superior, this would preclude the possibility of early intervention on behalf of employees under his jurisdiction.

✓ The value of Policy Zero Thirteen notwithstanding and the tremendous contribution being made to the community as a whole, it is believed most sincerely that there could be a greater contribution made in the area of earlier intervention, medical referral with subsequently more positive prognosis for rehabilitation, if management at all levels of responsibility were responsible for implementation of the policy and procedures.

CANADIAN NATIONAL RAILWAYS

Canadian National Railways, serving each of the ten Canadian Provinces, from the Atlantic to the Pacific, is divided into five Regions; Atlantic, St. Lawrence, Great Lakes, Prairie and Mountain; with headquarters in Montreal, it employs some 82,000 people.

In the annual report for 1972, made public June 5, 1973, C. N. Chairman, N. J. MacMillan, announced an operating profit of $48.3 million, with revenue increases in all aspects of rail operations including passenger service which reached $66.8 million. Employment rose to 82,095 for the entire system with earnings for employees showing an increase of 8.6 percent for an average of $9,636.

Initiation of Policy and Procedures

Canadian National Railway's policy and procedures for dealing with the behavioral health problem of alcoholism in the work force, initiated December 1, 1971, saw the crystallization of joint efforts between the Personnel and Labor Relations Department at Headquarters in Montreal, and senior management in each of the five Regions. Although it is difficult to credit any one person or group of individuals for the development of the policy and procedures, two Regions, the Atlantic and the Mountain, were the first to develop a special concern and to begin actions in 1970 which reinforced earlier discussions and the shaping of the policy. Of the two Regions which made substantial input of time and education, the Atlantic was perhaps the first to establish a team to study the problem in the area, examine applications in outside corporations both in Canada and the United States, and begin an alcoholism program in the Atlantic Region itself.

At approximately the same time, senior management in the Mountain Region was taking action. In September 1970, J. F. Munsey, Superintendent of Transportation, Mountain Region, met with S. H. Lindop, the Coordinator-Industrial Programs of the Alberta Alcoholism and Drug Abuse Commission to discuss the problem of alcoholism in industry. His specific interest was in the area of: 1) cost to industry, 2) what could be done to combat the problem, and 3) community resources available.

The subsequent discussion of this information with his superiors, G. H. Bloomfield, General Manager, and J. O. Pitts, Area Manager, resulted in a decision to schedule a senior management meeting for October, 1971. At this meeting approximately thirty participants, superintendents and department heads, were apprised of the estimated costs of alcoholism in the Mountain Region. They were also made aware of what similar corporations had achieved in rehabilitating their employees. Also stressed was how these corporations had achieved positive results in dealing with alcoholism through the initiation of specific policies and procedures.

The General Manager invited the Coordinator-Industrial Programs, Alberta Alcoholism and Drug Abuse Commission to the meeting to present background information and data on the progressive nature of alcoholism, how to recognize a developing problem with alcohol, how to motivate an employee to seek medical diagnosis and treatment. Of particular interest to the senior management representatives present was how a corporate policy was initiated and procedures implemented for dealing with alcoholism.

Such a policy was seen to represent a constructive alternative to the existing situation which, as in similar organizations, had meant coverup as long as possible, early retirements and terminations. "Rule G" explicitly requires that any employee found using alcohol and/or under the influence of alcohol on the job be terminated. Human nature being what it is, if it was humanly possible to protect an employee from termination, he was protected and covered for by fellow workers, shop stewards and supervisory personnel. With the best of intentions, those individuals covering up for their fellow workers were in reality conspiring to help the alcoholic destroy himself, perhaps his family, and in some instances, his fellow workers. There waş enthusiastic agreement among those present at the meeting that initiation of such a policy would provide a humanitarian alternative to the present "unwritten" policy of coverup and that representation should be made to headquarters to have such a policy implemented throughout the system.

Recommendations forwarded to Headquarters were well received as were similar recommendations submitted from the Atlantic Region. In an effort to ensure consensus from all regions, the recommendations submitted by the Atlantic and Mountain Regions were forwarded to the remaining areas for their perusal, comments and suggestions. In the interim, senior management in the Atlantic and Mountain Regions were to submit drafts of recommended policy and procedures which could be initiated. With ultimate general consensus from the other Regions in favor of adopting a policy for dealing with alcoholism, they also were requested to participate in the drafting of a system-wide policy and procedures.

Notwithstanding the lack of a formal policy and procedures, senior management in the Mountain Region, with the understanding and cooperation of the Regional Medical Officer, Dr. G. C. Pretty, initiated local procedures whereby employees whose overt, blatant behavior was clearly indicative of a problem with alcohol were confronted with the facts by their immediate superior. A further confrontation took place with Dr. Pretty, who, having outlined the medical ramifications of the illness, arranged for the employee to enter the Outpatient facilities of the Alberta Alcoholism and Drug Abuse Commission. Here the employee was given a further medical examination and evaluation in order to confirm preliminary diagnosis made by Dr. Pretty.

Following the medical evaluation, the employee was then

interviewed by Joan Howell, Director, Outpatient Clinic, Alberta Alcoholism and Drug Abuse Commission. Results of these two evaluations would decide future treatment regimen to be followed; i.e. treatment on an Outpatient basis or treatment on an inpatient basis for a twenty-eight-day period at Henwood Rehabilitation Center. Henwood Rehabilitation Center, an inpatient facility of the Alberta Alcoholism and Drug Abuse Commission, offers a twenty-eight-day intensive therapeutic environment where the employee is removed from tension of home and work milieu and is given the opportunity to come to terms with himself in a supportive community.

Concurrent with the initiative being exhibited by management, union representatives in Mountain Region were also taking action regarding problem drinking and alcoholism in the region. At a General Committee meeting, twenty local chairmen representing one particular trade, unanimously endorsed in principle the idea of a program directed to the rehabilitation of employees afflicted with alcoholism. The General Chairman was instructed, ". . . to use all influence and power to encourage or force the company to adopt an Alcoholic Rehabilitation Program similar to that on the Great Northern Railway, which had been in operation for twenty years." Concern and interest and commitment of senior management, Canadian National Railways, toward making the proposed policy effective when finally initiated and formally implemented, was exemplified in the dedication of J. F. Munsey, Superintendent Transportation, in the Mountain Region.

With the information and knowledge garnered first-hand by attending seminars, workshops and even by getting himself invited to Alcoholics Anonymous meetings, Jim Munsey undertook the task of confronting those employees whose problem with alcohol was obvious. In these initial confrontations, as he put it "to keep me from blowing my top," Munsey requested that Mr. Lindop, the Coordinator-Industrial Programs, Alberta Alcoholism and Drug Abuse Commission, whose responsibilities included counseling of employees and motivating them to seek medical diagnosis and treatment, to sit in on the initial interviews. This arrangement proved effective and resulted in several other management and union representatives utilizing the services of the Coordinator-Industrial Programs when dealing with individuals under their respective jurisdictions. Certainly the commitment, interest and concern of management at all levels, from N. J. MacMillan, Chair and President, George Lach, Vice-President, Personnel and Labor Relations, Dr. Peter Vaughn, Chief Medical Officer, G. H. Bloomfield, Assistant Vice-President Labor Relations, and A. T. Mathews, Development and Training, plus many others made the idea of a policy to deal with the behavioral health problem of alcoholism, a reality which became effective December 1, 1971.

Formal introduction of Canadian National's policy took place in the Mountain Region at a Co-Op meeting which comprised senior representatives of labor and management. The policy, effective throughout the system December 1, 1971, is as follows: The Company recognizes alcoholism as a health problem. To the extent that it affects the health, performance and conduct of employees on the job, and to the extent that alcoholism creates unnecessary costs to the Company, it is a problem of concern to Management which requires action. Alcoholism is a chronic disease, or disorder of behavior, characterized by the repeated drinking of alcoholic beverages to an extent that exceeds customary dietary use or ordinary compliance with the social drinking customs of the community, and which interferes with the drinker's health, interpersonal relations or economic functioning. Any employee whose repeated or continued overindulgence in the use of alcohol interferes with the efficient and safe performanc of his assigned duties and reduces his dependability must be considered a problem drinker. He may or may not yet be an acute or chronic alcoholic. Accordingly, it is Company policy:

1. To recognize that addiction to alcohol is an illness which may be treated and arrested.
2. To encourage employees concerned with problem drinking and alcoholism to voluntarily seek assistance and return to good health and improved work performance.
3. To train managers and supervisors to identify the early signs of problem drinking; to understand the attitudes and requirements of the problem drinker; and to refer such employees (who do not

themselves take the initiative) to the Company Medical Officer for diagnosis and treatment programs.

4. To require affected employees to accept certain conditions related to the problem of rehabilitation. If the employee refuses to cooperate, or if medical treatment and other measures fail, then removal from employment must be considered where there is continuing deterioration in performance. Such separation would be required, as in other circumstances, because minimum performance standards are not being met.

5. To grant sick leave, on the approval of the Company Medical Department, to the extent the employee is entitled for other illnesses.

6. To cooperate with and utilize provincial and community education and treatment organizations in order to assist employees undergoing rehabilitation and to educate supervisors toward a better understanding of alcoholic problems.

7. To inform union representatives and organizations of the policy and program, to seek active cooperation from them, and to facilitate access to the same training being given Company supervisors.

8. To recognize that there will be instances in which the employee is unwilling to acknowledge his health problem. In such cases, his retention in, or removal from, Company service will be determined in accordance with the presently established procedures dealing with the control of work performance and conduct.

9. To attempt to correct deficiencies in work performance, attendance or conduct of an unsatisfactory employee, preferably before it has resulted in disciplinary action. However, nothing contained in this policy is intended or should be construed to limit the continuing responsibility of Management to discipline employees. Alcoholics or nonalcoholics who drink intoxicants on duty or are under the influence of intoxicants on duty, will continue to be subject to disciplinary measures.

All Supervisory personnel are responsible for ensuring that employees under their jurisdiction having problems associated with alcohol are dealt with in accordance with the foregoing policy. If the matter cannot be satisfactorily resolved at that level, Supervisory personnel are to refer it to the next senior officer. The Chief Medical Officer and/or Regional Medical Officer is responsible for diagnosis and recommending appropriate treatment programs. The Vice-President, Personnel and Labor Relations, in collaboration with the Chief Medical Officer, is responsible for arranging training programs for supervisors, managers, etc., to assist them in identifying the early signs of problem drinking and alcoholism. Vice-Presidents and Heads of Departments are responsible for ensuring that appropriate training programs are carried out within their jurisdictions. Where an employee has a right of grievance under an applicable collective agreement, the grievance shall be handled in accordance with that agreement.

Although essentially unilateral in design and implementation, the policy and procedures initiated by Canadian National Railways had the implicit support of the majority of union representatives. The presentation of the policy at the Co-Op meeting was in keeping with Item Seven of that policy which states, ". . . to inform union representatives and organizations of the policy and program, to seek active cooperation from them and to facilitate access to the same training being given Company supervisors."

Responsibility for Implementation

Responsibility for implementation of the policy and procedures was the joint responsibility of the Vice-President, Personnel and Labor Relations and the Chief Medical Officer. This is explicit in the Policy and Authority regarding Problem Drinking and Alcoholism which states, "The Chief Medical Officer and/or Regional Medical Officer is responsible for diagnosis and recommending appropriate treatment programs. The Vice-President, Personnel and Labor Relations, in collaboration with the Chief Medical Officer, is responsible for arranging training programs for supervisors, managers, etc., to assist them in identifying the early signs of problem drinking and alcoholism. Vice-Presidents and Heads of Departments are responsible for ensuring that appropriate training programs are carried out within their jurisdictions. Where an employee has a right of grievance under an applicable collective agreement, the grievance shall be handled in accordance with that agreement."

Here is an example of a policy and procedures for dealing with alcoholism being supported by the "muscle" considered vital if any such policy is to be implemented uniformly throughout a corporation.

A special meeting of senior officers, Mountain Region-Canadian National Railways, was convened in June, 1972. The purpose of the meeting was three-fold: 1) to introduce J. W. (Wes) Peacock, Manager, Employee Relations, recently transferred from headquarters in Montreal, 2) to introduce J. R. (Jack) McNeil, Regional Employee Counselor, and 3) in adherence with the explicit direction of the new policy, to present a training program for the senior officers of the Mountain Region.

Peacock had made considerable input into the deliberations which resulted in the drafting of C. N.'s policy and procedures, and thus was able to contribute a great deal toward clarification of the various sections of the policy for the benefit of those present at the meeting.

J. R. (Jack) McNeil, a long-service employee of Canadian National Railways, knowledgable and well-respected by all in the Mountain Region was offered the opportunity of undertaking the responsibilities of the newly created position of Regional Employee Counselor.

Canadian National Railway's determination to take constructive action on a problem which had long been neglected is evident in the construction of the policy and the explicit reference to management's responsibilities for its implementation. Further evidence of this determination is readily evident in the creation of a new position, that of Regional Employee Counselor. In an effort to reassure confidentiality for any individual employee voluntarily seeking information and/or assistance concerning problem drinking or alcoholism, the Regional Employee Counselor's office is off Company premises. Recognizing that alcoholism is an illness which affects the whole family, a twenty-four hour answering service guarantees that any call for information or assistance receives a reply.

To date in the Mountain Region, in addition to the full-time Regional Employee Counselor, there are ten part-time counselors. These part-time counselors, many of whom are recovered alcoholics, have other full-time job responsibilities, however, when required to assist someone with a drinking problem, this takes precedence. Each of the remaining four Regions presently has a Regional Employee Counselor and, undoubtedly, will broaden its services, as did the Mountain Region through the enlistment of recovered alcoholics as part-time counselors.

Phase three of the special meeting for C. N. senior officers was introduced by G. H. Bloomfield, assistant Vice-President and General Manager, Mountain Region. In his introduction, Bloomfield emphasized the fact that ". . . this new policy for dealing with employee alcoholism is relevant to all employees, not just line, but staff level as well. We, you and I, have to observe our own behavior and example we set. This is not a 'we' and 'they' policy and we must ensure that the policy is implemented consistently throughout all levels of responsibility."

Guest speaker at the meeting was S. H. Lindop, the Coordinator, Industrial Programs, Alberta Alcoholism and Drug Abuse Commission who made a presentation concerning alcoholism in industry regarding what had proven to be effective in combating the situation and what the results had been in rehabilitation. Job performance, accidents and absenteeism were stressed as being the prime criteria in the recognition of a developing problem with alcohol. Two industrial films were included in the presentation, "To Your Health" and "Need for Decision."

J. R. (Jack) McNeil, newly appointed Regional Employee Counselor, outlined the duties and responsibilities of his job as he saw them. In appealing for understanding and patience on behalf of the alcoholic, McNeil stressed the need for a change in attitude toward the alcoholic.

The Regional Medical Officer, Dr. G. C. Pretty, outlined the role of the Regional Medical Department in the newly implemented policy for dealing with alcoholism. Stressing the confidentiality inherent in the doctor-patient relationship, he urged that anyone who had misgivings about their own behavior concerning alcohol to request an interview. "Elaborating on the criteria indicative of a developing problem with alcoholism," Dr. Pretty stated, "It is most important that proper documentation be maintained in order that a developing pattern can be observed. Such documentation need not be formal in nature just jot down the circumstances on a slip of paper, date it and file it. A review of these little slips of paper will present a pretty revealing picture if they have been consistently and diligently recorded.

Remember," he remarked in concluding, "we are dealing with peoples' lives, and the sooner we, you and I, become aware of a developing problem, the sooner we can deal with it with a more positive prognosis for rehabilitation of the employee and perhaps the conservation of a home and family."

The thrust of the procedures is to intervene in the progression of alcoholism early enough to preclude the necessity of disciplinary action. However, it was pointed out nothing contained in the policy was intended nor should be construed to limit the effect of Rule "G." The policy is explicit in stating: "Alcoholics or nonalcoholics who drink intoxicants on duty or are under the influence of intoxicants on duty will be subject to disciplinary measures."

Sickness, Pension Benefits and Relapses

In recognizing alcoholism as a health problem the policy ensures that sick leave and pension benefits will accrue as in other illnesses. It is recognized that with alcoholism, as with other illnesses, there could be relapses. Each case will be dealt with on an individual basis and merit.

It is also recognized that there will be instances where, despite the availability of medical assistance, individuals will be unable to acknowledge their health problem and take action toward its solution. In such cases, retention in or removal from Company service, will be determined in accordance with the presently established procedures dealing with the control of work performance and behavior.

Effectiveness of Policy and Procedures

Commenting on the effectiveness of the Policy and Procedures, Dr. Pretty indicated that during the period from January, 1972 through March, 1973, there have been some sixty employees motivated to seek treatment. Their disposition is as follows:

1. Twenty-five referred to various communities; Henwood Rehabilitation Center, Collingwood Acres, Maplewood (B.C.)
2. Three were terminated.
3. One retired early.

In evaluating the fifty-six who are still employed, Dr. Pretty estimates that ten continue to drink and are having problems. Thirty are considered to be making reasonable progress, having come to terms with their problem and endeavoring to do something constructive about it. It is interesting to note that these thirty, according to Dr. Pretty, have managed to remain abstinent for more than the past six months.

A. T. Mathews, Manager, Development and Training, at Headquarters in Montreal, in reply to a question concerning the success of C. N.'s program to date commented, "The best or perhaps most ready measure of success would be substantial increase in the number of arrested alcoholics in the Company. The number is increasing," he continued, "but at this stage we do not have any basis for saying how quickly or in what numbers such cases should emerge. We are trying to build up figure data; i.e. number of problem drinkers identified, undergoing treatment, rehabilitated, returned to job with illness arrested, etc., and hope to have some firm data in the near future."

J. R. (Jack) McNeil, Regional Employee Counselor, in commenting on C. N.'s policy and procedures in general, and in the Mountain Region in particular, stated "I believe that Canadian National's policy and procedures for dealing with the behavioral-health problem of alcoholism is second to none in Canada, perhaps in North America." To ensure wide dissemination of information concerning the recently implemented policy and procedures, McNeil prepared three pamphlets which were distributed to every employee on the Mountain Region initially and ultimately to every employee throughout the system.

Realizing the importance of complete understanding of the intent and focus of C. N.'s policy on problem drinking and alcoholism, McNeil has ensured that as frequently as possible, all meetings and seminars have representatives from both labor and management. These joint labor-management meetings have made it possible for each group to express their views frankly and has resulted in the retention of constructive confrontation "muscle" in motivating employees afflicted with alcoholism to seek medical diagnosis and treatment.

A review of the informational seminars and workshops held to date indicates that the participants have been Federation General Chairman, Local Chairman, District Chairman, pipe fitters, electricians, boiler makers, yardmen, labor relations officers, assistant station masters, office supervisors, operations supervisors, general foremen, shop foremen, senior clerks, a telex instructor, a Safety and Fire prevention supervisor, Roadmasters, purchasing agent, stores manager, etc. To date, approximately 12 percent of the some 8,000 employees in the Mountain Region have attended at least one informational workshop or seminar.

When it is realized that each of these workshops or seminars is presented by J. R. (Jack) McNeil, Regional Employee Counselor, J. W. (Wes) Peacock, Manager Employee Relations, and Dr. G. C. Pretty, Regional Medical Officer, it is increasingly evident that senior management are interested and concerned, and determined that the policy and procedures be fully understood and well implemented.

Strengths and Weaknesses

Once aware of the fact that alcoholism was a behavioral-health problem, an illness which was proven to be amenable to treatment and that other similar corporations had adopted means whereby employees afflicted with the illness were being successfully rehabilitated, Canadian National Railways lost no time in initiating a policy and implementing procedures for the welfare of their employees so afflicted.

Strengths of C. N.'s Policy and Procedures are believed to be as follows:

1. Explicit in the policy statement, recognition of alcoholism as a behavioral-health problem, an illness which has proven to be amenable to treatment.
2. Explicit in the policy statement that alcoholism, recognized as an illness will be treated as any other illness in respect to Sickness and Pension benefits.
3. Criteria of a developing problem with alcohol being job performance, accident rate, absenteeism.
4. Responsibility for implementation being the mandate of senior management in each region, discharged with the collaboration of the Regional Medical Officer.

5. Senior Management being responsible for arranging training programs for management, supervisory and union personnel; to assist them in identifying the early signs of problem drinking alcoholism; and for ensuring that appropriate training programs are carried out within their jurisdictions. Regional Medical Departments being responsible for diagnosis and recommending appropriate treatment programs.

6. Although drafted unilaterally, the policy is explicit in requiring that union representatives and organizations be kept informed on developments of the policy and procedures, to seek the active cooperation of union representatives and to ensure access to same training concerning problem drinking and alcoholism, as is available to management and supervisory personnel.

7. The building up of figure data; number of problem drinkers identified, undergoing treatment, rehabilitated, returned to job, etc., by the Personnel and Labor Relations Department, thus providing an ongoing evaluation and appraisal of procedures on each region and system as a whole.

The commitment of senior management to ensuring that C. N.'s Policy and Procedures achieve their maximum potential is evident in the clear delineation of responsibilities for implementation, training and medical diagnosis. Further evidence of this commitment by senior management and their determination that the C. N. Policy and Procedures realize their potential is the building up of statistical figure data right from the inception of the program. Such statistical figure data will serve as an evaluative appraisal tool which will indicate where management "muscle" might be required to ensure realization of the humanitarian and economic goals and objectives of Canadian National's Policy.

Weaknesses in C. N.'s Policy and Procedures are not readily apparent. However, there are two areas which have created some difficulty and concern for both union and management. These are the reinstatement and reallocation of employees suspended as the result of problem drinking or alcoholism, particularly those employees in "sensitive" trades.

It is suggested that, not unlike other similar corporations, these C. N. employees had during the progression of their problem drinking alcoholism been covered up for, hidden and shielded by fellow workers, shop stewards and various levels of supervisory personnel to the point where it was no longer possible, and suspension, early retirement or termination was inevitable. It is also suggested that, as in any corporation, instances of coverup, hiding and shielding of employees requires a certain degree of mutual understanding or "gentlemen's agreement" on the part of labor and management. There exists a much more important need for understanding and cooperation on the part of fellow workers, labor and management at all levels of responsibility if the afflicted employee is to be completely rehabilitated.

For the first time, through the C. N. Policy and Procedures for dealing with problem drinking-alcoholism, there is an alternative to such futile, devastatingly wasteful coverup procedures. Yet, unfortunately, those well-intentioned "friends" are the very ones who make it difficult if not impossible for the afflicted employee to be reinstated in his original job or reallocated in another Department. Here we have a situation which, unless resolved quickly, will seriously undermine the potential effectiveness of C. N.'s Policy and Procedures with regard to alcoholism. Not only is the employee denied the opportunity of returning to his trade for which he has specific talent and skills, he is frequently denied the opportunity of employment in any other Department. The rationale proffered by the heads of the various Departments being "that they are reluctant to take on their staff the 'culls' of some other Department." The feeling being that in so doing they are permitting one department to dispose of a problem employee at the expense of another department.

The problem of reemployment or reinstatement is not one that must be resolved unilaterally by management. The various locals compound the problem through the best of intentions in that they also have specific requirements concerning who shall be permitted to work in which trade. Certainly there would appear to be an urgent need for labor and management to sit down and work out some method by which a fellow employee who has comes to terms with his behavioral-health problem of alcoholism can be returned to suitable employment as rapidly as approved by the Regional Medical Officer.

If this employee, having conscientiously complied with the

requirements specified in the C. N. Policy and Procedures, has recognized his problem and availed himself of rehabilitative facilities, only to find that it was, in effect, for naught, he will certainly relapse and return to drinking. It is imperative in this critical stage of the rehabilitative process, that an employee be given the opportunity of regaining his dignity as a human being returned to work as quickly as possible. For those employees in the early phase of the rehabilitation process, it may be necessary to "bend" a few rules and regulations. And it is at this stage that "representatives of both management became self-righteous and sanctimonious about bending a few rules and regulations when it will contribute to the welfare of their fellow workers. Having been personally involved with some 10,000 alcoholics during the past twenty years or more, one factor has appeared in the majority of relapses—the loss of human dignity and feeling of worthlessness in not being able to obtain suitable employment.

Human nature being as perverse as it is, individuals tend to focus upon the negative aspect of anything new which will require a change in "normal" routine, attitudes and biases. Employees at Canadian National are no different and the longer the present situation concerning reemployment, reinstatement and the interdepartmental difficulties are allowed to persist the greater will be the negative response to the policy and procedures.

Summary and Evaluation

Canadian National Railways are to be commended for the manner in which they initiated their policy and implemented procedures for dealing with the behavioral-health problem of alcoholism. Once having become aware of the fact that positive constructive action was possible, no time was lost. In a relatively short period of time, the total resources of management and labor in each of the five Regions were marshalled in a concentrated effort to provide an alternative, a constructive, humanitarian alternative, to the practice of wasteful, destructive, coverup and termination, common to many corporations in dealing with problem drinking and alcoholism.

C. N.'s emphasis on the "pretreatment" phase of their policy and procedures augers well for the success of the program. Training seminars for management, supervisory and union personnel, at all levels of responsibility, will enable the capabilities of each group to be brought to bear on the objective of early identification and motivation to medical diagnosis and treatment.

J. D. Caldwell, Industrial Consultant with the Addiction Research Foundation of Ontario, in addressing delegates attending the annual meeting of the Canada Safety Council held at the MacDonald Hotel, Edmonton, Alberta in May, 1973, had this comment regarding coverup: "Employees with alcohol problems are being encouraged to continue their habits by futile 'coverup' practices by their fellow workers. Because of some taboo which persists in our society," he continued, "employees, and in many cases, the supervisors, work together to keep the problem out of sight."

Job performance is adversely affected by alcoholism. In the early stages of alcoholism there is a noticeable increase in the number of job related, as well as off-the-job, accidents. Attendance is adversely affected with more frequent absences being apparent for the days immediately following holidays and paydays. These, the accepted criteria for recognizing a developing problem with alcohol, are all evident in the pretreatment phase of any corporate policy for dealing with alcoholism. They are also within the responsibilities of supervisory personnel at all levels of jurisdictions.

C. N.'s clear-cut assignment of responsibility to all levels of management, supervisory and union personnel in the implementation of the pretreatment phase of the C. N. program, and of the responsibility of the Medical Department for diagnosis and recommendation of treatment facilities will do much to dispel any ambiguity as to whom the policy is applicable, line or staff. Certainly the statement made by G. H. Bloomfield, Vice-President General-Manager, Mountain Region, during a seminar for senior management, "This Policy is not a 'we' and 'they' policy. It applies to all levels of personnel in the employ of Canadian National Railways. On the Mountain Region," he continued, "the Policy applies to each and every one of us, you and I, in senior management. We, you and I, must be aware of our own attitudes and behavior as regards alcohol and the example we set to those under our respective jurisdictions will do much to dispel any ambiguity and doubts regarding the Policy and its applicability." The focus of the C. N. Policy and Procedures upon the welfare of the individual employee afflicted with alcoholism enables labor and management to cooperate at the departmental level in each Region without detracting from or impinging upon the rights and prerogatives of either.

It is hoped that having conceived, initiated and implemented a policy which is believed worthy of emulation, Canadian National will not permit it to be emasculated through inter-departmental differences when the question arises concerning the reallocation, reemployment or reinstatement of employees in the process of rehabilitation. The good will, understanding and cooperation of each and every individual are to achieve their optimum effectiveness. In the initial phase of the program, the actual confrontation of an employee will require an awareness of what "symptoms" or indices of a developing problem are being presented by the employee.

Canadian National would appear to have taken this fact into consideration; certainly it would appear so in the Mountain Region where there is one full-time Employee Counselor and ten part-time counselors, and the creation of a new position, Regional Employee Counselor, in each Region. These Regional Employee Counselors have as one of their responsibilities the initiation of information and training seminars for all levels of responsibility in management, supervisory and labor. Equally, if not more important, is the need for refresher seminars, at least on a semi-annual basis. It is in these refresher seminars that individuals will gain skill and competence in recognizing the significance of circumstances, events, details indicative of a developing problem with alcohol.

There is an area in which a majority of corporations default—follow-up. It is difficult to assess why. In other areas of concern —safety, introduction of more efficient procedures, etc.—repetition, follow-up, refresher and up-dating sessions are considered vital to corporate-wide acceptance and adoption. Yet, in this area, which has been proven to be effective in improving performance of job requirements, reduction of accidents (safety), improving morale and conservation of skilled employees, there seems to be resistance to doing what must be done. Perhaps here is an example of not recognizing the significance of the information being presented.

SUMMARY AND CONCLUSION

The foregoing trilogy of corporate policies and procedures are representative of the approach being taken by Canadian Business, Industrial and Labor organizations in an effort to resolve the behavioral-health problem of alcoholism in the work force. To date, unfortunately, relatively few business, industrial or labor organizations have undertaken similar positive, constructive action regarding a problem proven to be extremely wasteful in terms of economic and human resources. Nor is it the business community alone which is open to criticism for a seeming reluctance to take positive action toward resolving a costly, behavioral-health problem. Many governments, Provincial and Municipal, have not, as yet, taken any such similar positive, constructive action.

It is held that greater public education is necessary if the prevalence of alcoholism is to be contained and the incidence reduced. Yet, little use is made of the one group of individuals reognized as representing large and influential segments of public opinion—the leaders in management and labor.

Jellinek observed, "Labor and management form very large and influential sections of the public and thus their attitudes towards alcoholism represent an important part of public opinion; furthermore, the opinions of these groups may influence quite considerably the attitudes of other sections of the general public . . ." (Jellinek, 1960).

Trice (1970) made similar observations, "The work world holds great potential for the treatment of alcoholics. The potential present in the work world to do something truly effective about alcoholism continues to be overshadowed by the outmoded efforts centered in social work and colored by police court obsessions that reflect the "skid row" image of alcoholism.

Management and unions comprise two pivotal institutions in society which can be more potent in community effort than welfare agencies, medical facilities, or jails in their effect on the alcoholic."

In a majority of cases, government departments and agencies responsible for the delivery of community services for dealing with alcoholism, alcoholics, continue to focus their efforts in areas which have been, at best, only minimal in their effectiveness— treatment and rehabilitation. Little, if anything, is being done in the area of pretreatment, the early or precrisis stage in the progression of alcoholism. It is here in the area of pretreatment or precrisis that business, industry and labor, through corporate policies and procedures are able to achieve early intervention which precludes costly long-term inpatient treatment.

In this matter of early intervention, Trice (1970) observed: "Unions and management, by recognizing the existence of alcoholics in their own world, can counteract the characterization of the alcoholic as a police court inebriate, as they simultaneously ensure a much higher recovery rate that accrues to those who are treated while still on the job. The strategy is to attack the problem where and when there is a reasonable chance of success, that is, on the job."

Governments, Provincial and Municipal, along with business and industry being the major sources of employment, have, it is believed, a responsibility to ensure constructive, positive action being taken to contain the prevalence and reduce the incidence of alcoholism in the community. Where better to initiate such positive, constructive action, action which has proven to be effective in early intervention and subsequent successful rehabilitation, than with their own employees. Surely here is where a great deal of education could take place. Education which has proven effective in making possible early recognition of a developing problem; education which makes intervention possible prior to a crisis situation, education which precludes the necessity of long-term inpatient treatment.

Certainly, with the preponderance of evidence, information and data clearly indicating the high success rates being achieved by industry in rehabilitating employees afflicted with alcoholism, for leaders of government, Provincial and/or Municipal, and captains of industry, not to initiate similar policies and more important, implement procedures which focus on the pretreatment phase of alcoholism, it would not seem unreasonable to state that they are leaving themselves open to the charge of dereliction of responsibility as leaders, or, like Nelson, of using their blind eye when viewing a serious situation.

REFERENCES

Jellinek, E. M.: *The Disease Concept of Alcoholism.* New Haven, Hillhouse Press, 1960.

Trice, H. M.: *Alcoholism and the Work World: Prevention in a New Light.* Boston, Beacon Press, 1970.

Chapter 4

LONG-TERM EXPERIENCE WITH REHABILITATION OF ALCOHOLIC EMPLOYEES

Good

FERN E. ASMA, M.D.

ILLINOIS BELL TELEPHONE COMPANY

THE ILLINOIS BELL Telephone Company Rehabilitation Program for employees with alcoholism was started in 1950 and has gradually been expanded over the intervening years. The program was not started because of a certain knowledge that any specific number or percentage of employees suffered from this illness. As a matter of fact, in the early days of the program, it is highly unlikely that alcoholism was recognized as a real illness at all! The program was really started by a far-sighted management medical team who knew that the problem was significant. It was significant then in human loss, in loss of business efficiency, in increased sickness disability and in increased accident disability both off and on the job. We maintain our program today for the very same reasons. However, today we know that it is an effective program in partially solving these problems.

Our knowledge of the number of alcoholic employees in our 42,000 employee group is undoubtedly as rudimentary now as it was when the program was started in 1950. We have really made no effort to survey the problem. Because alcoholism is often a hidden disease, it is doubtful that any industry knows the real magnitude of the problem and its contribution to absenteeism, accidents and decreased job performance. Undoubtedly are all aware of the various statistics quoted about the incidence of this illness (Davis, 1970; Winter, 1970). Our company is probably no better or no worse than any other similar business. What we do know is that our program has demonstrated that we have enough sick employees to justify continuing and expanding our efforts.

The detection procedure we use to find the employee with alcoholism has undergone some changes over the years. The original concept was that of looking for the alcoholic employee. However, in 1962 we adopted our present concept of looking for the problem employee. We now look not only for alcoholism, but for any other medical reason that prevents the employee from doing a good job. We call this a Health Evaluation Program. The immediate supervisor selects the employee for referral to the Medical Department when that employee is not doing a satisfactory job and when the situation cannot be remedied by the usual management procedures. This being the case, the supervisor has a frank discussion of the job problem with the employee. The usual job problems are those involving the formal work contract such as frequent tardiness, frequent absenteeism, job performance not coming up to the standards, and difficulty in interpersonal relationships with co-workers, authority figures, customers, etc. In the discussion, it is indicated to the employee that this type of job performance—whatever it is—cannot be tolerated and that some effort must be made to change this pattern so that the performance will become satisfactory. A visit to the Medical Department is then suggested to the employee to determine if a medical problem is the basis for the poor job function. This is not a punitive visit in any way. It is explained to the employee that this is one more step our company will take in an effort to aid him in doing his job in a satisfactory way. The employee is free to accept this referral, or to decline it if he wishes. Should he decline the referral, he then must make a real effort on his own to change his job performance to that which is satisfactory to the employing department. Our management people have also been instructed that should the job performance still not come up to standards, that they again have a discussion with the employee and offer a Health Evaluation.

If the employee accepts the referral to the Medical Department, we view this as an opportunity to help a patient with a serious job problem. We do a complete history, thorough physical examination, and laboratory examination on every referred employee. We also arrange and pay for any outside consultations we feel are necessary. In other words, we do the best we can to aid in the rehabilitation of the employee. Of course, this has a company-oriented benefit too, in that it hopefully resolves the job problem as far as the employing department is concerned.

The Health Evaluation then is our case finder. With a detection procedure of this type, it should be quite obvious that the employees who are referred to us usually have an emotional illness, alcoholism, are drug users, or have undiagnosed or poorly treated physical illnesses. The great majority of the people we see on this type of evaluation have emotional problems. The next most frequent cause of job dysfunction is alcoholism.

Briefly the structure and function of our program for the employees with a drinking problem is as follows: The Assistant Medical Director is in charge of the Health Evaluations and supervises the Rehabilitation Programs. We also have an Alcoholics Rehabilitation Counselor in our Medical Department as a full-time employee. After evaluation by the physician, problem drinkers are referred to the counselor. At the time of the initial interview with the counselor, a plan of rehabilitation will be outlined. This will very likely involve regular counseling with the counselor on an individual basis. Arrangements will also be made for the employee to participate in meetings of Alcoholics Anonymous. The meetings of Alcoholics Anonymous are outside the company although we do have our own company sponsored Alcoholics Anonymous group and a Sunday Morning Breakfast group. The physician in charge of this program assists in the early rehabilitation and when it is determined that professional care above and beyond that which is furnished by the counselor is needed. Should hospitalization be necessary, this is also arranged for as indicated. We also frequently discuss our plans with the employing department. Without their cooperation any successful rehabilitation would be very unlikely. We feel very strongly that the constructive coercion thus initiated is necessary to motivate most employees to participate in the program. The job, after all, is extremely important to the employee and it is only by showing evidence of participation in a serious rehabilitation effort that the job will be secure.

It should be added that with any Alcohol Rehabilitation Program we should also be alert to any associated problems. Not only emotional problems, but all too often we may be dealing with multiple drug use or the use of drugs other than alcohol. Our Drug Abuse Program is handled in the very same way as the Alcoholics Rehabilitation. The majority of referrals are via the Health Evaluation Program. We also have a Drug Abuse Counselor in the Medical Department as a full time employee. Any employee using drugs other than alcohol is referred to the Drug Abuse Counselor. This counselor does individual counseling or may counsel two or three employees at a time. We also have our own company-sponsored therapy group which meets after hours once a week. Should hospitalization be necessary we arrange for this. If Methadone detoxification is indicated the referral is made based upon the employee's needs. It may be outpatient detoxification with a State program or in a therapeutic community.

Needless to say, with these types of programs available, it is important that the company be aware of the facilities available to them. Therefore, employee education of these facilities should be a constant ongoing part of the regular employee health education program. This education was and is accomplished in several ways. Members of the medical staff and nurses talk to many employee groups. Articles have appeared in the company magazine and newspapers. Motion picture programs are shown on company locations and adequate educational material is constantly made available in health education racks in easily accessible locations. In 1969, a brochure explaining our policy and program together with a condensation of the book, "The Drinking Game and How to Beat It" was mailed to the home of all employees. A videotape presentation was recently produced which is suitable for either management or employee group meetings. Our medical staff regularly present the Medical Department facilities at our management induction training programs. Education of our management is also accomplished by a published guide for supervisors. With the permission of Illinois Bell Telephone Company, it is presented completely to help in formulation of a similar education program for those who desire to do so.

ILLINOIS BELL GUIDE FOR SUPERVISORS

The Problem Drinker—How Great a Problem?

About 80 million adults in this country drink alcoholic beverages. Most of these people are able to indulge without harming themselves or anyone else. Many, however, are problem drinkers who are letting alcohol run, and perhaps ruin, their lives.

Two million or more of these problem drinkers work in industry. A number of Illinois Bell people may belong to this group, since it is estimated that 4 to 6 percent of the employees in any company are problem drinkers.

The problem drinker has a compulsive, uncontrollable urge to drink. His drinking interferes with normal living by creating problems in his daily life. He is physically and mentally unable to handle alcohol. To him, the importance of alcohol eventually outweighs all other considerations, affecting his family, his friends and his job.

Because compulsive drinking gets progressively worse, it's very important that we discover an employee who has a drinking problem as soon as possible. By identifying the problem drinker early enough, we may be able to rehabilitate him. We must remember that alcoholism can be just as relentlessly progressive and destructive as cancer if it is not treated in its early stages.

When Does Drinking Become a Company Problem?

Alcoholism can be defined as habitual poor job performance resulting from excessive drinking. This definition can be easily understood by a busy supervisor as well as the alcoholic employee himself. The problem drinker's repeated poor work in turn has a bad effect on smooth job operations as far as the boss, peers and union representatives are concerned.

Examples of when an employee's drinking becomes a Company problem:

1. His work is reduced in efficiency and dependability.
2. The employee's drinking affects his health.
3. The employee's drinking affects his personal relations on the job.
4. He has alcohol on his breath during working hours.
5. He is an attendance problem.
6. There are complaints from customers or other employees.
7. There are frequent on or off-the-job accidents.
8. There are unexplained disappearances from the work assignment.

Examples of behavior patterns exhibited by problem drinkers:

1. Frequent Monday, Friday, post-holiday and post-payday absence and tardiness.
2. A variety of poor excuses for frequent absences for minor illnesses. Such people claim to be suffering from colds, gastritis, flu, stomach conditions and other ailments more often than do other employees.
3. Frequent on and off-the-job accidents.
4. Moodiness and unusual sensitivity leading to arguments or disinterest in the job.
5. Decreasing reliability, evidenced by: an inclination to put things off; a tendency to neglect details formerly pursued; placing blame on other workers; a desire for different job assignments; seeking loans from the Company or associates.
6. A marked change in appearance, such as swelling of the face, flushed face, red or bleary eyes. These changes are often accompanied by increasing carelessness in dress and appearance.
7. Hand tremor.
8. Memory blackouts.
9. Drinking habits which differ from those of companions (faster drinking, sneaking drinks, drinking longer or heavy spending on alcoholic drinks).
10. Evidence of domestic discord or increasing financial troubles.
11. Marked sensitivity to suggestions that alcoholism is a problem.

What is IBT's Policy on Problem Drinking?

Illinois Bell's policy on employees with drinking problems has four basic premises:

1. The use of any drug interfering with safe and efficient job function is a matter of company concern and will be dealt with in an appropriate manner.
2. Alcohol is also a drug about which there is serious concern. Its excessive use will be considered in the same manner.

3. The company recognizes that drug misuse may be a serious medical problem. A rehabilitation program is offered in the Medical Department. Employees cooperating in a clinically supervised rehabilitation program may be eligible for benefits.
4. Possession or use of illegally obtained drugs or alcohol on the job or on company premises may be a cause for dismissal.

Remedial Steps to Be Taken

DON'T COVER UP. If you have a person with a job problem or suspected drinking problem in your organization, the sooner you face the situation the better. Don't cover up for him. No matter how well meant such an attitude is, it is a disservice to a person heading toward compulsive drinking. One of the underlying facts about this illness is that the victim can recover only with outside assistance. He cannot see the necessity for such assistance. The earlier the treatment, the greater the hope of rehabilitation. Alcoholism is like cancer. You can help by catching it early.

THE FIRST INTERVIEW. Instead of covering up, start as soon as possible with a down-to-earth discussion with him.

Plan the interview meticulously and be well-armed with facts and observations to back up the firm approach you'll take. Prepare a carefully written documentation of the interview. Keep your interview job-oriented. Do not discuss alcoholism unless the employee mentions it or unless the use of alcohol has been obvious on the job.

1. The employee should be told that he is in serious trouble on his job and his behavior will no longer be tolerated.
2. The employee should also be told that the Company has an excellent program for rehabilitation for illness and that he will be sent to the Medical Department for a health evaluation to see if his health is having an adverse effect on his job. This should be suggested in a genuine spirit of help and not as a disciplinary action.

Explain in detail the reasons you are concerned about his performance. For example:

1. The aspects of his work which are not meeting your expectations for a person with his amount of training and years of experience.
2. His personal record of tardiness and sickness absence, compared

with records of all employees in your own group, office or area, or in the Company.

3. His personal relations with other employees.
4. His safety record on and off the job.
5. Changes in his personal and physical appearance.
6. Alcohol on his breath.
7. Complaints from customers and other employees.

You'll need all the understanding, patience, perseverance and firmness you can muster if you're to succeed. Be firm about his job deficiencies and the fact that you will no longer tolerate them.

The first and perhaps the biggest challenge is to convince him that he has a job problem and that his job is in jeopardy.

Don't be surprised if he strongly disagrees with you, then comes up with excuses for his lack of job performance.

If the employee refuses to go to the Medical Department, be sure he understands that he must improve his performance. Watch the employee's performance closely. If he doesn't improve, talk with him again and insist that he go to the Medical Department.

If he refuses a second time, follow your usual administrative procedures dealing with unsatisfactory job performance which the employee refuses to correct. Also, call the Medical Department to see if they have anything further to suggest.

What the Medical Department Does

The Request for Employee Health Evaluation should include a complete written report of all the facts and personal interviews in the case. Include any suspicion or evidence of the abuse of alcohol. It is important to tell the employee that the information about his poor job performance will be available to the physician.

The physician will do a complete examination, evaluate the seriousness of the health problem, and recommend a plan of action. Consultation with outside specialists will be obtained when necessary.

The Medical Department has a trained Counselor who is responsible for coordinating rehabilitative efforts. If the examination indicates that rehabilitation should be attempted and if the employee agrees to cooperate, he will be referred to the Counselor. The Counselor and physician will then outline a program of therapy and follow-up for the employee. Basically, this program uses Alcoholics Anonymous and regular counseling in the Medical Department. Other specialized care will be suggested when needed. The Medical Department welcomes and seeks, the cooperation of the employee's family, his personal physician and his clergyman. The importance of the cooperation of the employee's supervisor is of utmost importance.

Application of Benefit Plan

An employee who is absent because of a drinking problem may be entitled to sickness disability under the "Plan for Employee's Pensions, Disability Benefits and Death Benefits." Sickness disability will be granted if the employee is cooperating in following a medically prescribed course of treatment, and if the Medical Department advises that he is cooperating but is unable to work. Based on facts in each case, the Benefit Committee will determine whether or not the employee will receive benefits.

Your Responsibility Continues

Once the decision is made to attempt rehabilitation, your role as a management representative continues to be a vital factor. The Medical Department will continue to need your close cooperation. You must remain an understanding friend of the employee, alert to his changing state of mind and moods, and prepared to take the initiative when personal problems arise relating to the course of treatment. For example, it may be necessary to assist by getting the help of the employee's family or church. Your assistance may also be needed in persuading the employee to seek aid from a local clinic, Alcoholics Anonymous or some other selected agency.

You should keep in close contact with the Medical Department and immediately report any new evidence of drinking.

He Has a Responsibility Too

As you try to help the employee, you should make it clear to him that:

1. It is his responsibility to gain complete control of his drinking problem.

2. The Company expects he will make favorable progress toward complete rehabilitation.
3. The Company will not tolerate continued unsatisfactory job performance.

If a relapse occurs, an understanding attitude should be shown if the employee is cooperative and continues to demonstate a sincere interest in his rehabilitation.

Action in Difficult Situations

When the employee is not cooperating in the program outlined for him, disciplinary action may be necessary, such as warnings, suspensions, leave of absence, etc. Final disposition of all cases rests with the employing department after consultation with the Medical Department.

It's important that the employing and the Medical Department cooperate in close supervision of the employee at all times.

Documentation

Frequently, in the administrative handling of an alcoholic case, the alcoholic will deny that anyone has ever talked to him or her concerning the problem.

In handling an alcoholic case, it is very important to keep complete records concerning each episode, interview or conference. Also include the facts relating to the supervisor's contacts with the Company's Medical Staff or other interested parties. All of a supervisor's records must be detailed, complete, dated and signed. It should be explained, for example, that the employee spoke incoherently, was unsteady in stance or walking, was untidy or shaky—rather than stating the simple conclusion that the employee was intoxicated. If disciplinary action is taken, there should be a written record of the reasons for such action. This record should describe the warnings given to the employee about his future with the Company, as well as evidence indicating that the employee understood these warnings.

Some Final Thoughts

Rewards to the Company, to the individual alcoholic employee, and to his or her family and friends, can be great when rehabilitative efforts succeed. Conversely, the penalties can be severe when rehabilitative efforts fail.

The earlier rehabilitative efforts start, the greater the chances for their success.

When the supervisor procastinates or does nothing, individual cases may "go too far" to accomplish rehabilitation.

Time alone will not "cure" the alcoholic—it requires the marshalling of all the rehabilitative forces outlined in this booklet.

Our program can best be summed up in the following summary chart. The chart follows the problem case through circumstances that may develop either to the successful conclusion of rehabilitative measures, or to ultimate disciplinary action.

A written statement of policy has been presented throughout the company also. This was accomplished through a letter from the Personnel Vice-President and through publication of the company newspapers. We find the general policy statement to be workable and can be adopted to suit most any individual situation in any industry. A successful, operating program needs the complete cooperation of all levels of management in a commitment to recognize alcoholism as an illness. In this way it can then be treated as such under disability and insurance programs and in the offer of rehabilitation. Since the disease of alcoholism is endemic in our employee population, by meeting it as such we can protect ourselves against the actual and hidden costs.

EVALUATION OF THE PROGRAM

Statistical studies are helpful in evaluating the program. The following statistics have already been reported in the *Journal of Occupational Medicine* but are included here for the types of statistics we feel are essential. These are the statistics on 402 employees on whom we had adequate records. In the early days of our program most records were not adequate for statistical follow-up. In the cases reported, we have records of five or more years before and five or more years after referral to our program.

Summary Outline of Possible Courses of Action

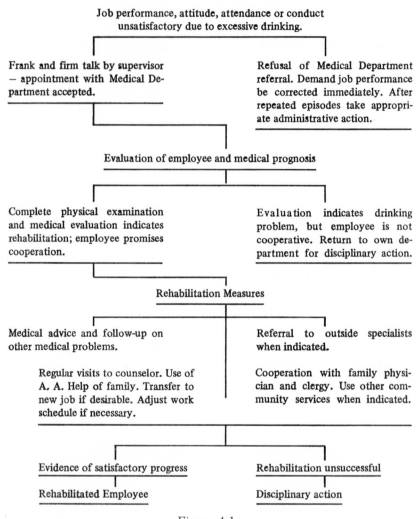

Job performance, attitude, attendance or conduct
unsatisfactory due to excessive drinking.

Frank and firm talk by supervisor — appointment with Medical Department accepted.

Refusal of Medical Department referral. Demand job performance be corrected immediately. After repeated episodes take appropriate administrative action.

Evaluation of employee and medical prognosis

Complete physical examination and medical evaluation indicates rehabilitation; employee promises cooperation.

Evaluation indicates drinking problem, but employee is not cooperative. Return to own department for disciplinary action.

Rehabilitation Measures

Medical advice and follow-up on other medical problems.

Regular visits to counselor. Use of A. A. Help of family. Transfer to new job if desirable. Adjust work schedule if necessary.

Referral to outside specialists when indicated.

Cooperation with family physician and clergy. Use other community services when indicated.

Evidence of satisfactory progress

Rehabilitated Employee

Rehabilitation unsuccessful

Disciplinary action

Figure 4-1.

First let us consider how these employees were referred to us. Ninety percent were referred by the employing department, the majority of these were on a Health Evaluation basis. Four percent were discovered while other examinations were being done in the Medical Department and 6 percent were self-referrals. These statistics show the need to educate all levels of management in the art of case-finding. Since management and goals change, this is a continuing effort that must be constantly adapted to these changes. For instance, the concept of educating our management to look for the problem employee rather than employees with a specific problem such as emotional illness, alcoholism or drug abuse.

The characteristics of these employees are shown in Table 4-I. In years of service, the greater number of employees had between ten and twenty-nine years of service at the time that alcoholism interfered with doing their job efficiently. Only seventy-seven had less than ten years of service. As Table 4-II indicates, these employees were most often between the ages of thirty-five and fifty-four years of age. These, of course, are normally the most productive years in the life of the employee and the years in which they could hope to progress in the business. The length of service and age distribution indicates to us that alcoholism had really been present and unrecognized for a considerable time before it finally resulted in a job crisis of sufficient magnitude to demand corrective action. The obvious remedy was to alert our employing departments to have Health Evaluations much earlier and repeat them again and again if

TABLE 4-I

YEARS OF SERVICE WHEN REFERRED TO PROGRAM

Years Service	Women	Men	Total	%
Under 10	19	58	77	19
10-19 years	23	99	122	31
20-29 years	27	77	104	25
30-39 years	23	56	79	20
40 or over	1	19	20	5

TABLE 4-II

AGE WHEN REFERRED TO PROGRAM

Age	Women	Men	Total	%
Under 25 years	2	7	9	2
25-34 years	4	56	60	15
35-44 years	30	95	125	31
45-54 years	50	106	156	40
55 or over	7	45	52	12

necessary. These statistics alerted us to the subtle nature of early alcoholism so that we became more efficient diagnosticians.

The great majority of men were married as compared with only about one third of the women. The incidence of divorce or separation was much higher in women. This could either indicate a difference of the view of society toward alcoholism in women or indicate that the married dependent woman is willing to endure more to hold on to her marriage. We know that there was severe discord in the marriages of many male patients. We might add that closer contact with the families of the alcoholic employee is essential. We have found that oftentimes the spouse also has a drinking problem and our rehabilitation efforts would fail without involving them.

We made an effort to estimate the major area of life stress in all 402 employees. In 86 percent it was our opinion that the life stress was within the employee himself. Home stress accounted for 25 percent, while job stress accounted for only 9 percent. It should be noted that some patients had more than one area of life stress. Where job stress was definitely encountered, we made every effort to alter the job situation as best we could.

We have found that it is important to make a diagnosis of the type of drinking in order to be most effective in our rehabilitation efforts. As shown in Table 4-III, 21 percent were heavy drinkers. These people were not true alcoholics but drink in a serious, damaging, recreational way. They are able to control their drinking much easier than the other types. However, some of these deteriorated into the chronic alcoholic category. Sixty-three percent were typical "chronic" alcoholics. These are the people in whom drinking is compulsive and self destructive. Six percent of the people were reactive drinkers. They react to life situations by drinking; that is, going out on a "binge," but between the episodes could maintain themselves to some degree. Ten percent were symptomatic drinkers. These patients were suffering from emotional illness primarily and alcoholism was simply a manifestation of the emotional illness.

What success have we had in obtaining the cooperation of these 402 people and in changing their drinking habits may be seen in Table 4-IV. Of the 402 employees, 230 referrals were

TABLE 4-III

DIAGNOSIS OF TYPE OF DRINKING

	Women	Men	Total	%
Heavy drinker	17	66	83	21
Chronic alcoholic	54	201	255	63
Reactive drinker	7	16	23	6
Symptomatic drinker	15	26	41	10

TABLE 4-IV

SUCCESS IN REHABILITATION IN 402 REFERRALS

	Women	Men	Total	%
Rehabilitated	52	178	230	57
Improved	20	40	60	15
Accepted help	17	75	92	23
Not controlled	4	16	20	5

rehabilitated—this is 57 percent. By rehabilitated, we mean that these employees have stopped drinking completely for one year or more. Fifteen percent were improved. By this we mean that these employees were able to function satisfactorily on the job although their drinking had not been completely controlled. This means job rehabilitation was accomplished in 72 percent of employees counseled. Twenty-three percent had accepted our help. This is the group of employees in whom we are unable to predict what will happen. Some will undoubtedly fail and will not be controlled. Others will be improved or even move on to the rehabilitated group. Five percent of all employees were not cooperative and our rehabilitation efforts were a total failure. Of all employees referred to us, 87 percent have accepted counseling by our Rehabilitation Counselor. A smaller group participated in regular activities of Alcoholics Anonymous. However, this group consisting of 55 percent was composed almost entirely of chronic alcoholics who benefit most from this fellowship.

Now the question of whether our efforts really helped to make the company run better which is the fundamental purpose of our Medical Department. The following data should answer the question of whether we changed job performance, reduced sickness disability absence, and reduced off-the-job and on-the-job accidents. Let us consider our success in changing job performance. We had the employing department estimate job efficiency for the five years prior to coming on the program and for the five years after rehabilitation efforts started.

In all, 46 percent of women were rated poor before entering the program whereas only 22 percent were subsequently rated poor as Table 4-V indicates. Only 10 percent were rated as good employees before coming on the rehabilitation program while 46 percent were rated as good employees after being rehabilitated. Clearly, we were able to change the job efficiency of these employees. Table 4-VI shows approximately the same results were evident in men. The employees rated poor were significantly reduced while the good employees were substantially increased after rehabilitation. The combined effect on job efficiency shows that poor job performance dropped from 28 percent to 12 percent. Table 4-VII shows that good job performance was only present in 22 percent prior to rehabilitation and increased to 58 percent after participation in the program. These results indicate that a significant change in job behavior can be accomplished by rehabilitation.

TABLE 4-V

ESTIMATE OF JOB EFFICIENCY

	5 Years Before		5 Years After	
	Women	%	Women	%
Poor	43	46	20	22
Fair	41	44	30	32
Good	9	10	43	46

TABLE 4-VI

ESTIMATE OF JOB EFFICIENCY

	5 Years Before		5 Years After	
	Men	%	Men	%
Poor	69	22	31	10
Fair	158	51	89	29
Good	82	27	189	61

TABLE 4-VII

ESTIMATE OF JOB EFFICIENCY

	5 Years Before		5 Years After	
	Employees	%	Employees	%
Poor	112	28	51	12
Fair	199	50	119	30
Good	91	22	232	58

It is well known that the alcoholic employee has many more days of sickness disability absence than does his counterpart who is not alcoholic (Asma, 1971; Observer, 1959; Stevenson, 1942). In Table 4-VIII, the statistics presented are for the number of cases—these are cases that lasted for more than seven days of reported illness. We do not have statistics on the first seven days of absence. These 402 employees had 662 cases of sickness disability absence in the five years before participating in our program. In the subsequent five years, the same employees had only 356 cases. This is a significant reduction in sickness disability. However, these employees still are not quite as good in this regard as employees who are never alcoholic. Nevertheless, cutting our sickness disability rate in these employees by nearly 50 percent is certainly worthwhile.

We are also very interested in our ability to change the accident process. The number of off-duty accidents are presented in Table 4-IX. Again, these figures indicate only those cases in which the disability lasted more than seven days. In the five years before rehabilitation, there were 75 cases of off-duty accidents as compared to 28 cases after employees were referred to the program. This is certainly a significant reduction. We are all well aware of the importance of alcohol as a contributing factor in these accidents. We are not all aware that a significant

TABLE 4-VIII

NUMBER OF SICKNESS DISABILITY CASES*

	5 Years Before	5 Years After
Women	229	75
Men	433	281
Totals	662	356

* More than seven days of reported illness

TABLE 4-IX

NUMBER OF OFF-DUTY ACCIDENTS*

	5 Years Before	5 Years After
Women	32	6
Men	43	22
Totals	75	28

* More than seven days absence

reduction in accidents can be obtained by an effective rehabilitation program. Alcoholic employees also have many more on-the-job accidents. Our employees were no exception. Table 4-X indicates the number of any on-duty accidents requiring medical treatment. Severity is not indicated in these statistics. In the five years before these employees participated in the program, there were 57 on-duty accidents. This number was reduced to 11 in the five years after rehabilitation. This is a dramatic decrease. There is no doubt that the control of alcoholism will produce a favorable change in the accident process.

The final disposition of our 402 referrals is presented in Table 4-XI. When this study was completed, 63 percent were still working, 9 percent had been dismissed, 6 percent resigned, 20 percent were pensioned and 2 percent were deceased. In the pension group it should be mentioned that some of these were forced pensions, some were voluntary and some employees had simply arrived at mandatory retirement age.

In summary, our statistics on 402 employees referred to us for rehabilitation indicate that job efficiency can be increased, sickness disability absence can be reduced and both off-the-job and on-the-job accidents can be reduced. When these advantages to the business are added to the social advantages to the employee

TABLE 4-X

NUMBER OF ON-DUTY ACCIDENTS*

	5 Years Before	5 Years After
Women	4	1
Men	53	10
Totals	57	11

* Any accident requiring medical treatment

TABLE 4-XI

FINAL DISPOSITION IN 402 REFERRALS

	Women	Men	Total	%
Working	51	204	255	63
Dismissed	9	27	36	9
Resigned	8	17	25	6
Pensioned*	22	56	78	20
Deceased	3	5	8	2

* May be forced, voluntary or mandatory

and his family as well as to society in general, it is quite obvious that a rehabilitation program is most desirable.

REFERENCES

Asma, F. E.; Eggert, R. L., and Hilker, R. R. J.: Long-term experience with rehabilitation of alcoholic employees. *J Occup Med*, 13:581-585, 1971.

Davis, W. W.: Practical experience with an alcoholism program in industry. *Ohio State Med J*, 66:814-816, 1970.

Observer, Maxwell M. A.: A study of absenteeism, accidents and sickness payments in problem drinkers in one industry. *Quart J Stud Alcohol*, 20:302-312, 1959.

Stevenson, R. W.: Absenteeism in an industrial plant due to alcoholism. *Quart J Stud Alcohol*, 2:661-668, 1942.

Winter, R. E.: One for the plant. *Md State Med J*, 19:97-99, 1970.

Chapter 5

FORMULATION OF AN ALCOHOLISM REHABILITATION PROGRAM AT BOSTON EDISON COMPANY

Iver S. Ravin, M.D.

When the idea of formulating a Company program for employees with real or potential drinking problems was first proposed at Boston Edison Company, we approached it in the same manner as any other proposal submitted to us which might promise to solve any other "purported" Company problem. We wanted to know and evaluate the following:

1. Is there, in fact a problem of employee alcoholism in the Company?
2. Where is the problem located in the Company, and to what extent does it exist?
3. What are the various possible methods to solve this type problem, and how do we determine the best solution for our particular circumstance?
4. What, if anything, are we doing now?
5. Should the Company proceed to install a new alcohol program, and if we do, what other related peripheral problems might exist which we should consider in implementation?

In evaluating a proposed employee alcoholism program from this same perspective of other Company proposals, the approach and methodology were clearly evident. We needed three special projects. The first thing we needed was a study and definition of the problem, which consisted of an overall general survey to decide whether an employee drinking problem existed, and a feasibility study on the merits of establishing a formal Company program to handle the condition. Then secondly, if conditions so indicated, we needed a systems study to evaluate the various available methods and design a detailed description of these three major projects, however, it is most important to preface this entire presentation with three preliminary remarks to establish the proper frame of reference.

First of all, we consider that our program represents the new an Edison Company program; and finally, we needed a special project to install the new alcoholism program. Before we begin "informed approach" to the problem of alcoholism. It is based on the principle of "constructive coercive" which we describe later in detail, and it differs in varying degrees from other approaches. The pure "Alcoholics Anonymous approach" used by a few programs in industry and in the community consists of either just a mere suggestion to (obvious) alcoholics to go to AA, or at the very most, the employment of a successfully recovered AA member to consult with alcoholics and introduce them to the AA program. This restrictive approach lacks many of the "constructive" and "coercive" features we describe later; and even though we readily admit AA is the only effective method for almost all alcoholics to personally recover from the sickness, a successful industry program needs additional features such as a formal policy on alcoholism, a definition of the supervisor's role, and other supportive measures. For some of these same reasons the standard "medical approach," the "community approach," and the "teamwork approach" are also not satisfactory or effective because they primarily exclude the "coercive" features, and only focus on the constructive aspects of dealing with alcoholism.

Thirdly, there are some duplications and overlapping in each of the three following sections of this report. This is unavoidable due to the method we use for the presentation, but to a certain degree it is also desirable as it serves to reemphasize some of the major features of our program.

DEFINITION OF PROBLEM

Since alcoholism is primarily a health problem according to all recognized authorities in the field, we assigned this first project to our Medical Department. We requested them to review all current and recent cases where alcoholism was indicated either during regular physical examinations or other medical services, and to check absence records and related data sources for any additional signs of the problem. The Medical Director alerted his staff of examining physicians and nurses to the assignment at hand, and assembled a task force to attack the problem. Everybody involved made extensive, in-depth studies; all reported a positive finding. The Medical Staff reported that several physical examinations revealed the effects of habitual excessive alcohol ingestion; and other experiences at routine sick call visits and medical services such as poison ivy and flu shots reinforced the finding.

The Personnel Department reported that a significant number of employees showed a very definite pattern of absence which was suggestive of those with problem drinking; and the Labor Relations Department estimated that 90 percent of their disciplinary cases were concerned with the problem of drinking as a direct contributing or associated cause. We will not detail the results of our study because it is worthy of a separate paper in itself. The undeniable conclusion, however, was that Boston Edison Company did in fact have a problem of employee drinking in several areas of the Company and that a program was needed to deal with the condition. We did not feel, however, that our incidence of involvement was any greater than the industrial community in general which was estimated at 5 percent; but 5 percent of the 4,200 employees at Boston Edison is over 200, and thus, a king-size problem.

In addition, the direct costs attributable to employee alcoholism for sick pay, overtime coverage, travel pay, hospitalization and other benefits were of sufficient magnitude to cause us some high degree of concern. But the thing which really surprised us was the existence and enormity of the indirect hidden costs, which we had not previously considered or even known. We learned about the "half-man on the job" operating at only a fraction of reasonable performance and costing us heavily through gross inefficiencies, poor judgment, and accident-prone situations. We also learned of the costs of alcoholism to Boston Edison attributable to our nonalcoholic employees: many of these people, due to the effects of an alcoholic spouse or parent, showed the same absence patterns and "half-man job performance" characteristics as the alcoholic employee. They were frequently at home taking care of an alcoholic mother or husband and doing other household chores including care of the children; or they were physically at work but mentally absent, worrying about the house being blown up or serious accidents to the home and the children.

Our study, in addition, revealed a very serious dilemma in handling the alcoholic employee. We were confronted with the conflicting views of considering alcoholism as a medical or a legal problem. Could a man be absolved from the consequences of his drinking and his acts by legally claiming that he had a medical illness? A historic arbitration case at the Chrysler Corporation came to our attention about this time. Chrysler was ordered to rehire a rehabilitated employee who had been discharged because of alcoholism, and even though we at Boston Edison Company had not discharged anyone for alcoholism, but rather the things that alcohol caused, i.e. absenteeism, poor work performance, etc., it was evident that the basic underlying cause of these cases was problem drinking.

Another interrelated problem we found was the considerable "covering up" of the alcoholic and his behavior by both his fellow workers and his superiors. There was almost complete avoidance of the problem of alcoholic behavior whenever possible. Only in the most extreme cases was the alcoholic confronted with the consequences of his actions, and even then it was frequently with great reluctance. Most management people felt that to suspend or fire an employee for drinking was to deprive his wife and children of support and spell doom to the man himself. They preferred the "ostrich method"—if we close our eyes maybe the problem will go away.

Then there was the union problem. The union officials had just naturally assumed they must perform their traditional role of "protecting the alcoholic worker from the injustices of management." Our union locals stoutly defended every alcoholic case regardless of the particular merits of each individual case involved. They felt that failure to support the alcoholic worker would be tantamount to an abdication of their basic responsibility to their membership and also incidentally, might jeopardize their own reelection to union office.

In summary, our study of employee alcoholism at Boston Edison concluded the following:

1. There was in fact a drinking problem of sufficient magnitude to indicate the need for a Company program; the problem was located in several areas of the Company including office and management personnel, male and female.

2. Supervisors and fellow employees were extremely reluctant to interview and confront an employee wtih the reality of his drinking situation, even in the most extreme circumstances, under the mistaken notion that drinking is a "personal" matter and most embarrassing to discuss.

3. The union locals were "certain" their proper function was to maintain the traditional role of "protector" and "defender" of the alcoholic employee in all disciplinary matters related to alcohol regardless of the ultimate consequences to the individual concerned.

4. We, ourselves in Edison management, had several questions on the best way to handle the medical and legal aspects concerning the alcoholic employee; and we recognized the need for more education on this subject.

It was the collective judgment of our project group, at this point, that we had satisfactorily completed the definition of the problem and its parameters in sufficient depth to provide an adequate base for the next phase of the project—the systems study. Just as with any other new Company program, we recognized there may be a need some time later, to further refine certain segments of our problem definition. But we were definitely convinced however, that all signals were a positive "go," and we enthusiastically proceeded into the second phase.

SYSTEM STUDY

Before we could start the actual design of an alcohol program for Boston Edison, we recognized the need and began an intensive study of all the available literature on the subject. We studied descriptions of the programs at DuPont, Con Edison, Allis-Chalmers, Eastman Kodak and several other large companies including two in the Boston area—Raytheon Company and Massachusetts Bay Transit Authority. We also studied papers and reports issued by the National Council on Alcoholism, the National Industrial Conference Board, the Yale School of Alcohol

Studies, Alcoholics Anonymous, and several other nonindustry sources.

The one document of most benefit to us was "Alcoholism in Industry—Modern Procedures" developed by Professor Harrison M. Trice and issued as a public service by the Christopher D. Smithers Foundation. This report outlines and comments on the essential "basics" of any successful alcoholism program in industry; and it is based on an intensive study of numerous programs in a wide variety of industries and on personal interviews on site with scores of medical, personnel and other company and union officials.

The several company programs we examined were most interesting and informative for both their similarities and their variances; and the actual operating details with which we became acquainted were of immense benefit in designing and implementing our Edison program.

We found that some company programs are very formally structural and others are extremely informal. Many programs are highly "AA-oriented" and some include the use of recovered alcoholics as employee counselors; other programs rely upon the old traditional approach of community alcoholism programs utilizing one or more of the standard professional disciplines of psychiatry, medicine, sociology, psychology and religion. Some programs were designed and installed by company personnel; other programs utilized outside agencies for this function. The initial motivation for some company programs originated from a union proposal and in one case from an alcohol program within the union local itself; other company programs were initiated from various segments and levels of management including the chief executive officer (but most frequently from the company medical director); a few programs were initiated by a proposal from an outside source.

There were several other factors where we noted similarities and variances, but the items above are sufficient to illustrate the point. Also, between the various extremes we mentioned were some modifications and other "shades of gray." We studied the pros and cons of the different approaches as they applied to our individual situation at Boston Edison, and we made our own evaluation of the "best" methods. This is where Professor Trice's manual assisted us so very much, in particular, the principle of "constructive coercion" which he expounds.

After many long discussions between the Medical, Legal, Personnel, Labor Relations and the Operating and Service Departments, we finally agreed that alcoholism would be considered as an illness, but that it be more specifically and correctly defined as an unique illness, and not an acceptable defense for the improper acts and behavior of the alcoholic. We adopted the work world definition of alcoholism as "recurrent poor job performance and/or unsatisfactory attendance attributable directly or indirectly to the use of alcohol." Our Medical Department would treat alcoholism as an illness and use all medical and related means to rehabilitate the alcoholic or problem drinker. The medical plan would be used for hospital benefits and pay purposes as in any other illness. However, the diagnosis of alcoholism did not place an umbrella over an individual and excuse him from disciplinary control. An abuse of the sick plan, insubordination, excessive absenteeism and poor work performance were all matters to be judged individually and were not excused because they were alcohol related. We were cognizant of cases pending before the U.S. Supreme Court at that time which indirectly challenged this point; however, we based our judgment on the tried and proven experience of industry and of AA in this regard and proceeded accordingly.

We knew from the experience of long-established industry programs that the large majority of the "new" referrals to the alcoholism programs came from the individuals themselves, either directly or indirectly as a result of their knowledge and contact with other employees who were recovered alcoholics. Just as in the community at large, the best motivation is this "power of example" of another recovered alcoholic who has successfully arrested his illness and regained control of other related problems. Therefore, one of the first things we did was contact as many of these employees as we could locate. Many of them were very active in the AA programs in the community, and some had also been conducting an unofficial (Company) program for fellow employees for several years. We explained our plan to this group of dedicated men and they were most enthusiastic. They gave us a pledge of full cooperation and even more. On their own initiative, with no suggestion or hint from the Edison Company whatsoever, they immediately formed a special AA Group to supplement the official Company program and handle employee referrals. These AA employees proved to be our greatest ally in every aspect of the formulation and adoption of the Company program. They were strategically located in all areas of the Company and were able to speak with authority and conviction to everyone: supervisors, union officials, top management and fellow employees.

We defined the role of the supervisor within the context of his traditional function. We referred to our officially adopted definition of alcoholism in the terms of attendance and work performance; and we emphasized that the immediate supervisor has the primary responsibility to document and evaluate these factors. We did grant that alcoholism itself was an illness and that its diagnosis was beyond the scope of the supervisor. We agreed that the medical doctor was the only one to make this judgment. We did not agree, however, that a doctor was the only person who could recognize the symptoms of alcoholism. Ask the distraught parents or the suffering wife and children of an active alcoholic if a doctor is the only one who can recognize alcoholism. Accordingly, we defined the role of the supervisor as a dual responsibility: first, decide if the job performance or attendance of the employee is satisfactory; and second, determine if there are any related symptoms of alcohol involvement.

The function of the Medical Department in dealing with both the chronic and acute aspects of alcoholism problems and the interrelationship with Personnel, Labor Relations and the employee's assigned Department were the next clarifications we undertook. According to the way we had defined alcoholism for our Edison Company purposes, the primary function and responsibility of each area was very clear. It was obvious the Medical Department should process cases of acute alcoholism just as any other acute illness; that Labor Relations should handle disciplinary matters related to alcoholism the same as any other disciplinary matters; and that the employee's own department and immediate supervisor had the primary responsibility for identifying the alcoholic and initiating the proper action indicated by the circumstances. The questions confronting us here were: how to coordinate the activities of the individual Company departments into one comprehensive, interrelated, interdepartmental activity; how to provide for special handling in special situations, and a follow-up program for dealing with the chronic alcoholism condition; and how to clarify the "gray areas" and ambiguities which are prevalent in a large majority of cases.

Our study of the various company alcoholism programs convinced us that the traditional legalistic approach of Labor Relations to alcoholic employees, while satisfactory for disciplinary purposes, had not achieved any significant success in actually rehabilitating the chronic alcoholics; and, neither had the purely medical approach even though they were continually rescuing employees from the dangerous effects of acute alcoholism, nor the laissez-faire approach of the employee's assigned department. The principle of "Constructive Coercion" was obviously the answer. We agreed that Labor Relations would still invoke discipline, but, they would also refer the alcoholic to the new alcoholism program. Medical would extend its role by instituting a new alcohol program to cover not only the acute but also the chronic alcoholism condition; and the employee's assigned department would initiate action and make the proper referral to the new alcoholism program as soon as alcoholism was first identified, hopefully, long before the employee's condition deteriorated to the point where the need for formal discipline was indicated.

The majority of the company alcoholism programs we studied were structured and operated as part of the Medical Department; and the more successful of these had created a new job position of Rehabilitation (or Alcoholism) Director to coordinate and direct the function. This is the approach which best suited our Edison need and which we decided to adopt. Those company programs structured in the Personnel Department, or the various hybrid structures including one alcoholism program reporting directly to the Chief Executive Officer, were either too dissimilar in purpose and definition from what we were planning, or for other special reasons were ineligible for us to consider as a pattern for the new Edison program, even though they might be satisfactory under the individual company circumstances of their own operation.

The concept of using an AA member, who has successfully resolved his own alcohol problem, as coordinator of the Company alcoholism program and/or rehabilitation counselor was pioneered by the DuPont Company over two decades ago; and this was, and still is, the very greatest single contribution to the success of industry alcoholism programs. The general idea of "constructive coercion" has always been a cornerstone of the AA program itself, and "AA Counselors" just naturally incorporated this into their company programs. The founders of AA proclaimed from the very beginning in 1935 that alcoholism is a sickness, but it is a unique illness which does not respond to traditional treatment methods. It is a three-fold sickness of the body, the mind and the spirit; and it only responds when the alcoholic himself cooperates in a coordinated treatment of all three areas. AA admits the alcoholic has no control over intoxication, but they insist he does have control over whether or not he takes the "first drink." Accordingly, he is responsible and must be held accountable for all subsequent drinks and related actions, sick or not sick. This original AA concept of responsibility and accountability for alcoholism and their three-fold coordinated recovery program, which DuPont and other companies adopted, is the main distinguishing feature between the successful programs of industry and the traditional, vari-discipline, professional approach of community programs where the results achieved are far, far less than acceptable. We do not mean to infer here that just any AA member can operate effectively as an alcoholism counselor in industry. The only point we are emphasizing is the basic concept—an AA member who possesses the basic skills required of a counselor or who has the capacity and potential to develop these skills, can work with alcoholic employees far more effectively and with much greater acceptance than a nonalcoholic counselor, regardless of formal education and professional training.

We defined the Rehabilitation Counselor (and the new alcohol program) as the primary treatment resource for employee chronic alcoholism at Boston Edison, and we assigned him the key role in our new, coordinated, interdepartmental approach to the problem. We structured our program along the general lines adopted by DuPont, but installed modifications to assure stronger control and more accurate Company communications. We also established an "open door" policy for the Rehabilitation Counselor so that anybody in any area of the Company could consult with him directly, on an alcohol-related problem, with no intermediate parties or records involved.

In considering the relationship we should try to establish between the Company and the union locals concerning the new alcohol program, we were again immeasurably benefited by the Smithers Foundation Manual and by our contacts with other company programs. We were in full agreement with the approach outlined by Professor Trice and decided this as best we could. We decided to seek the cooperation of our union locals in the very early stages of development, and if possible, to agree on a unified approach to the alcoholic employee. And here again we are deeply indebted to our several dedicated AA members—employees who volunteered to pave the way as unofficial ambassadors of good will by endorsing the newly proposed Company alcohol program to all officials and members of the four union locals, and by explaining the increased benefit which would accrue to everyone—employee, union and Company.

At this point we met with Edison top management to report on progress to date. We reviewed the results of our study and definition of the drinking problem; and then we explained the details of the system study recently completed and our outline of the specific features we recommended for inclusion in the proposed Edison Company program. For all practical operating purposes we received complete approval of the proposed program as designed and submitted, and obtained authorization to proceed with the final stage of the project—implementation of the program.

INSTALLING THE PROGRAM

At the very outset we recognized a very grave need for extensive education and training for everyone involved—first-line supervisors, union officials, Labor Relations and Personnel Department management, and the employees themselves. Therefore, before proceeding with the more formal implementation of our new alcoholism program, we agreed that related documentation should be prepared to avoid as much misunderstanding and apprehension and reluctance as possible. We developed the material listed below based on the findings (and decisions) of our problem definition and systems study:

1. An overall Company "policy on problem drinking" to explain our definition and philosophy and approach for alcoholism.
2. A general description of the actual program itself and its component parts.
3. A procedure for the Rehabilitation Counselor in handling alcoholic employees and in consulting with others concerned such as supervisors and other management personnel, union officials and the family members of alcoholics.
4. A job description for the Rehabilitation Counselor.
5. Forms (5) for the Rehabilitation Counselor to use in the program operation.
6. A Supervisors' Manual.
7. A general "Union Steward's Manual" which could be modified and adopted by each of the four locals for their own individual use.
8. Supplementary training material for use in the program operation.

We will not attempt to describe each of the eight items above because this presentation is only concerned with the "how and why and wherefor" in the actual formulation of an alcoholism program and the related approaches, methods, measures, techniques and other circumstances directly involved. However, a general idea of the program itself and its features and operation is obviously gleaned, even though somewhat segmented, from our descriptions of the "system study" and "installing the program" reported herein. And for anyone who may be interested in more detail, we will be happy to provide copies of all our material.

The new policy statement on problem drinking which we

developed was a joint venture in conjunction with the Legal, Labor Relations, Employee Relations, Medical and Administrative sectors of our Company; and it was authorized and issued by the President for distribution to all management employees and for inclusion in the Company policy manual. Shortly following this issuance we scheduled a full day seminar for certain key management personnel and union officials, to explain in general the various company alcoholism programs operating in the area, and to explain in detail our plans for an Edison alcoholism program.

The seminar was conducted off the Company property but at Company expense, and it included coffee service in the morning and afternoon, and a formal luncheon in the motel banquet room with a talk on the "sickness of alcoholism" by the Massachusetts Commissioner of Public Health. The entire seminar program was primarily designed to inform union officials on the subject. Our purpose in inviting selected Labor Relations and other management employees for this simultaneous (rather than a separate) presentation was to encourage an atmosphere of co-sponsorship, and to assure that everybody directly concerned with the problem received identical information; thus minimizing possible misunderstandings and misinterpretations. We also invited our dedicated AA volunteers who were able to intermingle freely with everyone and assist in melding the two traditionally antagonistic groups into a more receptive unit. Although we did not achieve complete recognition and endorsement of our proposed alcoholism program from all the parties involved, we believe the seminar presentation at this early date and the participation of top management and union officers in the seminar went a long way toward removing the fear of the alcoholism program and helped gradually accomplish this ultimate goal.

We did not establish any official data for installing the new alcoholism program. Prior to the formal issuance of the new Company policy on alcoholism and the seminar program, the Medical Department had already begun processing all alcoholism cases according to the new plan and approach. And the Medical Director and another management employee were functioning as part-time alcoholism counselors and program coordinators. Therefore, we consider that the alcoholism program was implemented on a gradual basis over a period of several months, beginning with the quasi-preliminary approval of our first draft of the policy on problem drinking and finally achieving complete implementation when the employee appointed to the newly authorized position of Rehabilitation Counselor actually reported for duty. Naturally there was a preliminary period during which some work time was devoted to training the counselor. However, the man selected was of such high calibre and possessed the basic counseling skills and knowledge of alcoholism programs to such a high degree that regular training requirements were minimal.

The training program we designed for first-line supervisors and higher management consisted of a dual approach. First we developed a special personalized program for supervisors who were presently involved in an active alcoholism case requiring immediate action. And second, we scheduled a formal series of meetings throughout all the departments of the Company for small groups of twenty to thirty people. At this time we issued a copy of the supervisor's manual to everyone and explained all of the contents in detail. We described the purpose of the program and how it operates, the function of the Rehabilitation Counselor, the new definition of the supervisor's role, the relationship with the union, and the interrelationship with Medical and Labor Relations Departments. We also developed a teaching kit which we distributed in conjunction with the film "For Those Who Drink" by Dr. R. Gorden Bell.

Almost all of these management people individually subscribed to the broad general concepts of rehabilitating the alcoholic. But when it came to the specifics of their new role they felt "caught in the middle." Where previously they could avoid the issue until extreme conditions developed and then refer the situation to Medical or Labor Relations for at least the appearance of a joint action, they were now on their own. Many of these supervisors had been promoted from the union ranks and felt a close kinship with the men. They felt a strong emotional reaction from "suspensions" and "firing"; and it was, and still is, most difficult to convince them that "early treatment" for alcoholism is the most humane and effective approach just as early treatment of cancer or tuberculosis or any other sickness.

There were some few management people who took a different view. They felt we were "coddling the drunks" and were going to let them "get away with murder." They just could not see this "hospitalization" and "special treatment" for "these people."

The reaction of the union officials and stewards was quite similar to management, but just the opposite. Some few expressed the feeling we were "starting a purge" to rid the Company of "loafers" and "troublemakers" under the guise of medical treatment. The majority, however, were in agreement with the general concept of rehabilitating the alcoholic but were hung up emotionally when it came to specific cases of suspensions and firing. They had extreme difficulty in reconciling this new approach to alcoholism with the traditional "protective" role.

Our own approach in installing the program and conducting the education was one of understanding and compassion for all these various reactions. And here again, we were forewarned and prepared for these conditions by our study of the experience of other companies. We accepted the reality of the various degrees of resistance from everyone concerned and realized this would gradually diminish as our sincerity of purpose emerged in proportion to the successes we achieved with the alcoholic employees treated under the new program.

In order to inform all the Company employees about the alcoholism program we prepared features articles for the Company magazine "Edison News" which is mailed to all the employee homes every month. We explained the program in detail and role of the new Rehabilitation Counselor including his "open door" policy for direct access. We were very pleased with the response to these insertions. Not only did we get several direct referrals from the men themselves, but we also received an unanticipated secondary benefit of much greater long-range importance. We received several direct inquiries from the wives and the families of alcoholic employees, and we counseled these concerned relatives by telephone and also personal interview whenever possible. Through the direct efforts of the alcoholics' relatives who learned about the program from the "Edison News," we gradually began to receive more "personal" referrals. And later, as a result of this experience, we revised the structure of our alcoholism program to include consultation with the family members of everyone in our alcoholism program, whenever such was favorably indicated.

When an employee is now referred to the alcoholism program through any of the normal intake channels (the Labor Relations or Medical Departments, Union, Employing Department, or the employee himself), we schedule meetings with the family to explain the program, our purpose and function. We also try to interest them in the community Alanon programs and accompany them to a meeting if practicable.

Although we mentioned previously we considered the program formally implemented when the Rehabilitation Counselor was appointed and started his duties, this is not fully accurate. We will not be totally satisfied with the program until all employees and their families are completely informed on the subject and we have gained general acceptance and cooperation in the great majority of cases. We recognize this may still be a long way off. However, based on several of the remarkable individual successes we have had thus far and the overall gradual decrease of opposition to the program and increase in supervisory level response, we are encouraged to proceed.

We expect to continue all phases of our alcoholism education and training projects on a permanent revolving basis and to continue and expand the personal involvement of our Rehabilitation Counselor in all aspects of the program. This combination of numerous "living examples" of proven success and happiness in the alcoholism program when disaster was obviously imminent otherwise and the increased awareness of our effectiveness and sincerity of purpose, is certain eventually to prevail.

SUMMARY AND CONCLUSION

The basic, primary, underlying principle and the very heart of our alcoholism program is this (relatively new to industry) concept of "constructive coercion." It has long been practiced informally and proven by the program of Alcoholics Anonymous, and more recently formally promulgated by Professor Harrison Trice in his Smithers Foundation Manual on "Alcoholism in

Industry—Modern Procedures"; but it has yet to be widely adopted by company programs.

This new industry approach is a happy and effective blend of the two individual, traditional approaches of "constructive" and "coercive," neither of which has ever produced any significant results. The various standard community programs represent the "constructive approach" which states alcoholism is a sickness and says, "We will treat you and make you well," but which ignores the human behavior factors and has never been successful. Conversely, the standard industry programs represent the "coercive approach" which states alcoholism is a behavior problem and tells the employee to "Quit drinking and do the job, or else." This does not consider the sickness factor including "how to quit drinking," and likewise has never been successful.

In summary, the most important decisions and factors we considered in formulating the alcoholism program at Boston Edison Company are the following:

1. Assignment of employees to the Project Task Force who are in complete accord with the purposes and objectives and who are able to make an unqualified, dedicated commitment to the project.

2. Initial approval and endorsement of the project by the highest level of Company management available, at the earliest time possible, and regular liaison through informal progress reports as the project develops.

3. Establishment of an unofficial "support group" of employee AA members if practical under the circumstances.

4. Issuance of a Company policy by top management which defines alcoholism in terms of job performance and specifies the condition as a "unique" illness which will be treated medically as any other illness, but, which requires the full cooperation of the alcoholic employee for successful recovery and provides for sanctions including job dismissal for failure to cooperate with the treatment prescribed.

5. Involvement of the union as early as practicable in the development of the project.

6. Utilization of employee AA members in the key roles of program coordinator and alcoholism counselor, if such are available and satisfy the other basic requirements.

7. Preparation of formal documentation and wide dissemination of

the information, including provision for continuing education sessions for everyone directly concerned.

8. Consideration and development of the project in the same manner as any other regular Company project and avoidance of any attitudes of urgency, undue importance, crusading, moralizing or other special considerations.

EVALUATION OF THE ALCOHOLISM REHABILITATION PROGRAM

In 1973 we decided to perform a study of the program in order to analyze its performance during the ten years of its operation. The analysis was carried out in two phases.

Phase I

The objective of this initial study of the Employee Alcoholism Program was to examine the major functions involved in the process and to determine whether the established goals are being achieved in a reasonably effective manner.

The scope of the study consisted of an evaluation of the following major activities conducted by the Rehabilitation Counselor:

1. Informal group therapy sessions conducted every morning at Massachusetts Avenue Medical Department from 7:15 to 8:00 AM prior to regular work hours.
2. Private personal counseling by appointment for all employees undergoing the formal one-year Rehabilitation Program.
3. Counseling for supervisory personnel and union officials in the functions of the Rehabilitation Program, and the most effective methods for referral.
4. Arrangements for hospital admissions for detoxification; and follow-up personal counseling each day during the remainder of the hospital period.

In addition, we also analyzed selected data for the following:

1. General overall effectiveness of the program.
2. Source of referral to the Alcoholism Program since implementation by the year 1963 to 1972.
3. Hospitalizations for the five-year period 1968 to 1972.
4. Absenteeism for program participants prior and subsequent to program entry.

We did not include in this study any activities of the Rehabilitation Counselor for employee dependents, nor did we cover related areas, such as hospitalizations for specific medical complications but directly attributable to alcoholism (e.g. hepatitis, liver, etc.) due to the six-week limitation established for this initial study.

Findings

1. The group therapy sessions conducted every morning are enthusiastically attended by an average of six to eight employees. Most of these are relatively new in the program and participate on a purely voluntary basis, before starting their regular work day. This has proven to be an excellent daily supportive device for the participants and has also become an expedient for attracting new members.

2. The private personal counseling session is the very heart of the program for the new person. During the first two months (Phase I) he meets with the Counselor every week. Many elect to continue on a weekly basis through Phases II and III, even though the program design only requires biweekly and then monthly meetings during the second and third phases.

3. Counseling for supervisory personnel and union officials has only been conducted on an emergency basis, when a crisis situation occurs, due to the time limitations imposed upon the Counselor by other priority demands for his services.

4. Hospitalizations are primarily arranged at Mt. Pleasant Hospital in Lynn, Massachusetts. Their facilities are excellent, the rates are somewhat lower than comparable institutions, and their effectiveness is excellent. The one area which could be improved is the period of hospitalization immediately following detoxification. The hospital conducts a formal group therapy session every morning from 11:00 AM to Noon; but that is the extent of the rehabilitation program they provide. Consequently, our Rehabilitation Counselor makes visits to the hospital every afternoon to provide personal counseling for employee patients during this period.

Our analysis of operating data and related statistics indicated the following, and are supported by schedules attached hereto:

1. The program demonstrates an overall recovery rate of 77 percent. As Table 5-I indicates, there have been 196 referrals to the program from 1963 through 1972, but 62 of these are currently

in process. Of the remaining 134 referrals, there are 103 employees who have successfully completed the program, and whose work performance and attendance are currently satisfactory.

2. Table 5-II shows that most of the referrals to the program come from either Medical or voluntarily.

3. As shown in Table 5-IV, hospitalizations for the five-year period 1968 to 1972 were somewhat comparable. The average number

TABLE 5-I

PROGRESS REPORT ON THE REHABILITATION PROGRAM

Of the 196 employees referred:

1. Completed Program requirements successfully		103
	Total	103
2. Less than one year completed in Program		
A. Alcohol problem—presently active in Program		
Phase I		16
Phase II		2
Phase III		12
B. Alcohol problem—not active—no progress		23
C. Alcohol problem—not active but improved by association with Program		9
	Total	62
3. Referred to Program during 1963-64-65-66. Investigated but not further action deemed necessary at that time		10
4. Terminations:		
A. Death		3
B. Retired		5
C. Resigned (in lieu of discharge)		6
D. Discharged (*)		7
	Total	21
	Total Case Load	196

There have been approximately 116 hospitalizations because of alcoholism. This number includes both employees and their families.

---

* Discharge modified

TABLE 5-II

SOURCE OF REFERRALS TO PROGRAM

	Quantity	*Percent*
Medical	69	35
Voluntary	47	24
Supervisor	33	17
Family	24	12
Labor Relations	13	7
Union	10	5
	196	100

of admissions per year was twenty-four; and the average period of hospitalization was fifteen days. During 1972 there were twenty-six admissions, involving a total of 336 hospital days and a cost of $33,958. Other direct costs for payroll during and immediately preceding hospitalization are estimated at $17,760 for a total direct cost in excess of $50,000. This does not include replacement substitution payroll costs, nor the indirect costs for waste, loss, accidents, inefficiency, etc., which is conservatively estimated by recognized authorities in the field at five to ten times the direct costs.

4. Table 5-V illustrates an analysis of twenty-three employees who had been successfully rehabilitated for at least two years, showed an average decrease in absenteeism of seven days per man per year. This is not a pure scientific conclusion, but it is a reliable indication of trend. At an average hourly rate of $6 for 1972 this amounts to $336 per man per year. If projected for the 103 successful rehabilitations and the estimated 77 percent success for the 62 men in process, this amounts to $50,000 annual saving.

Other findings, based on our analysis of specific exceptional employee cases, indicated the following undesirable conditions, which, although very rare, should be remedied. Appropriate corrective action is in process:

1. There are some known cases of serious employee alcoholism which have never been referred to the Medical Department (see Appendix I).

TABLE 5-III

REFERRALS TO ALCOHOLISM PROGRAM
BY YEAR AND SOURCE

Source of Referral

Year	Medical	Voluntary	Supervisor	Union	Labor Relations	Family	Total Referrals
1963	11	2	1	1	0	0	15
1964	9	0	0	1	2	0	12
1965	9	8	2	3	1	3	26
1966	10	6	4	0	1	5	26
1967	7	4	3	0	0	5	19
1968	5	8	3	2	1	2	21
1969	2	4	3	1	1	6	17
1970	6	5	5	1	3	1	21
1971	4	2	7	0	1	2	16
1972	6	8	5	1	3	0	23
	69	47	33	10	13	24	196

TABLE 5-IV

ANNUAL DIRECT COSTS FOR EMPLOYEE ALCOHOLISM
DETOXIFICATION

1968-1972

Year	No. of Admissions	Total Days Hospitalized	Average Rate Paid	Total Costs for Hospital and Physician
1968	26	526	$ 49	$26,200
1969	22	312	55	17,226
1970	24	339	61	20,885
1971*	23	349	75	26,508
1972	26	336	101	33,958
	121	1,862		
Average	24	372		

* Actual data increased by ⅓ to annualize due to 3 months strike in 1971.

TABLE 5-V

REPORT OF 23 SUCCESSFULLY REHABILITATED EMPLOYEES

Employee	Absenteeism Prior to Alcoholism Program			Alcoholism Program Absenteeism Subsequent to			Average Increase or (Decrease)
	2nd Year Before	1st Year Before	Average Before	1st Year After	2nd Year After	Average After	
1	7	12	10	1	6	3	(7)
2	6	7	7	9	3	6	(1)
3	12	53	33	2	7	5	(28)
4	150	17	84	94	56	75	(9)
5	55	54	55	10	61	36	(19)
6	7	8	8	2	2	2	(6)
7	10	36	23	19	4	12	(11)
8	0	4	2	0	6	3	1
9	0	8	4	1	0	1	(3)
10	4	11	8	5	1	3	(5)
11	16	52	34	0	0	0	(34)
12	5	20	13	4	6	5	(8)
13	5	8	7	76	3	40	33
14	19	6	13	1	5	3	(10)
15	7	87	47	4	7	6	(41)
16	13	37	25	29	1	15	(10)
17	8	15	12	6	47	27	15
18	4	13	9	0	2	1	(8)
19	2	0	1	3	3	3	2
20	7	4	6	2	2	2	(4)
21	2	7	5	3	6	5	0
22	2	1	2	1	2	2	0
23	37	11	24	4	23	14	(10)
24	17	7	12	(Entered Program in 1971)			

2. There are other serious but exceptional cases which are processed to Medical, but for various reasons are not processed into the Alcoholism Program (see Appendix II).

CONCLUSION AND RECOMMENDATIONS The findings above indicate conclusively that the Alcoholism Rehabilitation Program is operating effectively and achieving the goals originally established at implementation; i.e. "to provide a supportive medium for employee alcoholics to expedite their recovery from the acute illness phase and to facilitate their entry into standard community rehabilitation programs to assure continued permanent sobriety." Based on the newer developments in the field of industrial alcoholism programs during the past ten years however, we believe that the effectiveness and efficiency of the Boston Edison Company Program can be enhanced and improved and very significant savings realized through adoption of the following:

1. The Medical Department should develop and conduct a formal training program to inform supervisory personnel on the functions of the Alcoholism Rehabilitation Program, the most effective referral methods for them to fully utilize the service, and the adverse effects on job performance and attendance due to untreated alcoholism. A study of hospitalizations and referrals proves conclusively that:
   A. Most of the referrals require hospital detoxification, which means they are not getting to Medical until the very late stages, after the Company has incurred great losses due to poor attendance and work performance. From a purely theoretical viewpoint, the entire $50,000 in direct costs in 1972 could have been avoided through earlier referrals. However, from the more realistic approach, an effective supervisory function re alcoholism could easily save $25,000 annually.
   B. Most of the referrals are not coming from supervision, where the primary responsibility for work performance and attendance is assigned. This reinforces Item A above.
2. A follow-up function, similar to a "compliance audit," should be instituted outside the Medical Department to assure that supervisors carry out their assigned responsibilities re alcoholism, after an adequate training program has been completed.
3. An almost immediate savings of $17,000 per year could be realized if the contention of other hospital facilities located

distant from Boston, can be substantiated. Several claim to do a comparable detoxification process and a better rehabilitation function at less than 50 percent of the local rates charged. We should evaluate these claims as soon as practicable to effect the savings. In addition, if true, this would make available two to three work hours for the Rehabilitation Counselor to undertake the supervisor training function.

4. The basic rehabilitation program should be restructured to formally provide for relapses and other exceptional conditions. In addition, all current documentation and procedures should be reviewed and updated.

Phase II

The objective of this second phase of the Employee Alcoholism Program Study was to examine all program operations in depth, and to make such revisions as may be indicated to increase the effectiveness, improve participant controls, and effect additional savings.

The second study consisted of the following:

1. A detailed analysis of the time required by the Rehabilitation Counselor for each of the functions listed in #2 below, as originally posted in the personal daily logbook of the Counselor.
2. A detailed examination and evaluation of the following functions, including the related forms and reports utilized:
   A. Group therapy sessions conducted each morning prior to regular work hours.
   B. Personal rehabilitation counseling for alcoholic employees conducted in the Medical Department, and at other Company locations or at employee homes.
   C. Counseling management personnel regarding employee alcoholism program.
   D. Personal counseling for nonalcoholic employees, whose job performance is adversely effected by alcoholism at home.
   E. Inpatient counseling each day for employees during hospitalization period.
   F. Coordination with community programs such as: Alcoholics Anonymous, Alanon Family Groups, etc.
   G. Family counseling and supportive therapy.
   H. Travel to hospital, employee homes, other system locations, AA meetings, etc.

  I. Record-keeping for program participants, etc.

  J. Other functions (weekly staff meeting, etc.).

 3. A special study and evaluation of certain "unusual cases" (pertaining to the "outreach" function) which came to our attention during the course of our regular study.

 4. A special survey in selected areas on Company-wide methods and procedures for recording and controlling absenteeism at the local level.

Findings

1. From the daily logbook postings, we made ninety-six monthly summary schedules for the years 1965 to 1972. We then prepared annual summary schedules for each of the eight years and finally, an overall eight-year summary. We found that the Rehabilitation Counselor averaged a sixty hour work week for the eight year period; consisting of fifty-two hours average Monday through Friday, and eight hours average for Saturday and Sunday activities. The schedule below is a further analysis, by function, for this sixty hour average work week.

Function	Avg. Hrs. Per Week
Group Therapy	5.00
Personal Rehabilitation Counseling	7.50
Counseling Supervisory Personnel in re Alcoholism	2.50
Personal Counseling for Nonalcoholic Employees	2.00
Inpatient Counseling at Hospital	10.00
Coordination wtih Community Programs	5.00
Family Counseling and Supportive Therapy	2.50
Travel to Hospital, Employee Homes, etc.	10.00
Record-Keeping	5.00
Other Related Functions	2.50
Total	52.00
Average additional time on Saturdays and Sundays, not included in logbook	8.00
TOTAL	60.00

2. All of the program functions, as designed, are operating in the manner expected. We found some weaknesses, however, in the design of the program participants weekly report; and we revised the form to include the detail "by day" for the period, absence record with reason, and a statement concerning abstinence. In addition, we found other control deficiencies, and we designed new forms for the following, to improve program effectiveness:

  A. An overall control to reflect weekly progress and current status.

B. Control for reporting unsatisfactory progress.

C. Control for termination of employee from the Rehabilitation Program.

D. Control for rehabilitation counseling "appointments missed."

3. During the course of our study, eight specific cases of serious employee alcoholism came to our attention which concerned problems of "early identification and referral." We investigated six of these with the Departments and Divisions involved, utilizing existing documentation; such as employee health records, absenteeism records, department and division operating records, etc. In all cases, we were most welcome by local management, and they were anxious for our assistance with the overall problem. We satisfied ourselves, beyond any question, that local management want and need help whenever they have specific cases of employee alcoholism, and we have supporting documentation upon which they can initiate action and justifiably intervene in the case. These six cases were typical examples of the "outreach function" adopted by private industry during very recent years.

4. During our initial six-week study of the Rehabilitation Program, we made a special survey of participants' absenteeism prior and subsequent to entry into the program to determine whether savings could be documentated in this area. It was desirable, at that time, to contact the three Office Divisions in Operations and Engineering Organization and the Stores and Service Departments, concerning their methods for recording and controlling absenteeism. During this current three-week study we summarized and analyzed the data methods obtained during Phase I. We found that Company-wide methods, procedures and controls have not been formally established for "recording and controlling employee absence at the local level"; and that each area handles this problem somewhat differently. Two of the five areas requested assistance from us but we limited our commitment to a formal referral of the matter to the Employee Relations Organization for their direct action or further referral to the Procedures Department.

CONCLUSION AND RECOMMENDATIONS. All of the program functions are operating as originally planned and in accordance with the structure and parameters established during the program design and implementation. There were only minor changes needed to improve effectiveness and control.

The basic program structure, however, is more than ten years old and does not include the standard functions of second generation and third generation rehabilitation programs such as "outreach" (for early identification and referral) and "program management" (for ongoing evaluation and optimum cost control).

We recommend that the overall rehabilitation program structure be revised and updated to provide for these "outreach" and "program management" functions. Just as we ourselves have proven it is more economical to provide for rehabilitation counseling than to disregard the problem and allow the related costs to go uncontrolled, other private industry programs have proven it is more economical to provide for "outreach" and "program management" than it is to wait for late referrals and (periodic) program evaluation, and thus allow these costs to remain uncontrolled. In addition, the "outreach" test made during this current study (see Finding #3) has proven the effectiveness and generally receptive environment for this function; our previous initial study estimated potential annual savings at $50,000 for hospital and related direct payroll costs and $250,000 for indirect costs (according to the Industrial Division, National Council on Alcoholism which conservatively computes indirect costs at five to ten times the direct costs according to the industry and composite population involved). Finally, concerning the "program management" function, it is safe to state that during the past eight years significant savings of $200,000 to $400,000 could have been realized if program performance, measurement and optimization had been authorized and undertaken at regularly scheduled (two-year) periods.

It is important, before closing, to emphasize that for purposes of this specific study we have intentionally limited the scope of coverage to program effectiveness and directly related financial benefits and costs. We assume that after ten years of excellent operations, the costs and benefits in terms of "human values" are generally accepted by both management and labor. However, we have extensive documentation in our file on this aspect if any questions should arise.

In closing, we should emphasize we are not recommending that two new positions be established at this time, to provide for "outreach" and "program management." It may be feasible, at least for a start on controlling these costs, to revise and reschedule some of the present rehabilitation counselor functions and to relocate other functions utilizing outside agencies. This would enable the two new functions to be implementated on a limited trial basis. After a test period of approximately one year, a complete new evaluation could be initiated to determine the ultimate desirable course of action.

Summary

A program was set up in 1963 as described above and reviewed in an in-depth study in 1973. It was found to be working extremely well, with a 77 percent recovery rate (150 of 190 referrals). The expenditures of money, balancing the costs of the program against actual cost savings from diminished absenteeism and preservation of skilled workers in their jobs, are entirely within reason. Revisions suggested by our study have been listed, which are expected to improve performance, increase the number of cases found early, and reduce hospital costs.

APPENDIX I

COORDINATION BETWEEN THE LABOR RELATIONS AND MEDICAL DEPARTMENTS IN CASES OF ABSENTEEISM WHICH MAY BE DUE TO ILLNESS OR INJURY OR ACCIDENT

The following guidelines have been established for processing cases where unsatisfactory attendance of an employee may be indicative of a health or personal behavior problem, such as alcoholism, drug addition, financial irresponsibility, compulsive gambling, or other personal or health problems.

1. Labor Relations and Medical Departments will consult on each individual case which comes to the attention of either Department.
2. Labor Relations will confer with the employee's department and make arrangements for the employee to be referred to Medical Department for diagnosis and evaluation.
3. Medical Department will institute such diagnostic and evaluation procedures, including complete physical examination, as their

professional judgment may indicate desirable under the individual circumstances.

4. If the medical diagnosis does not indicate a treatable health problem, the employee will be so notified, and return to Labor Relations for further processing .
5. If the medical diagnosis does indicate a treatable health problem, the examining physician will prescribe the desired treatment and so inform the employee.
6. The employee may elect to either accept the prescribed treatment, or return to Labor Relations for further processing to resolve the condition.

APPENDIX II

GUIDELINES FOR COORDINATION WITHIN THE BOSTON EDISON COMPANY MEDICAL DEPARTMENT FOR THE DIAGNOSIS AND TREATMENT OF CHRONIC ALCOHOLISM

1. The examining physician and the Rehabilitation Counselor will consult, in advance, on each case which comes to their attention, in order to both be fully informed on all applicable data.
2. The examining physician will utilize whatever available diagnostic procedures he may consider beneficial in each individual case, including the standard symptoms developed by Johns Hopkins University, and also including a complete physical examination if such should be indicated by the specific circumstance.
3. The examining physician will inform the employee of the finding, specifying in his judgment whether:
   A. a positive condition exists—definitive diagnosis
   B. a probable condition exists—presumptive diagnosis
   C. a possible condition exists—impressive diagnosis
   D. a negative condition exists—diagnosis of chronic alcoholism is not indicated by available data at this time.
4. The examining physician will determine whether hospital detoxification is desirable and will so inform the Rehabilitation Counselor to make the necessary admission arrangements.
5. If hospitalization is not required the examining physician will refer the employee directly to the Rehabilitation Counselor for entry into the alcoholism program, provided the employee accepts the diagnosis and agrees to the prescribed treatment. Otherwise,

the employee will be referred to the Medical Director for further processing.

6. The Medical Director will describe the diagnostic findings of the examining physician, and the recommended treatment program conducted by the Rehabilitation Counselor. He will also explain the alternative measures available to the employee beyond the Company health function, including referral to the Labor Relations Department.

7. The Medical Director will request a decision from the employee, and will make the necessary arrangements for the course of action selected:

   A. Employee accepts prescribed treatment.

   B. Employee elects to submit formal report from personal physician and to proceed according to the Union agreement in effect for medical examinations.

   C. Employee denies a health problem and elects to process case as a pure labor relations matter outside the area of health.

Chapter 6

COUNSELING THE ALCOHOLIC EMPLOYEE IN A MUNICIPAL DEPARTMENT

Rev. Msgr. Joseph A. Dunne, M.P.A.

ESTABLISHMENT OF POLICE DEPARTMENT COUNSELING UNIT

Discovering the Problem Drinker

Whenenen this author was appointed Police Chaplain in 1958, he learned that the duties of this office included the supervision of policemen placed on probation for disciplinary violations. A review of charges against these men revealed that a majority had drinking problems resulting in misconduct, excessive sick time, accidents, and marital difficulties.

The chaplain sought the aid of Alcoholics Anonymous and found an AA group already in operation within the City of New York, established primarily for policemen. He attended the meetings regularly and sought the assistance of recovered members of the department. He found too, that the New York City Transit Authority and the Chicago Police Department had ongoing programs for their personnel. This knowledge stirred up his determination to establish a program for the New York City Police.

Organizational Problems and Conflicts 1958 to 1962

There were certain factors mitigating a formal program in the Police Department: 1) the Chief Surgeon had little or no empathy for alcoholics and his attitude was communicated to the subordinate district surgeons; 2) departmental regulations forbade men on sick report to leave their homes for an AA meeting; 3) when a policeman was diagnosed as intoxicated by a surgeon, he was immediately suspended from duty. Often, his guns were also removed, as the medical report would indicate that he was depressed, incoherent or manifested underlying personality disorders. This harsh treatment then resulted in policemen being transferred to a limited duty status, doing clerical work without firearms. There was little hope that these men would ever be restored to full duty; 4) fines for intoxification during this period were excessively high and almost automatic. The usual fine was thirty days pay and one year on probation. These fines worked a great hardship on the families of the men concerned. In view of these punitive measures, superior officers were reluctant to report alcoholics, resulting in "organizational coverup."

Retirement of the chief surgeon in 1961 gave new hope for the proposed program. However, more rigidity was phased into the bureaucracy of the Police Department, particularly from those in public relations who feared that a counseling unit would impair the image of the Department.

Police Department Conference on Alcoholism February, 1962

At the Chaplain's request, a line-staff conference was held on February 10, 1962, with Deputy Commissioners, Chaplains, Chief Inspector and headquarters officers.

The Deputy Commissioner for Disciplinary Trials reported that in the previous eleven years, 121 men were suspended for intoxication and averaged 31.8 days on suspension. The new Chief Surgeon reported that a majority of the district surgeons were in favor of program and rehabilitation. The Chief Inspector, however, spoke of the adverse criticism should the press bring such a program to the attention of the public.

The recommendations of this conference were to be made known to the Police Commissioner by the Chief Inspector. However, since no official reports were actually submitted to the

Police Commissioner, the net result was no progress for the next two years.

Department Policy on Alcoholism May 12, 1966

After attending the Center for Alcoholic Studies at Rutgers in July, 1964, the Chaplain was convinced of the necessity of obtaining a clear cut policy at the top level of management. With this new approach to the hierarchy of the Police Department and aided by the appointment of a new and intensely interested Chief Surgeon, Dr. Stephen McCoy, the Chaplain sought and obtained another staff conference on November 23, 1964. Dr. McCoy then wrote an official request to the Chief of Personnel recommending the establishment of a "Counseling Unit," together with AA therapy and a program of hospitalization, promising the active participation of district surgeons.

In January, 1965, the Chaplain, faced with inaction following Dr. McCoy's recommendation, coordinated his new effort with Captain James McEvoy of the Employees Relations Office who assisted in drafting a memorandum to the Police Commissioner through channels. This communication outlined the current enlightened view of alcoholism in industry, the official efforts in the past within the department to assist problem drinkers, and the sincere concern of the Chief Surgeon and the Chaplain that the medical and welfare problem be met honestly. This memorandum remained in the office of the Chief of Personnel for one year.

Finally, in January, 1966, the Chaplain, using his privilege to go outside of official channels, visited the office of the Police Commissioner and discussed the proposed program. The contents of the memorandum of the previous year was rewritten to include confidentiality. Thus, on May 12, 1966, in the presence of the Chief Surgeon and the Chaplain, the Police Commissioner, Howard R. Leary, signed a departmental policy memorandum on alcoholism.

MEMORANDUM FOR THE NEW YORK CITY POLICE COMMISSIONER CONCERNING A PROPOSED PROGRAM FOR THE IDENTIFICATION, TREATMENT AND REHABILITATION OF PROBLEM DRINKERS AND ALCOHOLICS

Background

There is an ever-increasing awareness on the part of leaders of industry, business, government and religions of the gravity of the problem drinker or alcoholic. The subject of alcoholism is emerging from old taboos as a topic of discussion since it is now recognized for what it is—the fourth largest socio-medical problem in the nation.

Steps are currently being taken by the National Council on Alcoholism and by certain religious and secular leaders to seek solutions to the problem of alcoholism on a national scale. One group hopes to induce the President of the United States to hold a conference on alcoholism. This, it is supposed, would ultimately result in treatment of the problem similar to that recently announced in connection with heart disease, cancer and strokes.

The medical profession by and large now regards alcoholism as a disease as evidenced by a statement by the American Medical Association in 1965 which concept brings with it the realization that alcoholic requires help in various forms. Chief Surgeon Stephen M. McCoy and the Chaplains of this Department concur in this view. Police Chaplain Monsignor Joseph A. Dunne has devoted a great deal of time and effort to become informed on this subject and in the various methods developed or under development to rehabilitate alcoholics.

Reliable estimates indicate that about 2 or 3 percent of the nation's work force suffer from alcoholism and it is also well known that those afflicted range from executives to unskilled laborers in all occupational groups.

It is estimated that about five hundred members of this Department are similarly affected, based on the reasonable assumption that the percentage of affected workers in the Police Department approximates that in private industry.

Alcoholism is reported to cost American industry $2 billion each year. From this it can be cocnluded that the cost of alcoholism to this Department each year is considerable. While this cost has not and probably could not be calculated in dollars and cents, its proportions are obvious in terms of lost man-hours stemming from sickness, injury, suspension and limited duty tenure. Aside from this is the very substantial man-hour cost of supervisory, medical and administrative effort expended on alcoholic members.

The social impact of alcoholism upon the wives and families of the alcoholic members can be attested by the Police Chaplains and by many other members of the Department.

There is, of course, the further problem of damage to the public relations and operating efficiency of the Department which is further complicated and aggravated by the dangerous potential inherent in the armed police officer, on or off duty, whose judgment and conduct are adversely affected by the intemperate use of of alcohol.

As in the case of other illnesses, early recognition or identification of the symptoms of alcoholism and early treatment are of vital importance. The most effective approach to the problem in many instances, has been "Alcoholics Anonymous" although medical and other therapeutic measures have also proved effective. "Alcoholics Anonymous" is a group of people for whom alcohol has become a major problem and who have banded together in a sincere effort to help themselves and other problem drinkers recover their health and maintain sobriety.

The National Council on Alcoholism states that based on experience of the past twenty years the recovery rate of those earnestly treated with some form of therapy is from 50 to 70 percent.

Since assuming this command over two years ago, the undersigned has interviewed numerous members of the force who have overcome the necessity for alcohol through the methods mentioned above. This success is impressive. Many of these members have been returned to full duty and also have reassumed their proper status as husbands and fathers. However, such successes, came about through the independent efforts of Chaplains or other interested individual members of the Department, rather than by a programmed effort. There is a consensus of opinion that a planned approach to the alcohol problem forefronted by a definite departmental policy would in all probability produce substantially more significant results.

Police Chaplain Monsignor Dunne and the Chief Surgeon, after discussions with Commanding Officers of the Medical Unit, Employee Relations Office and the undersigned, have proposed for consideration and implementation a policy to be followed for the early identification, treatment and rehabilitation of members of this Department who are problem drinkers or prone to alcoholism. This proposed program will be discussed below, but first, reference is made to objections or queries which may be advanced were this department to adopt it as a matter of policy.

It appears to the undersigned that the principal question would be: What effect may be anticipated upon departmental health, efficiency, discipline, morale and public image from the establishment of such a program? Concerning discipline, no departure from current policy and procedure is contemplated or recommended in the event that a member of the force is found to be unfit for duty by reason of intoxication. The means of referral of alcoholic members provided for in the proposed program are such that they will tend to eliminate the subjective factors affecting the decisions of Commanding Officers and other superiors when faced with the problem of disciplinary action against members of the force who are intoxicated. Insofar as morale is concerned, it is suggested that the net effect should be good in the sense that members would be aware that the Department was interested in the problem of the alcoholic and was taking positive steps to assist him. It should also be evident to the force at large that the unfortunate conduct both on and off duty which frequently accompanies alcoholism was not being condoned or neglected.

In terms of the Department's public relations or image it is not recommended that the proposed policy program be given any publicity, nor is it intended that any directive or other memorandum be distributed regarding it. If the program became known outside of the Department due to "leakage," which is entirely possible, it is suggested that the public is already aware that alcoholics exist among policemen as in other occupations and further, the segment of the public or press that might be inclined to comment is knowledgeable enough to distinguish alcoholism from drunkenness, per se. Assuming the existence of the program became public knowledge, any possible negative effect must be weighed against the very substantial benefits a planned program would produce to the department, to those members of it afflicted with alcoholism and to their families.

A counseling service is presently available at the Chaplain's Office in the Police Academy building on an informal and limited basis which has provided an effective referral of problem drinkers to volunteer "Alcoholics Anonymous" counselors. Additionally, through the Chaplain's Unit and in close cooperation with the Medical Unit, weekly AA meetings are held where group therapy is furnished to selected Limited Duty Section personnel.

Additionally, the Chief Surgeon has alerted the District Surgeons to the need for a more realistic and active approach to the problem drinker, with emphasis on early detection for referral to counseling and medical services as indicated. Commanding Officers too, have been urged to report problem cases to the Employee Relations Office for necessary attention but not to disregard disciplinary action where justified.

To effect the orderly and necessary transition from an informal program on alcoholism to a formal program it is recommended that the Department adopt and recognize the following policy statement.

Policy

1. Alcoholism is a disease and the alcoholic a sick person requiring skilled rehabilitative assistance.
2. Alcoholism is a departmental health problem and therefore a departmental responsibility.
3. Each case of suspected alcoholism or "problem drinking" shall be encouraged to seek adequate medical and counseling advice without delay.
4. Support and assistance will be afforded to any employee who cooperates and displays an honest rehabilitation effort.

5. Records will be kept strictly confidential.
6. "Problem Drinking" will be considered to exist for the individual:
    A. when his duty performance is materially reduced in efficiency and dependability because of drinking, and
    B. when such drinking is not an isolated experience but is more or less repetitive, and
    C. when such drinking results in recognizable interference with health or personal relations.
7. Each commanding officer will be responsible for the early detection of problem drinking on the part of any member of his command and prompt referral for rehabilitative assistance.
8. Our primary purpose is to rehabilitate the alcoholic to the status of a sober, reliable, productive employee, thus retaining his skills, training and experience.
9. Where all available rehabilitation attempts have failed, termination of employment on a consistent and equitable basis is in the best interests of the Department.

It is suggested, should this recommended policy be adopted, that a comprehensive departmental alcoholism program be initiated under the supervision of the undersigned who will coordinate the facilities of the Police Academy and the Employee Relation Office in a concerted effort toward education, motivation, early detection and rehabilitation. Close two-way communication will be established and maintained between the Medical and Chaplains Unit, as well as with other commands.

In a subject of this magnitude it is difficult to impose a formal detailed program. However, there is a common denominator which seems to be present in all effective industrial programs. This is a careful use of authority to insure acceptance on the part of the individual that he has a problem, to the point where he will take treatment for a sufficient period of time to receive the benefits that medicine and community education offer.

Basically, following policy adoption, the program would be initiated by a period of orientation and indoctrination of all command, medical and supervisory personnel through a series of conferences and lectures at the Police Academy. Lecturers or conference leaders will include the Chief Surgeon, the Chaplains and qualified medical personnel from within and without the Department, as well as representatives from the National Council on Alcoholism who have had extensive experience with "Alcoholics Anonymous" and the problem of alcoholism in general. The scheduling of conferences will be submitted to the Chief Inspector for approval. It is estimated that a series of three two-hour conferences for all supervisory personnel will be necessary to effect the training and educating needed for initial progress.

Initially, each commanding, medical and supervisory officer must be made aware of the Department's policy, the seriousness of a drinking problem, the necessity for early detection and rehabilitation and the need for their active and complete cooperation to insure the success of the program. Particular stress will be put on informing and instructing the immediate line supervisor, usually the sergeant, who is in the most favorable position to recognize and help the officer with a drinking problem. He must be reminded of his direct responsibiilty as a supervisor and additionally of his opportunity to aid not only the drinker but his family, society and the Department.

Briefly, the following basic procedures will be followed in the case of the problem drinker or alcoholic, but not to the exclusion of present disciplinary requirements:

1. The line superivsor will confront the individual with the indicated evidence of intemperate use of alcohol and advise of the rehabilitative assistance available.

2. He will also promptly confer with the Commanding Officer who will make necessary referral directly to the Employee Relations Office.

3. Commanding Officer, Employee Relations Office will review the employee's disciplinary, sick and accident records and effect an initial referral to the Medical Unit.

4. Commanding Officer, Medical Unit will interview the employee and obtain an immediate medical evaluation. Where it is indicated that rehabilitative measures should be attempted it will be essential to interest the subject in receiving medical guidance and recognizing the need for a proper course of treatment. Substance of interviews, treatment and results will be documented and filed on a confidential basis in the member's medical folder. The employee will be responsible for treatment cost except where departmental or medical plan services are available.

5. Where the supportive assistance of a department Chaplain and/or "Alcoholics Anonymous" is required, the Commanding

Officer Medical Unit will notify the Employee Relations Office where an immediate referral will be made to the Chaplains Unit. Qualified members of the Department experienced in the problems of alcoholism and its treatment have been acting, and will continue to act, as Staff Advisors under the aegis of the Chaplains Unit. Here too, documentation of treatment and results will be made on a confidential basis.

6. The Commanding Officer, Employee Relations Office will be responsible for causing a review to be made every three months of each case to determine if progress is being made. If it is evident the employee does not recognize his problem and shows little or no interest in rehabilitation, his commanding officer will be so notified. Concurrently the officer's commanding officer will report back to the Employee Relations Office every three months with respect to the subject's duty performance.

7. Reports or evidence of a drinking problem which emanate from other than the member's command will be channeled directly to the Employee Relations Office for the action indicated above. Included will be those cases disclosed from the combined routine examination of sick, disciplinary and accident records.

8. Where investigation at the Employee Relations Office indicates possible supervisory neglect has resulted in the ignoring of a drinking problem report will be forwarded through channels to the Chief Inspector for necessary attention.

9. Commanding Officer, Employee Relations Office will report monthly to the undersigned on the statistical results of the program. Additionally, he will make necessary recommendations for its improvement and expansion, as well as endeavor to determine the humanitarian and economic benefits accruing to the employee and the department from a properly administered program.

It is proposed to introduce the program smoothly, quietly and economically into existing procedures. It is not intended that it be a crusade but merely the application of sound management techniques applied to the areas of responsibility and authority in motivating and defining the role of the supervisor, as well as gaining employee cooperation in the early identification and rehabilitation of the problem drinker.

As an additional step it is proposed to distribute the attached booklet published by the Correctional Association of New York and the International Association of Chiefs of Police to all members of the force. Twenty-five thousand copies can be obtained at cost price of $.08 each for $2,000. It is not proposed to suggest that the booklet is, in any way, connected with the program. It will be distributed in the same manner as other informational data bearing upon problems encountered by the policeman in the course of duty. The information contained in the booklet will be imparted to the public by members of the force only upon request.

Among the benefits to be anticipated from a properly administered program are the following:

1. Reduction in absenteeism.
2. Improvement in morale.
3. Preservation of the department's vested interest in the employee.
4. Future potential of the rehabilitated employee.
5. Effect on the broader range of health problems.
6. Tightening of discipline in general.
7. Reduction in on and off-duty accidents.
8. Ease a supervisory problem.
9. Improvement of department's public image.

Should careful, periodic evaluation establish the value of this program further implementation and expansion will be proposed. In the past year a total of seventy-three cases were processed through the informal program now in existence, with highly favorable results. Eventual expansion of a formal program adequate to meet the needs of the department will require the inclusion of appropriate material into Police Academy refresher courses for commanding and supervisory officers, promotion courses and Command "E" courses attended by patrolmen prior to promotion in rank. Full use will be made of all available visual aid devices and techniques. Securing the enlightened cooperation of the line organizations should also be of substantial assistance.

To maintain the necessary impetus of the program request for staff and equipment necessary to meet the anticipated increase in case load will be made as the need develops. Review of the reports of dozens of industrial and public service organizations now maintaining programs disclosed unanimity of agreement in that the cost, while difficult to separate from the general medical budget, is minimal and completely justified by results obtained.

This proposed program for coping with drinking problems within the department is recommended for approval.

EARLY STAGES OF THE COUNSELING UNIT

Informal Stage

Prior to May, 1966, in an informal counseling program the sources of referral were limited largely to disciplinary cases, complaints from family members, the Medical Unit and a few supervisors.

Family conflicts are usually unwelcome to the supervisors; made often at the risk of violent reaction at home and frequently ignored at the precinct level. Police officers do not relish recording complaints against fellow officers.

Then too, job conflicts cause a morale problem. As his work deteriorates in quality and fellow members grow tired of "covering his mistakes," the problem drinker often goes through a personality change. His friends do not enjoy his company or his prolonged drinking; they resent his hostility and he himself becomes "a loner." He now drinks to relieve tension, resentment and loneliness, and in so doing actually perpetuates the addiction.

Hurwitz and Lelos (1968) studying thirty-six male employed alcoholics referred to the New York University Consultation Clinic for Alcoholism, examining interlevel conflicts of these patients and reported that 70 percent were in conflict over their dependency wishes.

In the informal stage for the year prior to formal policies being established, the Counseling Program held seventy-three interviews and thirty-two patients were hospitalized. Of these cases, thirty-four were referred by the Medical Unit.

Formal Program

In contrast, during the first thirteen months of the formal stage, a total of 216 interviews were recorded and of these 163 were referrals from the Medical Unit. Here, 104 admitted having a problem and 79 were hospitalized.

The explanation for this influx in the Medical Unit was

attributed to "better case findings," uncovering a large number of suspected problem drinkers from medical records, specifically from the "Chronic Sick List."

In this department, a policy of unlimited sick leave has been granted by the City of New York, due to the hazards of police service. To protect his important job benefit, an employee is considered "chronic sick" if he goes sick five or more times per year. By examining the medical folders of the "chronic sick" numerous instances of "Monday morning sickness," were noted, and we usually termed it 'gastroenteritis," or stomach disorder, which often signifies "coming off a drunk." These men were brought into the Medical Unit for examination and then were interviewed by an AA counselor.

Case findings also included a regular survey of accidents records by personnel officers. Particular attention was paid to bizarre activities, especially where an officer lost a gun or a shield; when a gun was discharged; or the lateness of the hour implied that the employee had been out drinking. Further, disciplinary records were also taken into consideration especially when a police officer was suspended or arrested in connection with intoxication on or off duty. Here a member of the Counseling Unit called him and arranged an interview in order to offer him hospitalization and rehabilitation. The sick member frequently saw a possibility of early restoration to duty as a result of cooperation with the department counseling service.

Thus a comparison of the first year of activity in a formal stage as compared to the informal stage would show that this department program had obtained a greater degree of penetration into the organizational problems of alcoholism.

TREATMENT PROGRAM

Initial Interview

The corporate effort of the program, illustrated by the combined efforts of trained supervisors and counselors and the medical referral of the suspected problem drinker, reaches his first test for effectiveness in the initial interview. The counselor is a patrolman in civilian clothes who is a recovered alcoholic and has been trained in counseling. All his talents and experience are brought into play as he greets his fellow officer who has been ordered to report for this interview.

Most problem drinkers are fearful of endangering their job, highly sensitive about the term "alcoholic," and quite resentful about being required to discuss "their private affairs." Even when an officer has been suspended for intoxication, he is not necessarily convinced that he has not been given "a bad break." The approach to the alcoholic employee must therefore be a delicate one. Wilcox (1968), writing in the *Ohio State Medical Journal,* relates that the counselor must realize that this interview will be unpleasant. He should expect to be confronted with denials, excuses, rage, remorse, lies and promises.

Tiebout (1948) states that the alcoholic is absorbed in his grandiosity and defiant individuality until he reaches a point of desperation. Because the alcoholic clings to those attitudes, he is usually stubborn about seeking help. However, when he feels beaten, he may give up some of his conscious or unconscious grandiose ideas of himself. Dr. Tiebout calls the process of getting the alcoholic to cooperate and accept treatment, "including therapeutic surrender."

After attempting to put the employee at ease and assuring him that records of his drinking experience will be kept confidential, in accordance with department policy, the counselor begins to trace the progress of the illness on a medical chart, adopted from Con-Edison Company.

A profile of advancing alcoholism is drawn on an age basis, beginning with social drinking and moving through problem drinking to the chronic stages. Various symptoms, are noted and pinpointed by the counselors. A line is drawn down the chart illustrating for the employee his life's story in terms of alcohol. When confronted by this evidence he himself has submitted he can become more aware of the seriousness of his condition.

In the second part of this interview, a publication of Alcoholics Anonymous, *The Twelve Questions,* is administered to determine the amount of insight the employee may have into his drinking problem.

The Chaplain, as Director, now enters the scene and reviews the work of the counselor in the presence of the patient. Here again the man must be put at ease, perceiving the role of the Chaplain to be friendly and dedicated in his ministry to assist policemen and their families. As a cleric-counselor (Dunne, 1964), he must restrain any desire to lecture or scold. The alcoholic has already lived with a deep sense of guilt, fear and desperation. The Chaplain can reinforce the findings of the counselor and lead into a discussion of the impact drinking has had on his family. He uses his position to advise the counselee to cooperate and accept whatever assistance may be offered as beneficial to himself and to his family.

Medical Determination

While the patient is often still undecided, the case is referred to the Medical Unit for interview with the Chief Surgeon or his Deputy. Here the doctor reviews the department medical record and then discusses the findings of the counselor with the patient. Where the problem drinker is cooperative or at least willing to consider joining the department Counseling Program the doctor can then send him to a hospital or in some cases merely refer him to AA therapy in the Counseling Unit plus AA meetings in the community.

Where the patient is completely lacking in insight and co-operation, a decision must be made regarding his welfare, independent of his reaction. If the man is not a chronic alcoholic and in good physical condition, he may be returned to his unit with an appropriate warning by the doctor to sustain from alcohol to safeguard his health and his job. On the other hand, where the uncooperative is obviously suffering from an advanced stage of alcoholism, both the Chaplain and the doctor will use the strongest moral persuasion to get him into a hopsital. Here the job may be used as a lever to get compliance, based on the terms of the department policy. A call to his wfie, however, usually robs him of his last defense, for she is happy that his problem has been brought to the attention of the Medical Unit and that he will receive help that is long overdue.

Detoxification

Medical authorities are aware that when the blood alcohol levels are falling after sustained intake, withdrawal syndromes may include tremulousness, hallucinosis, convulsive seizures and delirium tremens. Speaking of the treatment of alcoholism, the American Medical Association's *Manual on Alcoholism* (1968) says:

"Most clinicians agree that hospitalization is indicated in the early phases of most treatment programs, especially if there are apparent or suspected physical complications or when it is clear that intervention is needed to interrupt the drinking patterns."

The Police surgeon diagnoses the physical problems affecting the central nervous system and the digestive system. In recognition of the danger of sudden withdrawl, a five-day stay at Mount Carmel Hospital, Patterson, New Jersey, is usually recommended. Here the alcoholic is placed on a medically supervised plan of withdrawal and on a reduced program of nonaddictive medication. He receives a high intake of vitamins, including B-12, and can be expected to return to normal physical health during this five-day treatment.

During this hospitalization period, the patient has had good medical treatment specifically for alcoholism; a nutritious diet, a lecture by Dr. David I. Canavan, hospital director, explaining the disease of alcoholism, several AA meetings and group therapy sessions—all this to convince him that he has a problem with alcohol (Canavan and Lakes, 1964). Personal identification and admission to himself that his problem is alcohol is considered of paramount importance at this stage of treatment.

Most of the men who have returned to the Counseling Unit from Mount Carmel Hospital are convinced that their problem is not yet under control. They may feel better and have greater self-confidence, but they are advised to go to a halfway house for a period of four to six weeks. Here the recovering alcoholic is continued on high intake of nourishment, rest and light physical exercise. His knowledge of AA is deepened with a daily schedule of meetings at the lodge and in the community. His tutor in this AA way of life is the director, who, after eighteen years of sobriety, is qualified to give personal guidance and instruction in therapeutic sessions. Many problems and relationships lie at the root of his guilt, resentment and his tension. These obstacles to recovery are brought out in the discussion periods, in individual counseling sessions, and in eyeball-to-eyeball confrontations. Here is sought the all important removal of barriers to emotional and intellectual growth. Wasted years of drinking have taken a toll, in that reality has been pushed aside, and a fantasy world substituted. The alcoholic thus finds it hard to face reality in other people and even in himself without the help of fellow alcoholics.

The duration of the patient's stay at Glen Spey largely depends upon the progress he makes in the recovery program. The attending physician there and the director advise the Counseling Unit when they feel the maximum amount of benefits has been attained. In the meantime, the patient's family is often encourage to visit him over a weekend and to participate in appropriate conferences and social activities at the lodge. Many husband-wife relationships have been stabilized and normalized in this helpful setting.

Limited Duty Assignment

Thus far the patient has been administratively "on sick report" under the control of the Chief Surgeon and the Counseling Unit. His guns have been secured for the duration of the therapy. At the end of the stay, he must return to the Counseling Unit for further evaluation and assignment to Limited Duty status. For most individuals, immediate return to active duty is not yet indicated, even after long-term therapy. The fact that the person is no longer drinking may be considered a favorable condition, yet his reentry into the work scene requires strong stamina. For this reason, in view of individual needs, the patient is usually taken off sick status and placed on "temporary limited duty status," at the request of the Chief Surgeon for a period of ninety days. The Medical Unit retains administrative control over the patient and can extend or terminate the assignment whenever the Chief Surgeon considers him ready for full duty. The officer is then assigned to day tours in police headquarters units and will attend regular two-hour therapy sessions weekly at the Counseling Unit. He is also required to attend AA meetings each evening in the community and report this activity to his counselor. The record of meetings attended together with weekly reports of the attitude, appearance and cooperation of each patient is entered in his folder at the Counseling Unit for evaluation.

Restoration and/or Retirement

After ninety days, a determination may be made to return the recovering patient to full duty with firearms. The Chief Surgeon reviews the entire case and makes the final decision.

In most cases the police officer goes back to his former command. The policy here is to test his recovery in a realistic manner, with familiar faces and problems, and further, to impress his fellow workers with the effectiveness of the counseling program.

If, however, a patient returns to drinking at this period, a new effort must be made in his behalf, including additional hospitalization, psychological group counseling, and/or psychiatric assistance. Here this program is fortunate to have the services of a qualified psychologist and psychiatrist who are well-equipped to assist recovering alcoholics.

A useful tool in administering the problem drinker is the current policy of safeguarding firearms, rather than removing them permanently. The commander of the Medical Unit can safeguard firearms for problem drinkers when they are hospitalized and later, remove them permanently when these men may return to drinking despite departmental efforts. When a man's firearms are permanently removed he is then transferred permanently to limited duty and feels the sanction of the organization working against him, in view of his lack of cooperation.

Thus when a patient cannot recover from alcoholism in the opinion of the Chief Surgeon or has been on limited duty for more than one year, he becomes eligible for retirement for physical disability. Current pension benefits formerly denied a man with less than ten years service now authorize amounts based on years of service in the department. Alcoholism is considered ordinary disability in the personnel practices of the City of New York. The most encouraging part of a program is concerned with the success of a realistic, employee-centered approach to alcoholic employees. Here in this program three out of four who are enrolled in the therapeutic process were returned or have been returned to full-duty as police officers. We can also add the numerous benefits accrued to individuals entering the program as well as the wives, children and the community at large, including the department itself. The case study which follows recounts some of the benefits which accrued to a group of fifty men chosen for study as an illustration of what can be done. These accomplishments were achieved in the framework of an organization which has concern for its members through the functioning of the Counseling Unit.

A CASE STUDY: MAXWELL (1959)

A review of the literature revealed some significant work done by Dr. Milton Maxwell in 1959. This study examined the records of a company having 10,000 employees; selected at random a group of forty-eight problem drinkers, and compared them with a group without a drinking problem but of similar age, sex and years of service. The problem group had 2.5 times as many cases of illness (eight days or longer) and 2.5 times as many days of absence. The problem drinkers also cost the company three times as much in sickness payments, 3.6 times as many accidents as the matched controlled group. One basic limitation of this study, according to the author, is that it measures only instances of sick absences of eight days or longer. The company personnel policy of paying sick benefits only when illness extended eight days. Thus, absences due to alcohol related causes for less than eight days were not measured in this study. The case which follows, however, measures all sick absences before and after treatment.

Research Design

The case study treated here consists of an analysis of a sample of fifty patients, selected from the total of 130 men, were interviewed in the Counseling Unit during the year 1967. Using a table of random digits, a total of eighty-four men were picked in sequence, but thirty-four subjects were eliminated. In 1967, twenty-one men refused treatment. Of these, seven maintained that they had no problem at all, and fourteen, who may have had a problem, still refused treatment. In addition, thirteen were retired, dismissed or died during the three years of this study, leaving a total of fifty men to be analyzed.

The records of fifty patients who completed the therapeutic process were compared on the basis of before and after treatment. Their medical and disciplinary records were examined to obtain data describing their behavior before and after treatment in the Counseling Unit. Data was also gathered from the files of the Counseling Unit, based on information voluntarily given in the initial interview regarding age, years of service, and the point at which their drinking progressed to a chronic alcoholic stage.

Age Comparison

Data were obtained in an initial interview with each patient, listing the age at which he attained chronic alcoholism, and age at which they were admitted into counseling. This information was recorded in the interview form called Profile of Alcoholism.

The mean age at which employees suffered with chronic alcoholism was 28.6 years and most men were alcoholics for almost nine years before admission to the Counseling Unit. The problem of alcohol apparently was not recognized by the medical and supervisory personnel as a serious health problem for the employees in the group under consideration. The majority of men admitted to the program had reached the stage of chronic alcoholism between the age of twenty-one and thirty. The mean average for the men who became alcoholics was 28.6 years, but the mean age for admission to the Counseling Unit was 37.4 years, a serious neglect of a health problem.

Disciplinary Charges Related to Years of Service

The average years of service which members of this group rendered before coming into the Counseling Unit was 17 (range 0.5 to 25). This average, combined with the high incidence of disciplinary charges experienced by 38 of these men (mean 2.3, range 1 to 9), evidences that the Department was slow to take cognizance of problem drinkers in the ranks. These statistics seem to show, further, that supervisors attempted to cope with alcoholism on a disciplinary level, failing to recognize it as a medical problem. The average number of disciplinary charges per man is more than twice the rate of the entire Department.

Follow-up of this group of employees indicates that after return to duty on disciplinary charges have been placed against them—a significant contribution to organizational effectiveness.

Sick Absence Before and After Counseling

Perhaps the most interesting and useful comparison made in this case study is that of sick absences before and after treatment in the Counseling Unit. The mean number of days used for sick leave prior to counseling was 35.0, and in the 12 months after return to work, 16.8 days. It is also significant to note here that twenty men had no sick time recorded in their files after return to duty. These statistics represent sickness for all reasons, but not necessarily for alcohol-related illnesses. As previously indicated, supervisory staff tend to coverup incidents of alcoholism.

Statistics can be interpreted as time saved after counseling. Here lost time due to sickness was reduced by one-half for employee involved in the Counseling Service, for a period of one year after return to duty. This could be considered a significant change in the behavior and effectiveness of the employees concerned.

Comparison of Chronic Sick List of 1969

Another view of the contribution of the Counseling Unit in reducing sick time can be seen when the sick report of members of the case study is compared with that of a group selected from the Chronic Sick List of 1969. (Chronic Sick List is composed of members of the department who go on sick status more than five times a year.)

The average number of sick days taken by a random sample of fifty men out of a population of 561 placed on the chronic sick list of the department in 1969 is 30.8 days. In comparison, the alcoholic before counseling has an average of 4.2 days more than the chronic sick member. Thus reduction of sick time of the problem drinker to 16.8 days per year after counseling could be considered a significant improvement.

Alcohol-Related Illness Before and After Counseling

Although little information on alcoholism was available in the medical records of the department prior to May, 1966 when the Counseling Unit was formally established, nevertheless additional data from these records was extracted on the basis of lost time due to alcohol-related illnesses of fifty men in the sample group during the period of January, 1967 to December, 1968. A total of 2,758 days were lost by the fifty men in the sample group due to alcohol-related illness, before and during counseling, that is from January 1, 1967 to December 31, 1968, for a mean average of 55.1 days per man.

A total of 250 days were lost by the group after counseling in comparison with 2,758 days before and during counseling. Here the mean number of days lost by members of the group was reduced to 5.0 days after return to duty as compared with 55.1 days per man prior to and during counseling. Of note, too, is the fact that forty-two men did not lose any time due to alcohol-related illnesses after counseling.

Short-term sick absences were reduced from fifteen men before and during treatment to six men following treatment. It should also be noted that of thirty-one men of long-term sick report (twenty-one or more days) only four men fall into this category after recovery.

Conclusion

The first significant finding in the case study is that most problem drinkers in the sample had suffered from alcoholism for a period of nine years before receiving treatment. From an organizational viewpoint, this evidence points with serious neglect to a health problem. Granted, a lack of understanding of alcoholism, in industry, it still seems regrettable that an organization indulges in "scapegoating," when disciplinary measures seem to be utilized in lieu of medical help. The sample group averaged more than twice as many disciplinary charges as other employees. The same men, however, received no charges after treatment and return to duty. This evidence indicates that the establishment of a Counseling Unit for problem employees must be correlated with extensive supervisory training if the illness of alcoholism is to be handled effectively as a medical problem.

It might be countered that the problem drinkers probably deserve disciplinary measures for bonafide violations of discipline and for being a disruptive factor in the work situation. This view is defensible only if the superior and the sick worker have an alternative to solve their mutual problem. Until May, 1966, however, no counseling service was available either to the problem drinker who needed it or to the supervisor or district surgeon who were anxious to find a practical solution to the alcoholic employee.

This case study also documents a sharp reduction in sick absences for all illnesses and particularly for alcohol-related illnesses. The data reported demonstrates the possibility of meeting the needs of alcoholic employees. Such data served the additional purpose of showing management that such a goal is both possible and profitable as well as giving great satisfaction to management and labor alike. If Counseling Unit is credited only with reducing the sick report of fifty men by one-half, then the benefits to the organization are valuable. These men had sick records a little more extensive than those considered "chronic sick." By the small investment of a few trained and recovered employees, the problem of excessive sick absence was greatly reduced in the sample group. When these employees are returned to duty, the alcohol related illnesses were sharply reduced, a marked improvement which needs no justification. In terms of days, saved by this program, it is estimated that in this group alone the City of New York saved $100,000 in lost time benefits.

The recovery program as sponsored by the Police Department as previously described had a significant effect on the improvement of fifty men in the sample group. This study demonstrates that alcoholics can be helped and can be retained as skilled and useful employees.

FOLLOW-UP STUDY OF A GROUP OF FIFTY
ALCOHOLICS AFTER FOUR YEARS

A four year follow up study was done on a group of fifty men selected as a case study in the thesis entitled "Counseling the Employee in a Municipal Department." This group had been randomly selected from a total of 186 policemen and were counseled in their alcohol problems during the calendar year of 1968.

Case Finding

In January of 1973 efforts were made to locate each member of the group and it was established that thirty-six had remained on duty in the department; thirty on full duty and six on limited duty. A questionnaire and a covering letter was sent to the home of each active member inviting his cooperation. Names had been omitted from the questionnaire, but a code number was used for reference. This process was repeated thirty days later for those who did not immediately respond. Another month later, when six did not respond, they were brought into the Counseling Unit personally for interviews and thus all thirty-six members were accounted for.

Fourteen men from the original sample group had been retired from the police department. Two had been dismissed and twelve had been retired for physical disability (alcoholism) with a pension. Although several questionnaires were sent to the mail addresses which had been established through the Pension Unit, none of the retired men responded. The follow-up indicated that one had died of alcoholism; two were in hospitals; three were in correctional institutions; and five were simply unresponsive. Thus the bulk of the follow up data was limited to thirty-six members (72%) of the sample group on active duty.

Statistical Analysis

1. From the thirty-six-member group it was learned that; twenty-four (64%) had continuous sobriety; and twelve (36%) had had a "slip"; and of these, one had not stopped drinking.
2. The sobriety of the thirty-six member group ranged from two years and three months to four years and six months. The "slips" averaged three and one-half weeks and those who slipped averaged two "slips."

3. Twenty-nine (83%) attended AA meetings, averaging two meetings per week.
4. Seven (17%) did not continue affiliation with AA.
5. Eighteen (50%) consider themselves active in AA, that is holding meetings, speaking and participating in group activities.
6. In the entire sample group there were seven instances of members being hospitalized after initial introduction to AA.

Significance

Although this study was of comparatively short duration (four years) it may serve to encourage administrators of employee programs because of the high rate of recovery outlined below.

When the entire group of fifty cases is analyzed we have the following results to report:

Abstinent with recovery	24	48%
Early relapse but now abstinent	11	22%
Unimproved	6	12%
Death (due to alcoholism)	1	2%
Unknown	8	16%

It should be noted that "totally abstinent" and those with occasional early relapses, but now abstinent and working, constitute 70 percent of the entire group. This is a high recovery rate, but quite consonant with results reported by industrial programs. Perhaps the use of the job as a "lever to get cooperation" is not only effective but a valid approach.

REFERENCES

American Medical Association: *Manual on Alcoholism.* Chicago, AMA, 1968, p. 51.

Canavan, D. I., and Lakes, F.: The treatment of the acute episode in the chronic alcoholic. *J Med Soc NJ, 61:*504, 1964.

Dunne, J. A.: Counseling the alcoholic. *Social Digest, 7:*93, 1964.

Hurwitz. J., and Lelos, D.: A multi-level interpersonal profile of employed alcoholics. *Quart J Stud Alcohol, 29:*70, 1968.

Maxwell, M. A.: Study of absenteeism, accidents and sickness payments in problem drinkers on one industry. *Quart J Stud Alcohol, 20:*302-312, 1959.

Tiebout, H. M.: *The Act of Surrender in the Therapeutic Process.* New York, National Council on Alcoholism, 1948, pp. 8-9.

Wilcox, C. E.: The alcoholic in industry. *Ohio State Med J, 64:*78, 1968.

Chapter 7

INSIGHT: A PROGRAM FOR
TROUBLED PEOPLE

Otto F. Jones, M.S.W.

On July 1, 1970, the Utah Copper Division of the Kennecott Copper Corporation launched a program of help for troubled employees and their dependents and named is INSIGHT. The concept is simple—it is to provide professional counseling to 8,000 Kennecott employees and their 24,000 dependents who have problems and to help them get the help they need from Salt Lake County's 220 community service organizations. Program utilization is voluntary, confidential, available seven days a week, twenty-four hours a day, and obtained by dialing I–N–S–I–G–H–T (467-4448) on the telephone. The Kennecott Social Action Policy dated February 24, 1969, described the necessity and performance responsibility for such a program.

BACKGROUND

COMPONENTS OF METAL Mining Division, Kennecott Copper Corporation have been dedicated for many years to the principle that a corporation must be a citizen of the nations, states and communities in which it operates. Through the conduct of the Division and of its managers and employees and through generous contribution of corporate resources, Kennecott has established an outstanding record of concern and action.

Need for a Policy

The social problems arising out of racial discrimination and poverty in the United States threaten our society, our way of life, our economy and our national stature. These problems have been demonstrated to be beyond the capacity of government alone to resolve. Business and industry are being called upon to direct their energy and resources to help.

To assure that Metal Mining Division meets its obligations in this field, this Policy is intended to express the concern and commitment of the Division and to provide guidelines for the implementation of that commitment.

Statement of Policy

Like business and industry generally, Metal Mining Division, Kennecott Copper Corporation intends to do its part in meeting the social problems of the United States and, more particularly, of the states and communities in which it is located. The Division's effort will include:

1. Implementation of the Division Policy on Equal Employment Opportunity.
2. Allocation of a significant portion of its financial contributions or organizations, agencies and programs dedicated to resolving social problems in areas such as employment, housing, education, health and welfare, and law enforcement.
3. Encouragement of managers and employees to devote a portion of their time, talent and energy to participation in and leadership of organizations, agencies and programs dedicated to resolving such problems.

Implementation of Policy

Overall responsibility for implementation of this Policy rests with the executives and managers of the Division without regard to the nature of their assignment of business.

Financial contributions continue to be subject to the Corporate Policy on Contributions.

Interpretation of Policy

The Director of Employee Relations (in consultation with the Director of Public Relations) is responsible for:

1. Interpretation of this Policy and advice and counsel as to its implementation.
2. Keeping management informed as to the activities of the Division and of business and industry generally. (Kennecott Social Action Policy, 1969)

HOW INSIGHT WORKS

Insight is a program of help by referral made available to the employees and dependents (approximately 22,000) of the Kennecott Copper Corporation, Utah Copper Division. This service provides an easy way for a person in need to secure help through the proper community resource.

We sought a program that could offer not only a service, but confidentiality, self-determination and convenience. To accomplish this, we accept referrals from all sources; ranging from the employee relations department, unions and supervisors, to friends, family and relatives.

We have eliminated all "red tape"; one need only dial the letters I–N–S–I–G–H–T (467-4448) and a twenty-four-hour a day, seven-day a week counseling service is at their disposal. Anyone may contact Insight and report a problem affecting an employee.

We guarantee anonymity for the caller and the person referred. If the person accepts Insight's offer, help is given; if not, we politely back away.

The mechanics begin with a call to Insight. The caller is then referred to the program director for counseling. Problems are discussed and alternative solutions utilizing community resources are made available. The employee or dependent then makes a decision and a referral is made. Follow-up is very important to make sure the referred individual receives the necessary help. Sometimes another referral is required.

Insight performs a valuable service in many areas.

Labor-Management Relations

Employees who begin to develop chronic absenteeism or poor job performance patterns are offered help before the problem gets out of hand. To accomplish these goals, assistance is offered in the areas of alcoholism, drug abuse, family problems, marital problems, indebtedness, legal problems, etc. Whatever the reason, referral to Insight permits getting to the root cause, and, in many cases, solves the problem and saves the employee's job.

Disciplinary Procedures

Insight is built into the company disciplinary procedure, on the premise that the sooner an employee with a job performance or absenteeism problem gets help, the better his chance for keeping his job.

Normally, unsatisfactory job performance or excessive absenteeism will gain the employee a verbal warning with the first offense. If improvements are not made, a written warning follows. Continued misconduct warrants a hearing with the employee, his union representative and the employee relations department. Probationary terms are usually issued at this point. The next and final disciplinary step is termination.

With each of the above contacts with the employee, Insight is also notified. Our approach then is to offer our assistance—involvement in the Insight program is never mandatory. Each time a sincere attempt is made to help the troubled employee and in the majority of cases appropriate corrections are made.

Employee morale is greatly boosted when it is realized that the company will take an interest in a man's problem and offer him help rather than an insensitive mandatory stiplation of compliance or else. Loyalty towards the company and the man's job is the prevailing result.

Education

Of course, to make maximum penetration possible, information regarding the program and its potential must be effectively disseminated. This is accomplished through direct letters to the employees, special bulletins, company magazines, television spots, and presentation through lecture to the front-line supervisors and union personnel.

Explanation of program mechanics lowers anxiety and speculation regarding involvement. The best means of advertising, however, is through positive "feedback" from those having experience with Insight.

Community Organization

It is the responsibility of Insight to maintain a working rapport with community social service agencies and all other facilities that might be made available to our employees and their dependents for whatever problems they might have. To accomplish this, we must not only make ourselves acquainted with community resources, but become a part of community planning. There are some interesting public relations dynamics involved here. Every year the Utah Copper Division receives many requests for community project donations. Often in the past, these contributions were made and remained just that—contributions. Now, we consider these contributions more in terms of an investment, beneficial to both Kennecott Copper Corporation employees and the community at large.

We have a follow up procedure that indicates to us, through the participating persons, just how adequately they are being helped. This enables us to give valuable feedback information to community social service agencies and private facilities to whom we have referred our people. We, therefore, become actively responsible in upgrading existing resources and making recommendations for improvement.

Recording

An accurate, up-to-date recording system is self-explanatory. It provides us with a reliable means of measure for current response and evaluation. It assists us in making program adjustments and documents history (Appendix I).

Research

Closely related to recording rationale is the need for accurate research. We are currently trying to upgrade our own services and effectiveness in an attempt to not only accommodate but encourage program participation. Our research has included to date a preliminary study for program justification and comparison. It was followed by a study within the plants to check absenteeism and job performance improvements of those employees who were referred via the disciplinary procedure. Subsequently, a questionnaire was mailed to participants who had been in the program through July 1, 1971, and their responses were evaluated quantitatively. A further study was conducted after the program had been in operation over two and one-half years to determine long-term effects of the program. The results of these studies are described below.

RESEARCH PROJECT I

During the month of October, 1969, a study was conducted at the various plants in the Utah Copper Division to obtain, by sample, a means of measuring the extent of the alcoholism problem here. Because we did not want to cause undue concern among the men regarding a so called "black list" of alcoholics, we did not conduct a questionnaire-type research. For the purposes of this study, only the "well-known" problem drinkers were used. Each industrial relations supervisor from the four plants was asked to produce the names and payroll numbers of those men known to have a problem with alcohol to the extent that it affected absenteeism and job performance. Sixty-three names were produced.

It was our intention to observe the actual days lost by these men during the period October 1, 1968 to September 30, 1969. We also wanted to know the actual number of days paid in non-occupational sickness and accident weekly indemnity, to these men during this time. We realize that not all days lost nor all weekly indemnity paid would be due to alcoholism. Our interest was in comparing the known problem drinker with the average of the company as a whole. Because some of the men had been terminated during the designated year and others had not been working for the company for that entire year, we were only able to use thirty-seven men for this study. Several others from the total sixty-three were eliminated from the study because of their nonrepresentative status and lack of adequate absenteeism recording.

Although this program is not restricted to the production and maintenance personnel, the study was, simply because of the availability of records.

It was noted from the totals of the four plants, that thirty-seven men lost a total of 2,589 working days during the year observed. Of the 2,589 working days lost, 2,071 were paid weekly indemnity at the rate of $11.43 per day. A simple calculation then shows us that thirty-seven men who are having manifest problems with alcohol cost the Utah Copper Division $23,671.53 in one designated year for weekly indemnity alone. This is an average of $639.77 per problem drinker for the given year.

Just how much of this weekly indemnity and lost time was due to alcoholism is difficult to say. Perhaps the most reasonable approach would be to note that during the period from October 1, 1968 to September 30, 1969, the industrial relations report of absenteeism for production and maintenance employees noted an average of 12.27 days lost per man during the given year, or a monthly average of 1.02 days lost. These figures are based on the fact that there was a monthly average of 6,251 production and maintenance men working for Kennecott (UCD) during the designated year. According to our records, these 6,251 men lost 76,684 shifts (other than holidays and vacations) during the year. During the same given time period, our study revealed that the thirty-seven men chosen for the sample lost a total of 2,589 shifts for an average of 69.97 days lost per man in the given year. We see then that the thirty-seven problem drinkers lost on the average of 57.7 days per the given period more than the entire production and maintenance average, which would include the problem drinkers as well.

It is noteworthy to say that these are probably all men who are in or close to the chronic phase of alcoholism. They can not be used as a means for measuring all problem drinkers currently employed at KCC (UCD). The study does serve a worthwhile purpose, however, using these statistics and comparing them with statistics made available through national organizations, we can view the problem with better perspective.

The American Medical Association's *Manual of Alcoholism* cites "that major industrial firms have estimated the alcoholic employee will lose approximately twenty-two more working days per year than the nonalcoholic employee, and suffer twice the number of accidents." If we were to average all problem drinkers into the Kennecott study on absenteeism, I am sure that we would find the average very close to the estimated twenty-two days.

It is conservatively estimated by national organizations that the intensity of alcoholism will vary from 3 percent to 8 percent of the work force, depending upon the type of work and how heavily male-populated the force is. Using these criteria, once again conservatively, it is felt that 5 percent of the work force at the Utah Copper Division is having a problem with alcohol to some noticeable extent. If we were to use the 5 percent figure and multiply it times the approximate work force of 8,000 employees at Kennecott (UCD), we would see that there are some 400 employees with an alcohol problem that will cause them to lose on the average of twenty-two working days a year more than the nonalcoholic.

These figures can be multiplied to become extremely high (400 x 22 = 8800 shifts per year lost) and expensive, not only in terms of dollars, but in terms of mentality and social adjustment.

Hospital, medical and surgical (HM&S) costs are also contributors to the overall cost of alcoholism. Once again, during the period October 1, 1968 to September 30, 1969, thirty-seven men had claims paid to them for the amount of $32,539.27 (Blue Cross or hospital claims) plus $11,010.00 (Blue Shield or surgical, medical claims) for a total of $42,549.27. This is an average of $1,177.01 per man for Blue Cross/Blue Shield claims for one given year.

To better visualize total costs, it might be interesting to note that the total HM&S costs per given year per man ($1,177.01) plus the total weekly indemnity (WI) costs during the same period per man ($639.77) amounted to $1,816.78. This amount multiplied times the thirty-seven men in the study cost $67,220.86 (37 x $1,816.78 = $67,220.86) for HM&S and WI alone. This is not to mention all other areas that could be tabulated in the overall cost of the problem drinking employee. These are, however, the areas of greatest cost and concern.

Research Project I Follow-Up

The original study (October 10, 1968 to September 30, 1969) revealed that thirty-seven men lost an average of 5.83 shifts per month per man during the designated year. They received an average of $53.31 per month per man for weekly indemnity (WI), and an average of $98.08 per month per man for hospital, medical and surgical (HM&S) costs during this same time. This is to be compared with the production and maintenance absenteeism average for 6,251 employees during this same period of 1.02 days, WI costs of $10.81 and HM&S costs of $30.94 (calculated on a per month per man basis).

Of the thirty-seven men, twelve were referred to Insight (eleven from the employee relations department and one self-referred); eighteen were never involved with Insight; four were terminated by the company (one was involved with Insight); two were deceased (were never involved with Insight); one quit the company (never involved with Insight).

Those Involved in the Insight Program

Before Insight, we reviewed the absenteeism, WI and HM&S costs for the twelve employees who did eventually get involved in Insight over one year prior to their date of referral for a means of later comparison.

1. Absenteeism averaged 5.8 working days per man per month.
2. WI costs averaged $70.67 per man per month.
3. HM&S costs averaged $109.04 per man per month.

After Insight (12.3 months average time of Insight involvement):

1. Absenteeism decreased to an average of 2.93 working days per man per month.
2. WI costs averaged $25.33 per man per month.
3. HM&S cost asveraged $56.91 per man per month.

Those Never Involved in the Insight Program

We reviewed the absenteeism, WI and HM&S costs for the eighteen employees who never did become involved with Insight. This was for the period July 1, 1969 to June 30, 1970 (one year prior to implementation of the Insight program) to be used as a comparison for the year following the implementation of the Insight program (July 1, 1970 to June 30, 1971).

Before implementation of Insight:

1. Absenteeism averaged 5.25 working days per man per month.
2. WI costs averaged $66.71 per man per month.
3. HM&S costs averaged $122.31 per man per month.

After implementation of Insight:

1. Absenteeism averaged 5.41 working days per man per month.
2. WI costs averaged $93.35 per man per month.
3. HM&S costs averaged $132.01 per man per month.

Observations

Those involved with Insight showed an improvement in all categories: absenteeism, 49.5 percent; weekly indemnity, 64.2 percent; hospital, medical and surgical, 48.9 percent.

Those not involved with Insight tended to get worse: absenteeism, 2.9 percent; weekly indemnity, 28.5 percent; and hospital, medical and surgical, 7.4 percent.

RESEARCH PROJECT II

The following shows the results of a study conducted of eight-three employees referred for absenteeism problems by the employee relations department, unions or supervisors.

Before Insight

Average absenteeism was 3.81 days per man per month over a period of 11.6 months.

After Insight

Sixty-four decreased their absenteeism (77.1%). Eighteen increased their absenteeism (21.7%). One remained the same.

The sixty-four men were absent an average of 2.12 days per man for 7.2 months (the average time of Insight involvement) constituting a 44.4 percent individual improvement.

The eighteen men with increased absenteeism averaged 5.4 days per man per month over the same period for an increase of 37.2 percent.

RESEARCH III: FOLLOW-UP STUDY OF INSIGHT PARTICIPANTS

In February, 1971, it was decided to make a study to determine the effectiveness of the Insight program. A letter and questionnaire were sent to each individual family involved with

Insight. A total of 335 letters were mailed to those who were a part of the program from July 1, 1970 to January 31, 1971. Of this number, a return of 26 percent (eighty-eight letters) was received. For clarification, hereafter all statistics and information derived therefrom will be in reference to the questionnaire.

In response to the question of how they had heard of Insight, 53 percent (forty-eight) gained their information through company developed written communications, 20 percent (eighteen) through employee utilizers, and the remaining 27 percent (twenty-two) through supervisors, employee relations department, unions, Insight presentations, etc. One favorable comment shared was: "I know of one particular case other than my own where a man has received help from Insight and has made remarkable improvement. At least on the job, where I see him, this is the case."

When the participants were asked if they had found the Insight staff responsive to their requests, 94 percent (eighty-three) said that they had. Of the remaining 6 percent (five), two responded "yes" and "no" and the other one did not respond.

Frequent positive responses to this question were that the Insight staff was "responsive," "cooperative," "concerned," "eager to help," "fast," "understanding," and "willing to listen without recrimination."

Those who felt that they had not received sufficient help were seeking financial assistance or jobs for dependents.

After the particular problems had been received, 84 percent (seventy-four) felt satisfied with the suggested alternatives received, 11 percent (ten) were not, and the other 5 percent (four) did not answer the question. Those who answered favorably made comments like, "It's good to have them working round the clock," and "It's a good feeling to know there was someone to turn to."

Due to the confidential nature of some of our cases, we could not send letters to everyone involved with us.

The problems faced by those not happy with suggestions received were financial, absenteeism and need of work for dependents. A typical comment made in response to this question was, "I didn't like being sent somewhere else, I wanted help on the spot."

When asked if the services of individuals to whom they had been referred were helpful, we received only a 75 percent (sixty-five) response. Of those that did respond, 77 percent (fifty) did so favorably, 4 percent (three) were undecided, and 19 percent (twelve) were not satisfied. Response was low to this question because many people were not referred to outside agencies and therefore it was not applicable.

Those who were unsatisfied were referred to the Community Consumer Credit Counseling Service and found them to be "reluctant" and "evasive," to Legal Aid Society and found them to be "too busy to help," and the remainder to psychiatrists with whom they had communication problems. One favorable comment to this question was, "Insight made us feel like we were not the only ones who needed help."

In answer to the question, "Do you feel the Insight program helped you," 83 percent (seventy-three) said yes, 14 percent (twelve) said no, and 3 percent (three) did not respond. Again, those not helped need a home, a job, a loan or free legal representation. Negative comments were that Insight could not help in financial areas, jobs for the handicapped, or in real estate matters. Favorable comments included, "The program takes a personal interest," "Insight gave me a new attitude," and "Even though the problem is still here, they helped me realize why."

Ninety-three percent (eighty-two) responded favorably to the question of whether they would utilize Insight again, 5 percent (four) were undecided, and 3 percent (two) said no. Those who were undecided or who gave a negative response said it would depend on the type of problem. One positive comment which sums up many others is, "Insight provided me with a very much needed helping hand."

In responding to the question of whether or not Insight should be continued, 98 percent (eighty-six) said yes, and the remaining 2 percent (two) did not answer this question. There were no negative responses.

Our questionnaire concluded with a request to the participants to take the opportunity to make suggestions for improving the

Insight program. We have selected what we felt to be some of the more pertinent responses.

Requests were made for the company to make available through Insight protection from garnishment, legal facilities, financial assistance, recreation centers, and jobs and training for handicapped youth.

It was felt that there needed to be more publicity for the Insight program, literature and/or circulars available to all employees on major problems such as alcoholism and drug abuse, and Insight offices at each of the plants.

Suggestions were made for mandatory referral of those having problems on the job, more individual help and personal contact from Insight, less referral to other sources, closer follow-up made by Insight, and a program of prevention to be implemented along with Insight's program of help.

Some of the respondents found the program to be ". . . there when I needed it, twenty-four hours a day"; a program long overdue; a program which gives a whole new outlook on life; a program which helps workers make it on the job; and, ". . . the best benefit employees have." One specific comment was: "Many employees have many different problems. Happy employees are a good investment. This way Kennecott would receive back benefits back (sic) for their help. Make this program known to all employees and the surrounding benefits."

Another indication of the good feeling felt towards the program is that although signatures were neither requested nor were they necessary, 43 percent (38) of those responding signed their names. As one gentleman wrote, "Insight helped get the right help at the right time. Thank you."

RESEARCH PROJECT IV: TWO AND ONE-HALF YEAR EVALUATION OF INSIGHT PROGRAM

Our most recent study was completed midway through the program's thirty-second month, February, 1973. A sample of 150 men who had used the Insight program were observed on a before and after basis, i.e. calculating their absenteeism, weekly indemnity costs, and hospital, medical and surgical costs over a six-month period prior to their involvement with Insight, compared with a six-month period immediately following their program involvement.

On Tables 7-I and 7-II, the before, during and after periods are based on the criteria that before is a six-month period; during is generally a one-year period; and after is a six-month period.

Table 7-III, involving the nonparticipants in the study, covers calendar years 1971 and 1972. This is the closest breakdown we could conceive to compare with the information on Tables 7-I and 7-II.

TABLE 7-I
PARTICIPANTS

Health Medical Surgical	Before	During	After
Mine	$29,942.41 ($ 86.04)*	$33,671.16 ($37.94)	$15,822.32 ($45.47)
Concentrator	$31,817.23 ($123.32)	$36,626.76 ($57.94)	$ 9,606.18 ($37.23)
Smelter	$13,780.31 ($ 74.09)	$19,463.73 ($55.56)	$ 9,055.21 ($48.68)
Refinery	$ 8,355.42 ($ 77.37)	$ 5,320.52 ($31.44)	$ 2,975.05 ($27.55)
	$83,895.37 ($ 93.22)	$95,082.17 ($49.91)	$37,458.76 ($41.62)

55.35% decrease in health medical surgical costs after Insight

* All figures in parenthesis are computed on a per month per man basis.

TABLE 7-II
PARTICIPANTS
150 MEN AVERAGING 12.7 MONTHS IN INSIGHT

Absenteeism		Before	During	After
Mine	58 men/15.3 months	1,387 (3.98)*	1,370 (1.54)	580 (1.67)
Concentrator	43 men/14.7 months	1,009 (3.91)	927 (1.46)	422 (1.64)
Smelter	31 men/11.3 months	302 (1.62)	367 (1.05)	251 (1.35)
Refinery	18 men/ 9.4 months	163 (1.51)	193 (1.14)	128 (1.19)
	150 men/12.7 months	2,861 (3.18)	2,857 (1.49)	1,381 (1.54)

52% attendance improvement after Insight

Weekly Indemnity	Before	During	After
Mine	$12,260.45 ($35.23)	$13,114.99 ($14.78)	$2,985.96 ($8.58)
Concentrator	$ 8,542.10 ($33.11)	$ 6,822.84 ($10.79)	$1,456.42 ($5.65)
Smelter	$ 1,882.71 ($10.12)	$ 2,800.18 ($ 7.99)	$1,065.72 ($5.73)
Refinery	$ 788.57 ($ 7.30)	$ 965.72 ($ 5.71)	$ 455.71 ($4.22)
	$23,473.83 ($26.08)	$23,703.73 ($12.44)	$5,963.81 ($6.63)

74.6% decrease in weekly indemnity costs after Insight

* All figures in parenthesis are computed on a per month per man basis.

TABLE 7-III

NONPARTICIPANTS (150 MEN)

Absenteeism		1971	1972
Mine	50 men	428 (.71)*	495 (.82)
Concentrator	45 men	566 (1.05)	468 (.86)
Smelter	27 men	249 (.77)	259 (.80)
Refinery	28 men	195 (.58)	192 (.57)
		1,338 (.74)	1,414 (.79)

Absenteeism increased 6.33% during 1972.

Weekly Indemnity	1971	1972
Mine	$3,056.56 ($5.09)	$2,757.14 ($4.60)
Concentrator	$3,805.71 ($7.05)	$1,401.43 ($2.60)
Smelter	$ 982.86 ($3.03)	$ 870.00 ($2.69)
Refinery	$2,982.58 ($8.88)	$1,630.71 ($4.87)
	$10,827.71 ($6.01)	$6,659.28 ($3.70)

38.5% decrease in weekly indemnity costs in 1972.

Health Medical Surgical	1971	1972
Mine	$21,423.73 ($35.70)	$21,402.09 ($35.67)
Concentrator	$21,023.72 ($37.54)	$18,034.43 ($32.20)
Smelter	$ 7,261.53 ($22.41)	$12,237.35 ($37.78)
Refinery	$15,548.50 ($46.28)	$14,538.93 ($43.27)
	$65,257.48 ($36.25)	$66,212.80 ($36.79)

1.47% increase in health medical surgical costs in 1972

* All figures in parenthesis are computed on a per month per man basis.

Table 7-IV is a further refinement of Tables 7-I and 7-II. It demonstrates the percentages of those participants who improved, those who stayed the same, and those whose performance deteriorated.

Table 7-V is also a further refinement of Tables 7-I and 7-II. Table 7-V demonstrates, by plant, increases and decreases in attendance, weekly indemnity costs, and hospital, medical and surgical costs. In addition, it demonstrates the incidence of the various types of problems.

During the period of this study, other division activities have impacted upon the people utilized in the study. I will outline them under the headings of absenteeism, weekly indemnity and HM&S.

Absenteeism

Effective the third quarter of 1972, an accelerated program of absentee control was effected. Utilizing the Department of

TABLE 7-IV

PARTICIPANTS

Absenteeism		Improved	Same	Worse
Mine	58 men/15.3 months	45 (77.0% of 58)*	5 (8.6%)	8 (13.8%)
Concentrator	43 men/14.7 months	31 (72.0% of 43)	3 (7.0%)	9 (20.9%)
Smelter	31 men/11.3 months	19 (61.3% of 31)	2 (6.4%)	10 (32.3%)
Refinery	18 men/ 9.4 months	13 (72.2% of 18)	1 (5.6%)	4 (22.2%)

Weekly Indemnity	Improved	Same	Worse
Mine	29 (50.0% of 58)	26 (44.8%)	3 (5.2%)
Concentrator	20 (46.5% of 43)	21 (48.8%)	2 (4.7%)
Smelter	8 (25.8% of 31)	19 (61.3%)	4 (12.9%)
Refinery	6 (33.3% of 18)	11 (61.1%)	1 (5.6%)

Health Medical Surgical	Improved	Same	Worse
Mine	34 (58.6% of 58)	10 (17.2%)	14 (24.1%)
Concentrator	31 (72.1% of 43)	3 (7.0%)	9 (20.9%)
Smelter	17 (54.8% of 31)	2 (6.4%)	12 (38.7%)
Refinery	12 (66.7% of 18)	1 (5.6%)	5 (27.8%)

TABLE 7-V

PARTICIPANTS

Absenteeism

Mine	58.04% increase in attendance
Concentrator	58.06% increase in attendance
Smelter	16.67% increase in attendance
Refinery	21.19% increase in attendance

Weekly Indemnity

Mine	75.65% decrease in weekly indemnity costs
Concentrator	82.94% decrease in weekly indemnity costs
Smelter	43.18% decrease in weekly indemnity costs
Refinery	42.19% decrease in weekly indemnity costs
Mine	47.16% decrease in health medical medical costs

Health Medical Surgical

Concentrator	69.81% decrease in health medical surgical costs
Smelter	43.38% decrease in health medical surgical costs
Refinery	48.19% decrease in health medical surgical costs

Primary Problem Type

Familial	33
Alcoholism	29
Marital	18
Psychological	17
Legal	16
Financial	14
Absenteeism	10
Drugs	7
Job Performance	6

150

Labor formula for computing absenteeism, the absenteeism rate for 1972 was 4.69 percent compared to 5.24 percent in 1971. This introduces a variable into the absenteeism results of the study.

Weekly Indemnity

Effective the third quarter of 1972, an accelerated program to eliminate weekly indemnity abuse was effected. Impact was not demonstrated until the fourth quarter results were in. The cost per $10 of benefit in 1972 by quarter was as follows: First quarter, $1.70; Second quarter, $1.59; Third quarter, $1.73; and Fourth quarter, $1.45.

Meanwhile, on July 1, 1972, an improved liberalized weekly indemnity program was instituted. The weekly indemnity rate went from a flat $80 per week to a sliding scale of $85 to $115 per week, depending upon the individual employee's job classification. The cost of the liberalization on an actuarial basis should be 25 percent.

HM&S

The 1971 HM&S costs in the Utah Copper Division increased 7.1 percent over 1970. The 1972 increase in HM&S costs for the division over 1971 costs was 3.5 percent. However, HM&S costs in the Blue Cross/Blue Shield Book of Business, in the State of Utah, increased 5.7 percent. This again introduces a variable in the interpretation of this study.

It has been indicated that after an average of 12.7 months in Insight, these 150 men improved their attendance 52 percent; decreased their weekly indemnity costs 74.6 percent, and decreased their hospital, medical and surgical costs 55.4 percent.

It is evident that the Insight services are productive of results in relation to alcoholism and other personal and social problems. It is apparent that absenteeism can be reduced considerably by providing people with social services for problem-solving. This is accomplished by continuous up-to-date knowledge of community resources, shared with the individual according to need and interest. Such a program improves morale, enhances employee relations and better integrates industry into the community's activities. Benefits are realized by both the individual and the company.

Current Status Report

Periodically we inform the employees of the program's progress and utilization. This enables them to remain currently appraised and aware that the program continues to operate. Without such information, impetus falters and enthusiasm dwindles. It has been our experience that such notification to the employee and our managers encourages them to realize not only the effectiveness and participation of the program, but also that it remains viable.

Results have far exceeded expectations. Over a 48-month period, 5,264 persons had solicited help; 2,768 employees and 2,496 dependents had been placed in programs designed to help. The volume has not yet slackened.

The impact of Insight has extended beyond Kennecott. The National Institute on Alcohol Abuse and Alcoholism in carrying out its mandate under the Hughes Act, has adopted Insight's "troubled people" concept. We are informed civil service will use this approach. It is currently being effected for 120,000 civil service employees in the San Francisco Bay area and for the civil service employees in the State of Hawaii. The federal organization being established to expend $365 million annually for drug addiction rehabilitation is interested in this concept—particularly as it relates to penetration and utilization of rehabilitative community facilities. The city of Phoenix, Arizona is in process of establishing an Insight program. Pacific Telephone and Telegraph, San Francisco, has started an Insight program for its 21,000 employees. Hundreds of requests for information from both the private and public sectors have been received and answered.

Insight has attracted a great deal of publicity. It has been reported in the *New York Times, Business Week,* the Executive Voice series of *Fortune Magazine,* the BNA and various other management services publications.

Experience to date convinces us that the Insight program

represents significant breakthroughs in mental health and employee relations. We are further convinced return on investment exceeds by many times the cost of the program.

Up to this point, I have tried to give you an overview of the program, its concept, its results and its overall impact. Why and how this program came about will, I believe, be of interest to you.

The National Council on Alcoholism estimates that in a heavy duty, high male population industry that 5 to 10 percent of the work force is alcoholic. The Utah Copper Division is part of such an industry. The national problem alcoholism poses is demonstrated by the following:

1. Alcoholism ranks first in the nation as a major health problem.
2. Nine million Americans are chronic alcoholics.
3. Because of problem drinking, 35,000 were killed and two million injured on our highways in 1969.
4. The cost to industry approximates $7 billion a year.
5. Alcoholism is involved in 50 percent of all arrests.
6. Alcoholism accounts for 40 percent of all admissions to state mental hospitals.
7. Only 3 percent of the alcoholics are skid row; 97 percent are family centered.
8. Fifty percent of alcoholics attended or graduated from college.
9. Forty-five percent of alcoholics are professional or managerial people.
10. Seventy-five percent are men.
11. In Utah, alcoholism has increased 144 percent since 1965.

In the Utah Copper Division, using a thirty-seven-man alcoholic sample, over a twelve-month period, we learned their absenteeism exceeded the average more than 5 to 1; sickness and accident costs were more than 5 to 1; HM&S costs were more than 3 to 1. We also learned that the absence pattern of many alcoholics does not fit the classical chronic absentee pattern, thereby allowing many alcoholics to escape detection under the division's absentee control program.

We then naively set out to steal or copy an effective program from one or more organizations with experience. A comprehensive study of industry programs quickly revealed limited penetration—despite missionary zeal and dedicated effort on the part of program administrators.

We learned that industrial alcoholic rehabilitation programs' are strikingly similar. The standard program has the following common primary elements:

1. A statement of policy that in effect says "drinking becomes the concern of the company only where it adversely affects job performance."
2. The front-line foreman is the key element. He is the one who initiates the action to talk to the employee about this deteriorating performance and refers him to a company designated doctor for examination and recommendations.
3. Utilization of staff personnel (almost always a sober alcoholic) to follow up on rehabilitative efforts.
4. Threat of job loss for failure to achieve expected progress.
5. A dual standard, in that most programs are limited to blue-collar or lower echelon employees.

Analysis of these five elements made obvious why penetration is severely limited. The target or goal is usually limited to the blue-collar chronic alcoholic—a person approaching the end of the alcoholic continuum. Utilization of the front line foreman for discovery and initiation of action runs counters to human nature and "on-the-job" social and peer cultures. In short, the policy determining the target coupled with the procedure for discovery guarantees the progress of the illness to the chronic stage. This makes rehabilitation, recovery of health, reconciliation of marital and familial schisms, and maintenance of job very difficult.

My purpose here is not to downgrade the time, money and effort of other companies or to belittle the successes achieved in the rehabilitation of alcoholics. I do, however, want to point out what I am convinced are severe shortcomings in the standard industrial alcoholic rehabilitation program.

Concluding that alcoholism is almost always a manifestation of other problems and that employees have many other kinds of problems, we made the decision upon which our program rests. All the problems of employees and their dependents are cause for concern and reason for help.

Again the concept is simple. It is to make readily available through company-furnished professional counseling, on a confidential basis, the services of community organizations and other professional people to Kennecott employees and their dependents.

Successful implementation is based on the following prerequisites which, we believe, are structurally interdependent:

1. The right person on the job.
2. Voluntary and confidential.
3. Management, union and community organization support.
4. A nonidentifying program name.
5. Service, seven days a week, twenty-four hours a day.
6. A willingness to meet wherever the employee or dependent will be comfortable.
7. Every person seeking help must, in fact, be helped.

Over a 48 month period, for employees, the single greatest problem is alcohol abuse (511 cases), followed by familial, legal, marital, psychological, financial and drug abuse (130 cases).

For dependents, familial problems rank first, followed by marital, psychological, legal, drug (114 cases) and alcohol (78 cases).

Penetration of the employee alcoholic problem alone is vastly superior to any other program of which we are aware.

To date, we have conducted two measurements—one relating to alcoholics and one relating to absenteeism. Twelve of the original thirty-seven-man alcoholic sample enrolled in the program for an average twelve and one-half months. Their absences decreased 50 percent. Their sickness and accident costs decreased from $70.67 to $25.33 per month. Their HM&S costs decreased from $109.04 to $59.91 per month. The performance of the balance of the sample, for the same period, worsened in all categories. The second measurement consisted of a sample of eighty-seven chronically absent employees referred to Insight through our absentee control system. Sixty-seven improved their attendance. Overall improvement was 44 percent.

Definitions and methods of measurement have not as yet been developed for either alcoholic or drug abuse rehabilitation— nor for the other problems we deal with. Hopefully, the Department of Health, Education and Welfare, through its appropriate subsidiary institutes, will correct this situation.

We know our program has certain weaknesses, both in organization and administration, nor is our penetration and resolution of the various problem areas as good as we would like. However, we are convinced our policy of concern and program of help are correct and of mutual benefit.

The Insight concept has applicability in any area where community organizations exist. We are convinced it can be effectively promulgated by any large organization or a consortium of smaller ones). The cost need not exceed $1.00 to $1.67 per month per employee. So long as the program embodies the concepts of voluntarism, confidentiality, qualified administrators and is service-oriented, it should succeed and pay handsome dividends to all who participate.

AUTHOR INDEX

271

SUBJECT INDEX

A

Abstinence and normal drinking,
107, 108
Accidents and alcohol, 6, 7
Addiction Research Foundation of
Ontario, 146, 170
Alanon programs, 209
Alberta Alcoholism and Drug Abuse
Commission, 156, 157, 158, 163
Alcohol
Physical dependence to, 6
psychological dependence to, 6
Alcohol abuse
behavioral problems associated with,
xi
cost to occupational systems, 7, 8
economic costs of, 5
personal costs of, 6
Alcohol and arrests, 8-11
Alcohol-related problems
arising out of the context of social
interaction, 24
attitudes which prevent us from
taking positive action toward,
4, 5
general principles to be considered,
32-36
historical and sociological
perspectives of, 3-39
responses and attitudes toward, 26
ultimate solutions to, 25
Alcoholic Employees, rehabilitation of,
long-term experience with, 175-
193
Alcoholic Rehabilitation Program,
Illinois Bell Telephone Co.,
175-179
Alcoholic, Psychotic, Neurotic and
"Normal" employees, 52-54

Alcoholics Anonymous, 16, 24, 43, 44,
51, 60, 98, 105, 150, 158, 177,
189, 199, 209, 224, 228, 232
counselors, 203, 230
group, special, 201
meetings, 239, 241
oriented, 199
programs, 200
therapy, 238
Alcoholism
can be defined as, 179
consultation clinic for, 106, 107
definition of, negative results from,
18
different definitions of, 72
medical definitions of, 18
nature of the industrial problem,
48-62
pretreatment phase of, 153
"Alcoholism as a Self-Limiting
Disease," 47
Alcoholism Foundation of British
Columbia, 109, 116
Alcoholism industrial problem
cost of, 49-51
findings of, 50
implications of, 50
"Alcoholism in Industry-Modern
Procedures," 199, 209, 210
Alcoholism programs
activity of, 63
adequacy of, 65
appropriateness of, 65
commonly used designs, 67
definition of, 62, 63
design for evaluating, 66-72
efficiency of, 65, 66
industrial, three Canadian, 136-174
objective of, 63
resources for, 63-65